The Romantic Tradition in American Literature

The Romantic Tradition in American Literature

Advisory Editor

HAROLD BLOOM
Professor of English, Yale University

DISCOURSES

ON THE

CHRISTIAN SPIRIT AND LIFE

C[YRUS] A. BARTOL

ARNO PRESS

A NEW YORK TIMES COMPANY

New York • 1972

/10 /3/7

Reprint Edition 1972 by Arno Press Inc.

The Romantic Tradition in American Literature
ISBN for complete set: 0-405-04620-0
See last pages of this volume for titles.

Manufactured in the United States of America

∞∞∞∞∞∞∞∞∞∞

Library of Congress Cataloging in Publication Data

Bartol, Cyrus Augustus, 1813-1900.
    Discourses on the Christian spirit and life.

    (The Romantic tradition in American literature)
    1. Unitarianism.   I. Title.   II. Series.
BX9843.B29D5 1972   288   72-4951
ISBN 0-405-04622-7

DISCOURSES

ON THE

CHRISTIAN SPIRIT AND LIFE.

BY C. A. BARTOL,

JUNIOR MINISTER OF THE WEST CHURCH, BOSTON.

SECOND EDITION, REVISED,

WITH

AN INTRODUCTION.

BOSTON:
WM. CROSBY AND H. P. NICHOLS,
111 WASHINGTON STREET.
1850.

BOSTON:

THURSTON, TORRY, AND COMPANY,

PRINTERS, DEVONSHIRE STREET.

INSCRIBED

WITH LOVE

TO THE WEST CHURCH.

CONTENTS.

INTRODUCTION.

THE object of the Discourses, here put forth in a second edition, was practically to promote in the heart and conduct of such as might read them, that spirit and life of which they treat. A religious book, however, cannot now be published without being subject to examination in reference to the theological doctrines it expresses, or is supposed to imply. But, as I did not expect my volume to go beyond the circle of my friends and acquaintances, it did not occur to me to guard it with any explanation of my general views of Christianity. In sending it forth again, I feel it as a duty I owe to the truth, and to those who have given or may yield me in their minds a hearing, to set the variety of my special topics in the light of some larger expression of faith. Yet my motive to this is not mainly to disarm or to guide criticism, but to meet the scepticism about our religion, which, in a form so subtle, prevails at the present day ; and, if my words might have force and reach at all for such a purpose, to stir in some souls a fresh conviction of the momentous verity of the Gospel. I cannot with a good conscience withhold the offer of my utmost strength

1

to the slightest advancement of such an end. Leaving the unity of the first publication unchanged, save by such improvement as I have been able to make of words and phrases, I shall occupy this preliminary space with remarks upon the object, for which Christ came into the world, upon the lasting character of that object, or the duration of Christ's kingdom upon earth, and upon the accomplishment of the object proposed, or the method of Christ's influence. First, I will speak of the

OBJECT OF CHRIST'S COMING.

Let me begin with quoting to this point Christ's own words.

John xviii. 37. To this end was I born and for this cause came I into the world, that I should bear witness unto the truth.

Matt. v. 17. Think not that I am come to destroy the law or the prophets : I am not come to destroy, but to fulfil.

John xii. 47. I came not to judge the world, but to save the world.

John x. 10. I am come that they might have life, and that they might have it more abundantly.

The centre of all religious solicitude and the hinge of every theological difference is the object of Christ's coming. On this point his own authority is supreme. Nothing that he or his apostles say besides can be supposed to contradict his authentic statements. In fact, the whole New Testament only in diverse forms repeats them. They cannot be put into simpler terms or a more comprehensive formula. Christ came to attest the truth, fulfil the law, save the world, and enliven the soul, — or, varying the language with a personal application, to tell us where in the universe of being we are, what we have to do, how we are to be delivered from misdoing, and whence we are to get spiritual life. Here is the force of all other scripture phraseology,—faith, obedience, repentance, redemption, reconciliation or atonement, justification, sanctification, propitiation, the Holy Spirit, oneness in Christ and God, including every religious exercise and influence. I shall not enter into a minute analysis of texts, or that thorny style of exposition which converts the Bible from a well for the thirsty into a bramble-bush, but simply review Christ's own declarations.

He came to bear witness unto the truth, or to tell us where in the creation we are. We want first of all to know where we are, not as an animal in his narrow ring of observation knows where he is in his stall or pasture, and can find his way to the spring or the meadow, but where we are in the world. Our path runs a little way back and stops in mystery ; a little way dubiously forward, and stops in mystery. No blinding limitation or pleasant stupor of faculties shuts out, as with lower natures, this anxious query about our place, measured by our origin and destiny. Childhood, indeed, which is the slumber of the soul, protects us awhile from this solicitude. But when we wake from that slumber, we look around, curious and alarmed to ascertain, if we may, our position. We are not content with getting back to our visible home and parentage, in the street or among the hills, for the beginning, nor, after a little moving to and fro in a circle, with discerning the grave yonder as the end. "Dust thou art and unto dust thou shalt return," is an unsatisfying decree to us. A strangeness of sensation comes over us with our first distinct conception of being, and, contrary to Milton's imaginary account of the first man, we shudder at the thought of loss of being. But we have no natural assurance against this doom. Our life is like a running stream, all existence a fluctuating tide, our hold of it loose and slipping, and the heart cries out within us to know where we really are in reference to our cause and continuance. Here, indeed, is a substantial want of the mind.

They are poor observers and reasoners, who would persuade us that this uneasiness belongs to the feeble commencement or imbecility of the intellect, and that with increasing thought, or by the clearer pointing of instinct, we come to know where we are, as no revelation or resurrection could inform us. The precise contrary is the fact. Thought is the very thing which disquiets us, draws the shade of death upon our brow, hangs the cloud of uncertainty over our pilgrimage, and puts us upon this quest of our fate. In the ignorant childhood, or savage condition of the race, though there is a superstitious activity of the religious imagination, yet there is

not the same deep yearning to understand the spirit's origin and futurity. The senses act more
strongly, this world is more absorbing, the satisfaction of animal wants is the great interest, earth and
time give scope for busy pursuit, and, in their ignorance, men often die like other creatures, with no
gnawing thirst for knowledge of what is to come.
But when human nature becomes intelligent, when
it awakes, retires into its closet, holds itself off from
and compares itself with other things, then it wishes
to know where in the creation it is, whence and
whither tend its steps. It is not the Pacific Islander
or the African Boschman, or the wild Northman,
that is so much concerned to know who made him,
or to what end he travels. He is asleep,—watching in his woods, sailing with his canoe, or speeding
on his piratical track,—but spiritually asleep. And,
in his heavy ignorance, God kindly hides from him
the awfulness of death and withholds the sharp points
of fearful questions, while fancy guesses after some
vague and pleasing solution of the enigma of life.
It is the wise and knowing, those intellectually of
age, possessed of all their faculties, Socrates, Plato
and Cicero, that are anxious, with an unappeasable
desire, to understand their position between the
source of their existence and the prospect of eternity.
How they would have welcomed a teacher like
Jesus Christ to tell them where they were! and how,
as, in the increase of knowledge and the multiplying number of awakened minds, the want of this
information became wide and insupportable, God

1*

sent his Son to satisfy it, " the fullness of times " for
him being, as Greek and Roman history avouches,
the fullness of need for his instructions.   And
how sufficient for the case those instructions are!
what a wonder-working power in the world and on
the human soul from his few simple and glorious
words! Believing in him, we know our state,
though it be not only a joy-inspiring, but, to the
unfaithful, terrible knowledge.

This view may relieve us of a particular apprehension. The present danger to the Christian faith
is supposed to come from the intelligence, the critical and prying intelligence of the age. We need
not fear for Christianity on any such account. Human intelligence, we may be certain, wants Christ
even more than human ignorance does. The positive knowledge of nature and art in every attainment of human science, which the senses and
understanding may compass, can never long, never
fully or finally satisfy the soul. As the Magi with
the shepherds brought their offerings at Christ's
birth, — the sage more earnestly than the simple
will ever be Christ's followers, — for they more
consciously and profoundly, with a still greater
stake at every new development of their power,
want to know, as he alone can largely and lucidly
tell them, where they, their individual conscious
spirits, are. If a few of the able and learned for a
time wander off on the adventure of scepticism and
self-sufficiency, they will be likely, nay, how often,
by their own spiritual necessities, have the strongest

of them been constrained to return. Christianity, many-sided, many-handed, stretching out far her guards and co-workers, has encompassed, caught and rescued them, changing their infidelity at one human presentation of her into faith, as she beams upon them in another. She has, indeed, other apologists than those who have written and spoken eloquently in her behalf. Sickness, death, sorrow, sin, and remorse, if other witnesses can be resisted, are her sad, yet majestic advocates and defenders. Our weakness, our pain, our anguish, press upon us the indispensableness to our comfort and peace of knowing if we may, as in Jesus we may, — where, in this mysterious, surrounding immensity of existence, we are.

Christ's object is next to show us what, in the position thus defined, we have to do. So far from destroying or relaxing any just, existing law of human duty, he would only make it more perfect and imperative, the passing of heaven and earth, as he affirms, being easier than its failure in one jot or tittle. They mistake, then, who think the gospel a scheme for waiving the divine claims on the human soul, or providing any substitute in their discharge. Christianity has, in this respect, been too violently contrasted with both Judaism and natural religion, as not like them a system of law. It is not a ceremonial or simply moral law, but spiritual too, yet in no other religion or philosophy was ever proclaimed so high and strict a code. It is comparatively an easy thing to go to certain sacred places, to observe certain sacred times, to offer certain outward sacrifices, and practise certain reputable decencies; but a law running back of all this into the heart, girdling with its authority the motives, asking nothing less than the soul as a whole burnt-offering in love to God and regard for a fellow-creature, — summoning not crimes alone, but inclinations to its tribunal, considering a thought a sin, an imagination defilement, and the love of money the service of mammon, calling a look adultery, irreverence blasphemy, coveteousness theft, and hatred murder,— and fixing the eye of the Judge ever on the germs of conduct, — a law like this, not taking, like all human law, a few palpable things into its account, but arraigning every movement of our being for trial, may well startle and hold us employed.

There is a sublimity, a glory, even a most moving pathos in Christ's expectation that we shall keep this law. He does not, like human theologians, take it for granted that we are going to break it. He admits not for a moment the idea of our inability to fulfil it. He preaches no doctrine of human impotency, original depravity, or universal degeneracy. He makes no allusion to Adam, or to a fall of mankind, but to God refers us for our nature and obligation. If Pharisees and hypocrites, the worst of men, set on foot their cruel frauds, with tones of grandeur, and a severe goodness, we, in our passionate habits, faintly conceive, he styles them, in the intelligible idiom of the times, children of the devil and a generation of vipers, not meaning any absurd fancy of literal descent, or of real diabolic presence, — but the lying and malignity, whose living shape is worse than all we suppose in the apparition of demons ; while, in his requirement of the opposite disinterestedness and truth, he pays a tribute to our nature and capacity, which no fond discoursing about its dignity and divinity could ever equal. He does not say,—You cannot obey this law, and therefore, I am obeying it for you; but, instead of such discouraging scorn, shows men the enkindling respect of setting up before them the highest standard, bearing it on and calling on them, one and all to follow. If he had conversed all the day long on our endowments of will and affection, or talked with David of our being made " a little lower than the angels," he would not have sent so keen an inspiration into the humility and resolve of the human soul.

Shall we not treat with him in the same nobleness, and answer him with the manhood to which he appeals? We need his divine legislation to guide us. Natural conscience cannot alone, without him, tell us what to do. The inner light is indeed requisite, but not sufficient. Like a lamp in the hand, or over the stormy coast, it gleams in the breast, but flickers dimly and narrowly, compared with that lustrous law from above, which shines over our whole sphere and pilgrimage. Nay,— the conscience itself of right and wrong is not simply a native instinct of the race, invariable and equal in

all ages and among all tribes, but itself very much
a gift of our religion.   Compare the conscience of a
Hottentot or an Esquimaux with that of a refined,
cultivated. experienced Christian.   You could hardly
put together any two things of more marked diver-
sity.   The larger part of the conscience in the
world has been made by the Gospel.   Man's native
conscience, moreover, not only strays from the
moral law as it stands in God's mind, but is
often ignorant and perplexed, nor can decide for us
what to do.   Christ came to disembarrass as well
as to correct it.   Showing our relations to God, to
each other, and to a future existence, he shows the
duties they imply.   Worship, charity, meekness,
forgiveness of injuries, love of enemies, care for
strangers, humanity, broad as the earth for the suffering and oppressed, self-denial and self-sacrifice in
the cause of truth, of freedom and piety, ranking
the lightest obligation of a principle above the price
of comfort or life, and holding it cheap though our
arm should be palsied, our utterance exhausted, or
our blood flow, for the promotion of peace and
good-will among men, or quietly, with noiseless
martyrdom, consuming every day's strength, in our
toil and longing for such ends, — these are but the
plain obligations he sets in sunlight by his truth.
Thank God, we know what to do.   Shall we not
do according as we know ?   The way of duty may be
a narrow way, but it is as plain as the road dyked
above waters, walled over deserts, cleft through
hills.   The gate of life may be straight, but it is

as clear as the pass notched between gigantic mountains.

But I speak to the consciousness of every heart here, as well as from the consciousness of my own, in saying that this very revelation, so clear, deep, and vast of duty, only puts us the more sensibly into the condition of sinners. The breadth of the commandment is our conviction. The law comes, sin revives, and we die. A dull savage may be a much lower character, than a believing Christian. But he has nothing like the sense of sin that the Christian has. The pure perfection, that is the Christian's aim, glares dreadfully at transgressions and short-comings, which the savage, composedly and without remorse, outdoes in the evil purposes and delinquencies of every day. Conscience is very much a creation of Christianity ; and sin, too, or the knowledge of sin, is its creation. How live and tender this faith makes the soul ! A stain is a wound, — forgetfulness is fault, and the fear to have offended, remorse. The hands that seemed to be clean, are, in its light, spotted with iniquity. The long writing on the heart's tables, with the invisible ink of life's secret unfairness and silent meanness, starts out, black and legible in its fire, and actions that passed by as venial or customary, exciting no compunction in ourselves, and the sub- ject, perhaps, of no accusation from others, rise up from the dust into mountains to fall upon us and rocks to cover us !

Christianity, unearthing these wrongs, letting

nothing stay in the grave of oblivion, arming every past baseness, boldly committed, with a sting, and heaping up, with wretched aggravation, our completely unburied and exposed offences; it seems, according to the goodness and equity of God, that it should be not only a system of law, but also a manifestation of mercy. Equity, I say. For if the savage or the heathen has not the same miraculous assurance of pardon for the penitent, neither has he at the bottom of his heart the same wasting conviction of sin. Here is the marvellous union of law and love in Christ. He wounds to heal, bruises to anoint, and breaks to bind up. More touchingly than the Psalmist knew when he wrote, " Mercy and truth are met together: righteousness and peace have kissed each other."

Once more, then, on his own authority, we must say, the object of his coming is not only to tell us what to do in our by him defined position, but to deliver us from the remorse and death of our misdoing. How tenderly he expresses it ! " I came not to judge the world, but to save the world ! " Oh, if he had come to judge, to make God's face hard upon us, and the heavens brass over our heads, so that our prayers could not pierce them, — so " many thousand miles of clouds and air lying between us and God," — while at the same time his heavenly light transformed our misdeeds into monsters, and our neglects as bottomless gulfs, what flesh could stand ! Who would not be devoured in these jaws of ruin quickly ! But, in our compunction, the hand of mercy arrests us on the brink of the precipice, and scares away the ghastly pursuing spectres of our guilt. God holds forth his arms for the returning prodigal, Christ seeks and saves that which was lost, lives, toils, dies on the cross for the sinner, constantly affirming, *all is the work of my Father's forgiving love*, makes the scarlet of our transgression to be as snow, and turns the crimson fabric of our life like wool. We wash our robes and make them white in the blood of the lamb. His love and purity, an unction from the Holy One, a stream from the heavens, cleanse and quicken us with all holy purpose and self-consecration.

Thus he is not only teacher and lawgiver, but saviour ; as the angel said to Joseph, *" thou shalt call his name Jesus, for he shall save his people from their sins."* One of the most injurious mistakes of theology has been the notion that the object of Christ's coming is to deliver us from the consequences of sin, the retribution of the past, instead of from actual sin itself for the present and the future. That sin should have woful consequences is not cruelly, but mercifully, ordained ; the cruelty would be to exempt us from that fire of anguish which is the soul's baptism. Fending off a just and good Being's doom upon the guilty would be an equal affront to him and mischief to them. But to be redeemed from sin, to have the yoke of its slavery broken, the deep, fine roots of its dispositions plucked out, and the inveterate custom of its actions displaced for habits of virtue, — this is a deliverance. After light upon its condition, and law for its direction, freedom from its transgression is the great want of human nature.

We want indeed to be happy. We wish to lead a life as clear from trouble and annoyance as God in his wisdom may permit. From the pinch of distress, from the steeping of poverty, from the scourge of disease, and from driving helplessly through storm after storm of grief, we would, if we might in the decision of a better knowledge, be rescued. But not for any such liberation or defence do these immortal, self-acquainted souls so long, and pray the good Lord who delivers, as they do, to be emancipated from wrong desires, from low thoughts, ungenerous dispositions, impure imaginations, from the very seeds of iniquity, and all that is unworthy in those prevailing motives of our conduct, which wake with us at the touch of early morn, go with us through the day, prompt our words, move our hands, suggest our social bearing, and order our lonely mood, till at night they sleep with us again only to rise once more with our refreshment, "grow with our growth, and strengthen with our strength." To reach and rectify these subtle and profound motives, to pass them through some secret furnace and take away their baseness and dross, is our pressing and supreme need. Here, at the core of our existence, Christ came to help us. The work he does is no forensic work of vindication, getting us off from our deserts in the court of divine judgment, but a work in the vital part of us, by his searching probes and burning words extinguishing every mean or malicious impulse, and inflaming us with good affections to God and man, from the penetrating heat of his own. So far from preventing the wo that belongs to sin, his own energy conspires with it for our salvation, not alone from the hell to which the steps of iniquity outwardly travel, but from the pit of misery and death in the breast, and so of course from the final consequence and termination of persisting vice.

For this spiritual salvation, what toil and pain too great, or what display from heaven too marked! Let God send, — our souls cry, — if they have any dignity, or manliness in them, — let him send sickness and sorrow, and earthly straitening for it. Let him send, if such his boundless mercy, his own Son into the dress of our circumstances, the garb of our nature, the crowd of our temptations, and to the drinking of a cup all his own. Let miracles of power and love, combine with every sharp instrument used by Providence to emancipate the undying tenant of these bosoms from obstinate error and vile propensity, if, listening to Christ's teachings, following his example, beholding his deathly face, his gory cross, and communing with the spirit that ascended on the breath of his forgiving prayers, they may be formed in his likeness and restored to the image of God. For, teacher of truth, fulfiller of law, and Saviour from sin, Jesus does not end with mere Salvation, but crowns his mission with being in and beyond these things also a giver of life. So, again, summing up and completing the accomplishments in him of the divine purpose, he sets forth the object of his own coming. *"I am come that they might have life, and that they might have it more abundantly."*

We think not rightly of Christ when we regard him but as an agent, a divine factor, or a vehicle to convey a divine message. He is, too, the divine brightness, image, manifestation, God with us in the flesh, God's rectitude, purity, goodness incarnate on the earth. *"As the Father hath life in himself, so hath he given to the Son to have life in himself."* Saving, he enlivens us, quickens us into harmonious, everlasting growth, sets us upon the road which is eternal progress and eternal peace. Here is the glory and conclusive demonstration of our religion, in the life it imparts. If any other religion or philosophy, scheme of faith or negation of doubt, could animate the souls of men with a nobler life and flow out from their hands and lips in more cheering bounties, or benignant benedictions, if Mahometanism, or Buddhism, or Scepticism, or a speculative Transcendentalism could overtop with the monuments of its benevolence and devotion the gospel building, or show richer fruits than come from its vineyard, if any style of character could fairly surmount and shame that which Jesus has brought into the world, then we might fear for the foundation and permanence of his reign. But who requires to be informed that even the imperfect beginnings of Christian excellence outvie every other type! Who,

that looks back from this span of time and top of
civilization, to the first shedding of Christian blood!
What then shall be the ripening and culmination,
according to Christ, the inexhaustible model!
From the fountain of life he is a fountain, the way
of living waters, God's approach to man, man's approach to God, infinity of goodness, reduced from
the appalling abyss of inconceivableness into the limits of human apprehension, representing God not as
a formal ambassador, but as a partaker of his nature
and immeasurable possessor of his spirit, the Son
knowing, as no man does, the Father, — and with
his voice of gracious meaning and supernatural power, calling the dead in trespasses from their graves.

This bodily life, which we think so sacred, and
which is such a mystery, as it waits on the beating
pulse and runs through the throbbing, tingling veins,
is unutterably less precious than the other life of
God in the soul. The life of the body wastes like
the dropping sand, and is daily swept away, as the
dust of the floor, into the tomb, whose door swings
in a thousand turnings while we speak. But the other
life that Christ gives, is not consumed. The language
of Scripture lament, was not taken up over that. It
is no vapor, no fleeing shadow, or withering flower,
but firm, bright, and blooming with immortal vigor
and increase. Millions, from every clime come to
bear witness that he has given it to them. The
earth trembles at the tread of that living host, and
quakes as their generations over its surface rise from
their rent sepulchres. Nay, — myriads on high, ad-

vanced into the lines of cherubim and seraphim, with the vitality, he first gave, celebrate without end their fresh, grateful thanksgivings.

The end and sum of all this superhuman work of the Gospel is to participate Christ's life. To this our nature is equal, as he is not a supernaturalist, but an anti-naturalist who denies. No denaturalizing is needful, but a reaching forth of the nature God gave to the Son he has sent. Have we, then, any experience to understand Paul when he says :—"*I am crucified with Christ : nevertheless I live; yet not I, but Christ liveth in me : and the life which I now live in the flesh, I live by the faith of the Son of God, who loved me and gave himself for me.*" "*My life,*" said one, who was brought into question, "*My life must answer for me.*" True, our life must be our answer to man and to God, if we have any answer. Yet not our life, in a superficial sense ; the word has a larger and deeper meaning than is commonly supposed, embraces not only what may be fair and good-looking in human behavior, decent and current in what we call society, but the first springs of deportment and speech, what lives at the source of life, moves at the centre of motion, holds the helm of our course, gives the shape and momentum of our existence, and has the inner business of constituting our character and originating our acts. This is the two-edged sword for the spirit of the nominal Christian.

I have thus, under the leading of Christ's own words, spoken of the object of his coming into the world. Let us now proceed to inquire how this object, proposed, has actually stood and been maintained, or the

DURATION OF CHRIST'S KINGDOM.

Some of the views already given may be further vindicated, as I endeavor to clear up the grounds on which the object of Christ's coming has been historically maintained and his reign established.

It is the bold prophecy recorded in the gospel of Christ, that his kingdom shall be without end. He asks no apology on account of the time when, as men count life, he lived. Let us consider the elements of durableness in his kingdom. It is the year of our Lord, 1850. That the chronology measuring all else should be measured from him, is one signal of his permanent influence. In the opinion of some, Christianity is a partial system, showing tokens of obsoleteness and decay, ready to give place to more perfect expressions of truth following upon its outgrown creed, its exploded and abandoned narrative. This opinion is not novel or suggested by facts, but by a moral unbelief or a metaphysical speculation. All I have to say is, that the facts waive any excuse for Jesus, drawn from the age when he flourished. Indeed he did not *flourish* like other great personages, opening into temporary attractiveness, soon to fade, but with endless unfolding, — nothing in his existence needing to be palliated, charitably spoken of, or left out by reason of the lapse of time. He so predominates, that the wisest judges cannot yet agree whether he was God or man. He is not, in the phrase of the day, a "representative man," but representative of deity. The world recedes not from, but approaches him. He seems in the future, not in the past. He transcends all our transcendentalism. What vast changes in 1800 years have come over the scene, but he is fresh as the morning! The book published yesterday has nothing of beauty or originality to match the newness and force of his old instructions. There is no fault to scale off from his divine form, no glory of wisdom to supply to his person. Sap and weather-stain have crumbled the rock on which his feet rested, and the aged olive beneath which he prayed or wept is in its grave, but his religion is yet in the youth of its triumphs. "Time writes no wrinkle on its brow." Other religions have been periodical, or have lost their hold on the advancing human mind. But its last days have been its best. Christ's immediate followers hardly apprehended him. The author of the work on "Ancient Christianity," shows that the Fathers understood him more poorly than his disciples now ; and any one reading the history of the Popes, may see that Rome as well as Jerusalem ever fell short of the present discernment of his teachings. Bacon's maxim of general science, that antiquity is the ignorant childhood of the world, and the modern time its wise and experienced age, fits the Christian Church. It has not exhausted its author's resources, but ever grown upon his wisdom. We have discovered defects and gross violations of truth in other masters and leaders. We must apologize for Socrates, for Plato, and Aristotle, on account of their times, but not for Christ. We have not been able to see round him or over him.

It is not because Christianity has wanted antagonists. Judaism, with its forces of ancient tradition, and Paganism, with the arms of all its gods, fought against it. The world, a worse enemy, embodying the sin and folly of the human heart, has striven to deaden and extinguish it in a foul embrace. But, too vital to be palsied, too strong to be overthrown, too peculiar to be confounded, it has maintained its own firm and wholesome quality as "the salt of the earth." Distinct in its boundaries as it is vast in its proportions, it abides, the oldest institution retaining hold of human faith in the civilized and enlightened quarters of the globe, and the indications are that its frailest record, about leaving a cloak or bringing a parchment, will survive our most admired poems and philosophies. It is because Christ himself is the heart and soul of this living and increasing body, ever renewing and moving it with a divine and immortal energy. He asks no man's apology. His department, the religious, is the highest, and he chief in it, nor has the world outgrown the need of it; but only painfully stitched in a few threads of the incomparable pattern he set. He has a "second coming," and that without end.

Human invention has done wonders since the angels' song over the manger in Bethlehem. It has travelled over and into the earth, dived through the sky, weighed and measured planets and their central orb, explored nature and transformed it. The magnet, the leaden type, a bubble of steam, the electric spark and chemical force, wielded in man's fingers, have almost turned the world into another sphere. Rocks and sunbeams are taxed for our benefit and enjoyment. Ancient kings lacked the advantages of the modern poor. We have travelled far, but not from the cradle and the cross of Christ. We have distanced Judea, but not Jesus. With the marvellous fulfilment of the primal decree, "to subdue the earth and have dominion over it," the need of his influence has but increased. England and America, as well as Ethiopia, stretch out to him their hands with that inward hunger and thirst, for which all human labor, riches, refinement and advancement cannot provide. The original prediction then, that of Christ's kingdom there should be no end, has not yet failed. He is a king, though Roman Cæsars and proconsuls of Galilee are dead.

We may get further proofs of our point in considering what is the kingdom he reigns in. It is not a kingdom of outward office, or physical force, but, first, a kingdom of light or of ideas. His religious ideas, or revelations of God's truth, are still paramount. No rust of disease, no pall of oblivion, is upon them. No extenuating plea is to be made for them, as being of worn substance or an ancient fashion. They meet a permanent want. The cry of human nature, enclosed in this perishing form, is for light upon its origin and destiny. The sun in heaven lights up this world splendidly for its explorations, but also fatally spins off from his golden wheel the numbered divisions of its life. Whence it came into his beams it knows not, nor whither from them it goes. As a stranger it enters the room of existence, as a stranger it leaves. It wants a lamp to its feet, besides that of the sun or of science. Its own understanding searches and pierces for the source and the outlet, where the door closed on its admission, and where it should open for its release. But the secret spring baffles its touch, yields not to its pressure. It fathoms the sea, but not the grave, — drills the earth's strata, yet penetrates not through the superficial sand round a corpse, — traces out a web of material connections, but cannot fasten on the link which knits the spirit to another world, finds the solar system is an easier problem to it than the planks of a coffin, reaches every edge and corner of the earth, but cannot clearly set foot over its verge and horizon. Inspired by genius, winged by imagination, it soars where it seems to catch bright glimpses of higher regions, but, in its ordinary state, it sinks back into its limited bark on the ocean of time, and, like a weary bird stooping at dusk on a ship at sea, cries for light and rest.

Christ answers its cry. Here lies his power and the foundation of his kingdom. He has distinctly followed the way from God to man, and back from earth to heaven, crossing and recrossing, to show that we, timid and weak, can move after. He has lain down in the tomb, measured it with his own body, and returned in the figure of a definite existence to prove its dimensions unequal to our life. He has given ideas of God, heaven, and man's relation to God and immortality, — before which the host of heathen deities flee from their Olympus, and the fables of Elysium and Tartarus become trifling stories. He does not say much on these grand themes, but every word he says bursts with meaning. Wonderful how a few sentences about the Father, his Holy Spirit, the Comforter, the many mansions of his house, the angels of little children beholding his face, and the succeeding of more spiritual relations to these bonds of flesh and blood, the ties of kindred and marriage, — sentences spoken incidentally, for a purpose of correction or consolation, — should furnish symbols and pictures of the heavenly world, which no other delineations can obscure or rival, which, so far from growing dim, make our hearts at every perusal stand still in an awe of delight, and all additions to which, though made by the genius of a Swedenborg, of a spiritual mystic or metaphysical philosopher, are like modern daubs on an ancient master-piece. As every part of any animal frame implies, and might furnish means to restore the rest, and as the smallest segment could be produced into the complete circle, so his briefest sayings seem to involve the whole structure of the celestial city. .A few strokes of his pencil portray eternal life. We pause over the amazing depths and significance of his declarations, we mark the strength and dignity into which they withdraw from all other human speech, we survey his beneficent miracles as only the proper emphasis of such words, we see in all the ranking of other teachers in a list with him only presumption and profaneness, we bow the knees of our spirit before such communications, we own that Christ reigns in the kingdom of ideas, and believe that of his kingdom there shall be no end.

Not only in the kingdom of religious ideas does he reign, but also in that of moral laws. The world has not outgrown the gospel morality, any more than it has the gospel truth ; but with only a slow, panting and yet how distant step, its gigantic bulk follows after the Christian standard. It seems superfluous to argue the point, that no apology is needed for Christ's precepts, but only for our neglect and violation. The spiritual worship he prescribes, not necessarily on such a mountain or in such a temple, but in the closet and the secret soul, how far exceeding the conceptions of that age or the attainments of this ! How the pagan groves shook and the partition walls of supposed sanctuaries sundered at his voice, opening the world from every stream to every hill-top for the temple of the Most High ! His statutes of meekness, humility, self-denial, forbearance, forgiveness, love of enemies, devotion to the welfare of the needy and unfornate, — are they exhausted and buried without life or use in the forgetfulness of the past ? Look for the laws of Numa, Solon and Lycurgus ; and

3

obscurely guess at certain fragments of them, like single timbers from wrecks, wrought into the frame of existing legislation! Study the commonwealth of Plato, and apologize, as you must very largely, for the Greek sage as mixing with his wisdom such ingredients of folly, corruption, and cruelty, — but make no apology for those commandments of Jesus, the practice of which alone is required to bring back Eden, not as an Asiatic garden with limits and one river parted into four heads, but as the earth. Or, with introverted eye, consult your own conscience, and in its dullness, uncertainty, or variations, as of a clock or a compass, behold the necessity and blessing of a law of duty from above. For our guide in life, we want something which our passions or fancies cannot alter, our fingers cannot touch; as we need, not a mechanical instrument alone, but the North Star and the sidereal time of the heavens, to direct us on an earthly voyage. Conscience, independent of religion, of God's will, is not enough; all history in every land shows it is not enough. It is but like a lantern on the vessel's mast, casting a little light around, but swaying and turning with every motion of the waves, or eclipsed by the tempest, and incapable of illumining the whole course. The sailor must look beyond his candle to the steady, ever-shining pole. And while we move in the varying light of our own mind, and keep that inner, indispensable lamp carefully trimmed and burning, we must supply its deficiencies from the bright, high oracles of God in Jesus Christ.

But, once more, Christ's kingdom is durable as a kingdom of love. The law of duty, standing in conscience, nature, or revelation, is by man ignorantly or knowingly broken. He becomes a sinner, and a kingdom of mere light and law does not console, but alarms him. That God, the Supreme, loves us, simple truth as it seems, separate from revelation is but a half-solved mystery, a late and rare discovery. Philosophy alone, with its coolly tracing finger, never made it. The simply native religious sentiment of the human heart could not reach it, but commonly saw for its deity, a sagacious skill or a resistless force, to which it offered the tribute of fear, not confidence. The feeble idolizing soul, from Scandinavia to Rome, forged its gods out of every element of matter, or took for them its own magnified and reflected passions, till more of lust and wrath than of goodness sat on the throne of the universe. The most perfect idea, which, without divine help, ever got extensive footing in the world, was that in which the many objects of pagan worship were reduced into two rival deities, benevolent and unkind. The problem, like a hard substance in the chemist's hands, refused further analysis. Even Judaism, knowing God's unity from himself, was far from conceiving of him as pure benignity, and it was left for Christ to persuade us that he is only love, the Father. This once unknown conception, our unregarded commonplace, is indeed the most amazing fact. That the Being who made from his own essence all this

we see, the round solids that circle in this bewild-
ering infinity, the light and ether that play between,
the grades of life from the green blade to the conscious mind, and that this Being, dwelling in immensity through eternity, should love you and me,
— if the gospel, and that alone, had not made it the
most familiar of thoughts, — would mix emotions
of mystery with choking tears of gratitude. And
that to the eye of Christian faith his love shines on
uneclipsed by our sorrows, that the clouds and darkness round his throne do not mount to his bosom,
that his chastenings are affectionate, what we call
his anger only the faithfulness of his regard, and
all our various disappointment and trouble but
his way of weaning us from the world, — this belief
of our religion fills the soul with a satisfaction so
deep and distending, that waves and storms, chafing
and weltering by its vessel of mortality, find no
room for a drop of the threatened anguish to come
in.

The love of God, we bless him for the fast hold
which in his Son he lets us lay on that, not as a
caprice of his will, or alternation of his feeling, but
as the positive energy of his nature, and the informing principle of all his acts. To understand,
cling to, not let go, but be wrought upon by it,
alone is salvation. It may do to let many points
waver on the tossing sea of speculation, or sink
under the stress of argument and dispute, while this
one stands on the rock and throws light over the
tempest. Christ's kingdom is enduring and end-

less, the highest kingdom ever established, because
the only one of perfect, divine love. And the
crown and triumph of this heavenly royalty is, that
we cannot even sin away or mortally offend God's
goodness. He still seeks us, sends his Son to die
for us. More than earthly father or mother can
ever know, the Father's heart yearns for his children. The prodigal is among the husks and the
swine, but the calf is fatting, and the music is preparing, the ring and the robe, and the shoes for his
bleeding feet are ready, when he shall come to
himself. Nothing could show God's love but the
extremest and most incredible case. It was not
enough that the morning sun should punctually
every day relight his flame above our paths; it was
not enough, that the harvest should annually wave
its yellow signal in the breeze, announcing the supply of our wants; it was not enough, that beauty for
a finer taste should be poured over the earth and the
heavens, and sun, moon, and stars by the Almighty
hand be thrown as fuel into the fire to please
with all forms of lustre our imagination; it was not
enough, that the charities of home, kindred and
friends, should warmly swathe in our hearts, till
the common resources flow for the individual need;
nor did it satisfy God to comfort and bless us while
we might keep in the way of his commandments,
acknowledging and serving him; but when we
forgot him, and went wrong in our wilfulness and
self-seeking, when an oath was on the lips, and
profaneness in the heart, and many, hating their

3*

brethren, were murderers, then God sent the sinless,
wrapping him in the garment of our flesh, and the
inner clothing of our nature, exposed his beloved
one to temptation and all manner of want and distress, let him go forth to hunger in the wilderness,
to faint in the field, not to rest his weary head, but to
sweat the great drops of blood in Gethsemane, and
bear his cross to Calvary, that on its nails there he
might stand and pray, stretching out in pardon for
his murderers the hands they had stretched out in
revengeful rage.

"Herein is love!" Here the reconciliation and
atonement of man to God. We want no theory to
understand it, any more than we do to understand
the folding embrace of a forgiving, welcoming human
parent, or the tender looks and tears of an injured
earthly friend, forgetting all but his love. Violated
laws have their penalties, and wield their rod according to the aggravation and frequency of guilt.
Misery cleaves to transgression, as our shadow
follows swiftly as we may run. Nor did Christ
come to destroy the law of these dreadful wages, but
to fulfil. But while this blow of pain falls from
the hand of God, to look up in Christ, and see the
eye of God not hard and hating, but full of love
to prompt that blow as the severity of his goodness; oh, this vision makes the heart crave and
gratefully own the discipline. We can bear all, in
the scope of time and nature to inflict, if, through
all, we can only know that God loves us. This is
a charm against the stings of calamity, an anti-

dote for the poison of human falsehood and treachery, a healing ointment and salve for every wound
of misfortune, the soul's balm.

I have spoken of Christ's kingdom of light and
law, as lasting. Shall his kingdom of love come to
an end? While men suffer, while men sin, while
men live, shall the love of God, no where expressed
so clear and perfect as in his son, lose its power!
What is the kingdom of man's independent philosophy compared with it? Like an earthly kingdom
truly, with succession of princes and dynasties, a
history of ceaseless change and downfall. I see
the pale philosopher in his intellectually exploring
mood. On the walls of his chamber of thought he
writes strange characters in cold phosphoric gleam,
and, with doubting look and vague utterance, spells
out his fancies to his disciples. The broad night
of ignorance is about. The vapors of wordy strife
and the clouds of impenetrable mystery hurry by.
Death, a dark figure, hovers near. Feeble is the
blaze of knowledge with which he strives to pierce
the gloomy void, and uncertain the path in which he
gropes and guesses his way. I turn to the countenance of the most ignorant Christian believer, and
see it irradiated by his master's revelation of the
Father's love. As the best light in the world is
the warm light of the sun, so the best illumination
of life is not from the moon-like beams of human
speculation, but from the love of God. That love,
like the sun, opens the universe, turns even clouds
into glory, and lifts death itself to a mount of
transfiguration.

But the highest term in designating Christ's kingdom, the most comprehensive ground of its endless duration, is, that it is a kingdom of life. This is the final question and fatal test in regard to any system, not whether it informs, delights, or astonishes, but whether it communicates life, quickens what is deepest and best in us. There are those who fancy that the spiritual nature lives and grows, not on stimulus from without, but on the food of its own intuitions and abstract principles. But this is contrary to the analogy of our whole nature. From an imperceptible germ quickened by external nourishment, and played upon by the thousand influences of creation, lives and grows the body. No otherwise is it with the mind. Look at the sleepy infant, reposing in arms, without thought or proper will, reluctant to open its eyes, and when it does, seeing all things indiscriminated and close upon its witless gaze, and, uninterested, relapsing into its vacant doze, a glory of innocence on the earth, but ignorant as it is beautiful and spotless. Who would imagine the amazing faculties there dormant under those soft lids! The strong man, who shall hereafter traverse the earth, unbury its treasures, meddle with all the wonders of art and science, draw down the planets, and open the chambers of atoms with his lens, now helplessly slumbers. He cannot wake himself. He dreams not of his latent abilities and future achievements. He knows nothing of the nature in himself which shall hereafter become one of the subjects of his analysis and investigation. How shall the spell upon him be broken? By objects, coming to the babe, one by one, to solicit and stir it,— external objects : — its cradle and pillow, the floor, the chair, the fire, the hands that beckon or hold it, the face and eye of the mother, flushed and sparkling upon it, every sight and sound and motion. Daily its arousing goes on. Its sphere enlarges, its vision widens. Greater objects invite it. The earth and sun and moon take it into their attractions. With every new thing and fresh excitement, all that is going on in the street, the events and conversation of the family-circle, this inward development proceeds, till the mind, long fed with light, seems to become self-luminous.

Now the religious power can no more than the intellectual, educate and unfold itself by any intrinsic virtue. It can maintain no independent or original life. Objects suited to waken and bring out its energies must be provided ; and the best, the grandest, crowning objects are furnished for it in the Christian faith. Thus is Christ's kingdom a kingdom of life. Making real to our perception the sublimest things we can apprehend or conceive, it feeds into increasing strength the hidden man of the heart. Christ embodies these invisible things, concentrates and incarnates them in his person. He differed from a philosophic author, as the face of nature, in all her solid grandeur and beaming beauty, differs from a theory and system of physics, for he is the reality of which he discourses, the truth he illustrates, excellence alive. And, as life communicates itself throughout the vegetable and animal, so in the spiritual kingdom. It flows from the motion of his lips, from the touch of his hands, from the hem of his garment, from the record of his words and deeds, till the whole family of rational intelligences, with which he comes into connection, feels a renewing energy pouring through its ranks, age upon age, and can trace back its exhaustless current only to the life of God, the fountain of divine glories, infinite wisdom, rectitude and love.

Only looking up to what is thus above us, coming through him in measureless expression, endless descent, can we be enlivened. He who acts from his own centre, sees nothing above the height of his own thought, and never kneels, but assumes to be on a level with the Most High, can move with no warm and flowing inspiration, but must be cold and self-conscious, having and giving no spiritual life. He may be brilliant, original, and pure, but not wise or deep. He cannot go down the shaft of life's mystery to the bottom of the human heart, cannot reach the profoundest emotions of human nature, cannot stir the fountains of tears, or understand the mighty, pleading wants of the human soul, or of course weigh the worth of that religion by which they are met. As he cannot look up to God, and but names him as though he were a kinsman, he discerns not the relation of God to man, loses both the terms of all true knowledge, and, as the necessary result of his falsely taken premises, slights Christianity. As this real life of the soul is the one thing of most especial need to mankind, a need which can never cease through all the generations of the race, and as he, with unspeakable superiority to all others, imparts and sustains it, his shall indeed be a kingdom without end.

In fine, however, though the vitality of human nature must thus be touched and expanded from without and from above, this vitality is itself a real and individual principle within. Man has been said to grow like a peculiar class of trees, as the date and palm, from the centre and not from the surface. This does not prove him self-subsistent. For, as those trees require the same sunshine, air and rain that enliven every twig and leaf of the forest, — so man depends for his soul's life on the spiritual elements. Without them, he famishes and dies. With them, he maintains and enlarges not an accidental and perishable, but a distinct and lasting existence. Christ came not to intoxicate us with a momentary ecstasy of life in God, to be lost at death as the air from a breaking bubble in the general atmosphere, but rather to build up a firm and permanent character of life in every breast, which should soar unhurt from the wreck of the body, to thrive in new regions of nature, amid fresh manifestations of deity. If the theory of self-sufficiency is to be rejected on the one hand, the theory of pantheism, somehow strangely kindred to it, is no less to be rejected on the other. For, while annihilating man, it also robs God of his honor, the very honor it pretends alone to give. If the soul is not to grow with a real life and separate identity, but to be, at any time, merged and absorbed in Divinity, it of course can no longer love or worship the Divinity in which it is absorbed. The highest honor of God, beyond that of the reflection of his face in matter, is lost.

This philosophy therefore respects not God, but defrauds him. The more distinct his creatures are from him, the more they can enter into clear relations with him. So is it reverential to him, as much as it is cheering to our own hearts, to look up in faith's vision and see mighty natures, Michael and Gabriel, elders of heaven, and patriarchs from the earth, advancing through inconceivable degrees of knowledge and individual power, the greater they are, the nobler their offerings of service and ardent gratitude to him who has made them. So, too, a thrill of rapture runs through these mortal bosoms at the thought, that Christ's kingdom of life here is the threshold over which we may step into that upper state, of which the church below is but a suburb, and find that, so far from there being anything local in Christ's earthly time to attach to and sink him, his kingdom, past all time, goes on without end in eternity.

The respects, then, in which Christ rose above his own time and all human chronology, or the elements of durableness in his kingdom, I find in his bringing from God and heaven light for the mind, law for the conscience, love for the heart, and life for the soul. These are essential and sufficient conditions of a permanent spiritual reign ; — no more are requisite, no less would do ; — all of them Christ fulfils as no other historic character fulfils any one. But no such curious intellectual analysis is necessary to our becoming subjects of his kingdom and receivers of his influence. Neither can any subtle thought of ours solve his mystery, or bring the secrets of his sway into the circle of our definite comprehension. Enough that we can so far understand his claims as to see their supremacy, and yield ourselves to that yoke of his better than any other freedom. This self-surrender will, more than any reflection, teach us what we owe him, and when his hand shall have moulded our spirits, our highest tribute, in a flame of gratitude, will be paid.

METHOD OF CHRIST'S INFLUENCE.

Such being the object first proposed by Christ, and which, on grounds impregnable, has been for so many centuries maintained, let us now consider the mode of its accomplishment. He uses a three-fold instrumentality, the Bible, the Church, and the Spirit, a power from the past, in the present, and through the eternal. According as the writer to the Hebrews describes it, his influence is " the same yesterday, to-day and forever ;" of an invariable nature and force, in the age that is gone, that which is going, and through all ages. We hear our Lord's voice from afar, at our side, and out of the everlasting world. The voice from the past is a book, his biography ; that in the present is an institution, his Church ; that which embraces and exceeds

4

all times his Spirit. First is the Bible, disclosing the end and import of its sublime discourse of four thousand years, in the narration of Christ's life, of what he did and said, and of the commissioned acts and teachings of his Apostles. The necessary beginning of Christian faith and experience, the foundation of all we can truly think and feel for Jesus as our Master is evidently an authentic, trust-worthy statement of the fact of his earthly existence, as it stood in that old land of Judea. We must know what he wrought and spoke in Jerusalem, Galilee, and by the Jordan. We must see that sacred region of his divine descent and superhuman action rise, a clear, bright picture upon our mental vision, till, in imagination and soul, we are with him

> " ——— in those holy fields,
> Over whose acres walked those blessed feet,
> Which, eighteen hundred years ago, were nailed,
> For our advantage, on the bitter cross."

It is vain to talk about Christianity at all, or to be sensitive about giving or taking the name of Christian, unless we can believe that we have the substantial truth about Christ as an historical personage. No conclusions of faith or practice can be raised on a fiction, more than " a castle in the air," made of cloud and vapor, can stand to be occupied by us as a dwelling, or can hold our confidence and hopes. Therefore, thanks to those, who against ancient or modern scepticism, have shown us the firm ground of our religion by argument and testimony that no mind can reasonably resist.

Thanks to God rather, who made the facts themselves of the gospel too strong and vital to be buried or obscured; and gave to them an energy and importance by which they have propagated themselves through ages, and across the globe's longitudes and zones: though Christ himself made no record of aught that fell from his hands or lips, that which fell therefrom moving the tongues and pens of his disciples to a report whose letter has not faded, or its sound ceased, amid all the noises that have succeeded, or pages of voluminous literature that have intervened.

The biography of Christ is the basis of Christian faith. It is not, however, the essence of Christian character. A man may accept or assent to the facts as sufficiently demonstrated; he may entertain no infidel theory about the origin of the evangelical stories; he may admit both common event and miracle therein related, nor doubt that the dove descended, and the heavenly voice was uttered, that blindness saw, deafness heard, lameness walked, and that sickness, insanity, death fled away, and he whose holy escort through the world was these marvels of mercy, rose from the grave and reappeared to his disciples; a man may deny nothing of all this, yet not be essentially a Christian, because all may be but a mass of fact held in his understanding, from which he has not drawn the legitimate consequences to his disposition and life.

Yet the fact is the primary rock we must build on, the threshold we must pass over, the spring we must drink from, the premise of every conclusion. Indispensable is the attestation from the past, the book of our faith. How wondrous has been its working! As we look back through this glass of the human mind's memory to the distance of eighteen hundred years, what scenes from that border of Asia, where Jesus sojourned! From that one crowded year of his being, how all that is best in all these other years of the world's continuance, pour out! From that one city in Palestine, and from one life passed within or near its walls and breathed out on its Mount Calvary, what overflow of a tide to cleanse and sanctify the towns and populations of the earth! What peculiarity of influence, mixed and confounded with nothing else, extricating itself from all other combinations, and too potent to be destroyed, from that living fountain of the heart of Christ through the New Testament, into the bosom of hundreds of millions of men, and still as fresh and pure as ever for each breast, yours or mine, ready to receive it! The book, by God's grace ours, let us not give it up, or suffer it to be classed with other books of inferior quality, lower proof, of different import and from a different source; but hold it as having a divinity possessed by no Koran, by no oriental documents, which with their strange names decorate of late the fond speech of some, by no teachings of pagan sages, or proverbs of nations. Let us travel with the blessed Teacher, delighting to retrace the footsteps of his journey, finding the events ever new and marvellous, to disclose deeper meaning than at first we caught, till the sermon on the Mount, the talk with the woman of Samaria, the discourse with the sisters at the raising of Lazarus, the transfiguration, the feeding in the wilderness, and (but I should relate all, not knowing what to select,) yet till all, with the sweat of the garden and the tragedy of the cross and the glory of the resurrection, are printed as living tablets on our heart and brain, and the meaning and purport of all renewed in our love and our life.

But this first step, taken, leads to a second. Jesus Christ comes to us and moves us not only in this representation from an antiquity of many ages, but with a present power in his Church, through an institution as well as a book. His life is not like the life of Alexander or Hannibal, carrying us back simply to a remote period, where the events began and ended, and their whole significance was lost or undistinguishably mingled with the stream of affairs, and cannot now be recovered from the general composition of things, or any special, permanent weight in them be by any means noted; but in a way, of which no other earthly existence can afford the parallel, the life of Christ has continued, flourishing on and increasing to this day and hour, sinking in no sandy grave of oblivion, cut short by no fate of mortality, but surviving in countless hearts of believing and loving friends, who, ever since the stone was rolled from the sepulchre, have dated and derived their principles of thought, sentiment and conduct, from

4*

the crucified, the ascended One. He not only lived, but lives still, — lives not only in heaven, but more and more on earth — lives not in Judea only, but in England, in America, and the islands of the sea, — lives in all his Church, through all the communion with him of his followers; and whole nations, entire histories of Greece, Rome and Assyria, do not now at this moment let in such a current of life and power upon the human soul as comes from him, all single, all alone. Every temple reared at his first instigation and dedicated to his name, every Sunday that shines with the light first given to it by his rising, every voice of persuasion that preaches his word, amid the seats of civilization or in heathen countries and to savage tribes, every drop in baptism that touches the foreheads of children or flows over the forms of those consecrated to him and his Father, every affectionate and revering celebration of. the supper whose table he spread, every prayer offered in his name, every song of praise to God for his coming and consolation, makes a part of this present influence, shows that Christ is "to-day" as well as "yesterday."

Is this living and present Christ, any more than the past Christ of history, to be neglected? his sanctuaries to be deserted or entered idly, and occupied listlessly? his sabbaths to be wasted or devoted to the world? his ordinances to be despised and disused? or his devotions to grow slack and faint in our hymns and supplications? Lo, he not only

sailed over Gennesaret, or travelled through the
wilderness, but has gone further than is fancied of
the doomed wanderer that offended him, and is
here, as truly with us, if we open the door to him,
as we are with each other, communing with us in
the emblems we use, as really as we with him ;
(said he not, "Lo I am with you always, even to
end of the world ? ") the church that he founded
and purchased with his blood, still enlivened by
his Spirit. His Spirit, I say ; for Bible and Church
the first and second steps, must bring us to that,
the third, or they can neither of them be of saving
profit ; and his past and present must blend in that
eternal influence which is independent of and superior to fleeting time. The Bible and the Church
are indeed great necessary stages to reach the
" Spirit ; " they are organs by which the " Spirit "
speaks, channels through which the " Spirit " flows,
and, if you will, supporting hands to lift us up to
the " Spirit ; " but there is something in the " Spirit "
itself, of Christ, uncontained in words, unexpressed
by symbols, something measureless and everlasting.
It is round the believing soul as an atmosphere. It
overhangs our thought, it inspires our affection.
It is Christ's abode in us, Christ formed within, the
hope of glory. It is an incarnation or expression
through the flesh, through human life and nature,
of God's wisdom and goodness ; and therefore not
local or temporary. It is worn by no change of
circumstances, wasted by no lapse of years, works
upon us by divine right, makes a deeper demand

than human genius or any ordinary virtue of human character, being an influx of what is best in the universe for the assimilation of our souls.

We can reach no such position or height as properly to question the claim of this superhuman energy of the Spirit. As the thing made cannot find fault with its maker but by finding fault with itself, offering a suicidal quarrel through its own substance, so we cannot criticise or abate from the spotless and supreme excellence of Christ. It fills our highest thought of what is pure and good. It makes our ideal of all that is to be loved and followed. By a Christian birth and nurture, it is in us like the print of the Almighty's creating fingers, and is the best part of us. Even as the strength of these hands or the sight of these eyes involves and refers back to the mother's milk we in infancy drew, so whatever meekness, humility and self-sacrifice we can exhibit, we owe largely to Jesus Christ, to his word from the past, to his church in the present, to his eternal Spirit.

This three-fold method of Christ's salvation, the past, the present, the everlasting, begins to operate upon us without our will, but can be carried on and completed only by our voluntary seeking of Christ. As the sick of old took their station in the path along which he was to pass, so we must put ourselves in his way.

The Bible, as a mere book, will, for us, soon be closed ; the earthly church as an organization, will soon, for us, be dissolved ; and then the only question will be, whether, through these agencies, or by laying hold of the winged inspiration of God lifting us above them, we have come to apprehend and participate of that in Christ which transcends every process and all duration of time, which our dissolution in death shall not alter, nor the circling of Eternity reverse. Does our Saviour invisibly go with us, a holy companion? does he hover over us, a spiritual guide? does he descend upon us in the gentle flight of a dove? give the serpent's wisdom to our action and speech? and, " broad and general as the casing air," compass our walk?

Then is he Jesus Christ to us, truly so called,— the anointed, Jehovah's help, our healing Redeemer by a past, present, and eternal power; with his touch taking the pain from our wounded spirits, with the voice that once drove out demons expelling our evil passions, and with the breath of his devotion calling forth good affections in us, as, by a less important exertion of his power, he once raised the dead :— yesterday in our knowledge of him, to-day in our new sympathy with him, forever in our increasing experience the same. Our own heart's witness alone can verify the fact!

For, in fine, Christ's method of accomplishing his object is, through all the instrumentalities of his gospel, to regenerate the individual soul. This is the basis, centre, and end of all religion. The whole bible is hardly more than a conversation between God and the individual soul. The old Dispensation is a training of the conscience and will, and the New, moreover, of the affections of the individual mind. Jesus and his Apostles ever insist on the necessity of our being born again. Nor is this an irrational, arbitrary, or wholly mysterious injunction. The nature and need of regeneration are manifest. What is the too common fact with regard to human beings? We begin life and go on engaged in earthly things, fastening upon them our senses, pursuing them with our inclinations, transforming them into the means of our gratification, or promotion, making of all nature a ladder for self to mount upon. This is not all of human life and human nature, but it is a very strong and wide propensity and procedure. Selfishness is the grand, original, prolific sin of the human race. Every form of merely private, exclusive gain, pleasure, or aggrandisement is one of its steps. Moving slowly and winding cautiously, or striding hotly to its ends, —paving its way with falsehood and fraud, or wielding pride, anger, and revenge for its weapons, — boldly snatching its objects or cunningly secreting them,—appearing in its gross deformity, or covering itself with a decent and polished courtesy,—content with safe and petty indulgences, or rushing on to pollution and murder,—in every shape and motion selfishness is the first principle of human depravity, the progenitor of all wrong.

Now regeneration is the change of the selfish into the spiritual mind, by an unfolding, through the help of God, of devout and generous affections above all mean desires, and the substitution of heavenly objects for those of this world. God's being, goodness, and purity, with Christ's love, meekness, and self-sacrifice, regenerate the soul. The action of these divine realities is the holy Spirit. Meditation and prayer are the hands that open for it the door. All the institutions and ordinances of religion are instruments to invite its access. The truth of revelation is its voice, and the divine Providence, through every mode of human condition and chastening, its channel.

Nothing else in religion is to be proposed as the great end, nothing else will answer our Lord's demand, but this unfolding and consecration of the individual spirit. The most perfect, beautiful and orderly church-organization cannot stand in its stead. When this organization is offered as the saving power, it is displaced from its true office as a conductor of the soul to Christ and God, and made to choke and eclipse the spiritual energy which through it should shine and flow. We are not Christ's disciples and God's children simply by being members of any organization however sacred, but only as far as, in any ecclesiastic or other manner, we become conscious of and faithful to our relationship with God and Christ themselves. Moreover, this is the only way in which the church itself, in its unquestionable importance, can be truly constituted. It is not by merely putting certain individuals together under particular names and symbols to act and react on one another, that the church of God and Christ can arise in its reality and glory, but only when those, whom God and Christ have spiritually quickened, are united by the power of those affections which live and swell in each separate breast. Outward mechanical union makes not the church, without a bond of union ; and the spirit of God alone, descending as a dove into each solitary bosom, can weave this bond and carry its living thread across the gulfs that divide us, in its flight from heart to heart. If we have the same devotion towards that blessed Son and Father as a sincere principle in the very pulse of our individual feeling and will,—if any number of us, a hundred or a thousand, are exercised with the same holy, humble, and forgiving temper, then we shall indeed be together in the spiritual world, too close for the insertion of a dividing-line, a real Church, whose harmony can no more be broken than can that cohesion by which the ribs of the earth cleave together. The fountains of love sunk invisibly within, the streams of sympathy will flow into sight. Real Christians, meeting from abodes sundered by the earth's bulk, shall find themselves at one in their Master's company, as the Quaker, William Allen, and the Greek from Zante melted into fellowship at the sound in the Russian tongue of the word they could both understand, the name of God.

As one law marshals the myriad fine clouds in the sailing fleet of their lofty procession, as one instinct moves in a single line the ranks of emigrant birds athwart the sky, so will believing, loving souls, individually and inwardly alive to the glorious objects of faith and love Christ presents, form his inseparable Church, and the gates of hell shall not prevail against it. " Who touched me ? " asked Jesus when, in the pushing throng, he felt the finger of that modest woman on the hem of his garment. Those who touch him shall be one in him. More surely than kindred and countrymen know each other, by a better sign than those belonging to some secret body come into recognition, and with a holier tie than even that common nature which reveals man to his brother-man, shall they, whom the divine energy through the gospel has regenerated, be knit and built up, nay, grow into a living temple in the Lord. When the church abides and moves throughout with this internal strength, no portion will quarrel about a ritual, or ask of the law to itself a special privilege, or be anxious respecting the propriety of priestly ministration, any more than the invisible and everlasting church in heaven is troubled concerning the style of its observance or the formal qualifications of its members.

As no ecclesiastic formula, so, again, no nurture of the young can displace from the centre of Christianity this principle, the regeneration of the individual soul. Regeneration, with the children of Christian parents or the pupils of Christian teachers, does not indeed occur in the same sudden or flashing way as with the adult disciples who constituted the original church. Breathing an atmosphere of religious sentiment, early indoctrinated into evangelical principles, with the great example steadily

5

held up before them as the model of all excellence, they may almost imperceptibly verge towards a spiritual frame. But the gospel's design is not effected, till they are brought to that state, in which their own free and individual mind shall inwardly and independently move. Having led them to the sun, even we must stand out of their sun-light, nor interpose between them and God. We must put prayers upon their childish lips, but only that we may bring prayers out of their voluntary hearts, as a little water is thrown upon the valves to fetch water from the living well inexhaustible below. Our aim continually in religious education, should be, not to fill the mind with dogmas and moral rules, but to rouse it to a consciousness of its own relations to God and Christ, that it may love, serve, follow, and be like them. Oh, there is nothing in this world more beautiful than a youthful person, a son, a daughter, coming to recognize that filial relation which, beyond human parentage, links the spirit in that slender stature, to an everlasting Father. There is nothing so sublime in nature as that first dawning sense of obligation to keep the law, to do and bear the will of the Eternal One, which makes a child brother to the cherub, or sister to the seraph. Its acceptance and discharge is regeneration. This new birth universally of the rising race, will of course be the salvation of the world.

There is, again, no virtue in what we call the public mind, which can suffice for our help, without this individual regeneration. We talk much of public sentiment and public opinion, as an irresistible power, proceeding to all beneficent achievements. Yet what is public sentiment and public opinion, but a current formed from the contributions of private conviction and feeling, fed from ten thousand secret springs, while the tributary rills come not only from sources pure and sweet, but from those too that are foul and bitter. The sanctifying regeneration of the gospel must reach every separate fountain, before the strength and action of the public mind can be to us a trust and joy only, and not a care and terror; else there cannot be a public mind strongly and consistently acting to any proposed end, any more than there can be an electric battery, without first the fit construction of each separate jar.

Lastly, social reform can arise from nothing but individual regeneration, personal consecration to God and human good under the constraining motives of Christ's religion. Stormy indignation, and driving passion, cannot change society or better the state. It will be but as the violence of a summer-shower soon dry, or the noise of a sudden torrent, compared with that silent accumulation drop by drop, of individual moral power, which sweeps abuses away. There is a grandeur in that energy against wrong institutions and evil customs, which comes from no party-league, or temper of private rage, but from God's own persuasion, through his truth and Spirit, of the individual soul. There is a majesty in saying, for instance, in regard to such a thing as slavery,— Lo, it is not in a political band, or from a mere social sympathy, or at all by a selfish or sectional pride and jealousy, but by a moral necessity, that we oppose this wrong. Lo, the sword of the Lord pushes us into these straits where we strive against it. Wo is unto us if we witness not, in its contradiction, at his word of command.

Thus our individual being, and our nature shared with others, our separate Christian life and the life of the Church, our private motives, and the joint convictions which meliorate the condition of the community and the world, will not clash with or abridge, but only strengthen each other. The more sincere and conscientious we are, the more with all that are sincere and conscientious shall we be united, not by weak concession or politic compromise and mechanical or partisan conformity, but by likeness of mind. The flow of all gracious sympathies will be proportioned to the depth and beating of every heart, and the vigor of coöperation be determined by the strength and activity of each independent hand. As the mightiest earthly structures have been reared by myriads of individual toilers, so will countless solitary hearts swarm to raise the temple of the Most High. The more, not of conceited individualism, but of true Christian individuality there is, the more will there be of harmony, as the notes of a musical instrument accord by reason, not of nearness, but of fit distance and distinct, decided, melodious quality. Such is already the process and commencing triumph of our religion. As it goes on, roots of bitterness, the growth of ages, will more and more decay, the habits of the race itself be changed, social evils vanish, common goods be established and multiplied, the garden of the Lord reappear with no narrow Oriental bounds, and the fruit of the Spirit be in all his tabernacle with his children. Freedom and love, inclination and will, fellowship and duty, the Protestant and the Catholic, man with man, and mankind with God, shall be one. Placed in the light, put under the law, set before the love and life of Christ, — with the regenerating divine Word, Church, and Spirit all open,— let us consider what we, every one individually, owe to so sublime and universal a work.

5*

DISCOURSE I.

BUSINESS AND RELIGION.

Rom. xii. 11. — NOT SLOTHFUL IN BUSINESS, FERVENT IN SPIRIT, SERVING THE LORD.

Is there not something extraordinary in this injunction of diligence in business and devotion to religion, in the same breath? Is there not a common and a growing tendency to separate these things; to put religion by itself, and business by itself? But is not this disunion sadly making enemies or rivals of what should be friends; substituting, for the mutual blessings, religion and business ought naturally to confer on one another, only mutual injuries? For religion, when divorced from business, becomes a subtle theory, a mystical reverie, or a pompous show: it loses the weight proper to a law of life and a motive to righteousness, and is rarified, as it is raised above the earth, into a thin atmosphere, which few spirits even try to breathe. Business, on the other hand, divorced from religion, becomes a mere selfish and ungodly scramble, every man for his own gain and advantage, heedless over whom he treads, or whom he pushes behind. It becomes falsehood and fraud, low manœuvre and winding intrigue; and turns the exchange into a gambling-house, just so far as it forgets its obligations to the Most High, and its responsibleness to eternity.

Is there a business-man, of whatever religious repute in his sectarian or theological circle, with his name standing however high on the roll of believers or saints, who yet regards his religion like his Sunday garment, as a thing to be left out of his shop or counting-room, lest it be soiled there in the rough hands of the world? There will be a littleness and disingenuousness in that man's secular proceedings, exposing him, if not, alas! the religion he professes, to contempt.

Religion is not so dainty about herself as this subscriber of her creeds, and observer of her forms, is about her. *She* is ready to go, with the whole power and splendor of her celestial presence, into the commonest scenes, for the adjustment of the humblest matters. This separation of religion and business is no fiction, or supposed case for the sake of argument and moving appeal. I have known one in the very heat of religious enthusiasm, and with the most sacred names upon his lips, defraud a poor woman in the performance of a stipulated service, without seeming to imagine there was any inconsistency.

"I am told," said one friend to another, during the stress of a strong religious excitement, "that you have become a convert." His respondent eagerly acknowledged the fact. "Glad I am to learn the certainty of this," was the rejoinder.

" Suppose, then, we place Jesus Christ between us here, and make a settlement now of our small accounts." " Oh ! business is business, and religion is religion ! " Does not this little circumstance, whose recital may occasion a smile, speak volumes of the gravest meaning that the pulpit, in its most solemn moods, can utter ? The earnest convert was under a mistake, however honest. Jesus Christ would not have disdained to sit between them, and there expound to them the precepts of justice and brotherly kindness. No : he who " sat thus on the well," and talked with the woman of Samaria, — he who let fall some of his sublimest teachings in a fishing boat or by the way-side, would — how willingly ! — have seated himself by their desk, or leaned over their counter, and, when he saw truth and equity prevail between them, would have rejoiced in spirit over the fulfilment of the mission on which he came from heaven to earth.

We make a great mistake, brethren, in this matter, if we imagine that our Saviour wishes we should install him or his religion in a high and solemn place to render formal tributes of respect, such as are rendered to earthly princes and mighty men, on set days, for famous achievements. He asks not ovations and triumphs at our hands, like those which ancient nations gave to successful heroes. Oh ! no : the most humble and quiet daily service under his holy laws, in the ordinary transactions of life, he will accept as of more worth than great processions under his banner, than splendid architectural displays in his temples, or than imposing celebrations of manifold rites to his honor.

I entreat you to come to an understanding of this matter of the extent of religion's claims over you. Is it to give her a seventh day and a sanctuary, and certain specified ordinances ; while the rest of time and space and conduct runs into the domain of business, and is to be governed by the laws of business, — by a morality of the world's own contriving, which the preacher goes out of his place when he undertakes to criticise ? Is it even so, my brethren ? Is religion to be regarded as a thing of state and ceremony, drawn out periodically from the sequestration which, like the pompous retirement of an Oriental monarch, she for the most part maintains, and led forth in sincere solemn pageant for a few restricted hours of sentimental regard, and then sent back again into a vacancy like the six days' emptiness of this pulpit and these pews ; leaving the main current of human energies through the live-long week, the busy conflict of human wills as they struggle and writhe together, and the hive-like murmur of earthly actions that rises up from the ground for ever into the ear of the Almighty, untouched and unregulated ?

Undoubtedly, these special excitements of religious feeling, these appointed offerings of praise, we must have ; or the heated crowd of men would grow savage in selfishness, and rabid with every

evil passion.   But the reason of these regular exer-
ises is, not that we are thus to make and finish a
certain sacrifice, pay an exactly calculated tribute
to God beyond which he has no claim, but rather
to obtain strength and encouragement, from the
contemplation of eternal truth, for a divinely beautiful performance of every great and every small
action, with unswerving fidelity to our Witness and
Judge.   I grieve to confess, that it is in part the
religionist's own fault that religion and business
have been so injuriously dissociated ; time and
eternity, the higher world and this lower world,
having been too often by him arrayed against each
other as of course deadly antagonists, either gaining
any advantage only at the expense of the other ;
whereas, in fact, this passing world, in the busiest
pressure of its affairs and in the endlessness of its
wearisome details, is, and is ordained of God to be,
the best possible discipline and preparation for all
the glory and blessedness that shall be revealed.
It is ordained, beyond these immediate objects of
accumulation and earthly pleasure, by its education
of the intellectual and moral faculties, to send a
power and a joy into ages and regions far away
from these toil-trodden fields of mortality.

No matter how much outward respect is gained
for religion, — no matter now many festival-days
are rescued for her out of the calendar, — no matter
how magnified and majestic her rites may be made,
it is a radically wrong principle to separate her province from the province of business ; and the world

never can be Christianized, so long as this separation is speculatively and practically made. You may enlarge the peculiar sphere of religion as much as you please ; you may greatly multiply religious meetings, and thrust the public assembly, as we sometimes see it, into the morning and evening of every day ; you may place a religious sentinel, as it were, at every turn of the labyrinthine circles of sale and bargain into which men plunge ; you may break in upon men's thoughts, as often as you choose, with the summons to some set function of piety, the call to some appointed season of worship, — it will not all suffice to establish the sway of the gospel, until men's minds are made as religious in their business, in the intellectual operations and moral purposes involved in the simplest transactions in which they are engaged, — just as really religious and faithful to God in these as they are in the decent and orderly exercises of the sanctuary. And till you are as devout in " things earthly " as you are in " things heavenly," — on the common floor of the world as in the aisles of the consecrated temple, — formality, mockery, and hypocrisy will continue to seat themselves in the house of God and at the table of the Lord ; for what are formality and mockery and hypocrisy but the exact measure of the interval between a man's profession and his practice ? Until business, the serious avocations of men and women, their merchandise, their profession in life, their working for a livelihood, their household cares, — until these are Christianized, the great

river of their meditations and desires will run into
sin and selfishness; and all the specialties of religion, however solidly established and however
sacredly observed, will be but little obstacles thrown
into the bed of the mighty stream, over which for
ever it tumbles and foams.

The very nature of religion proves the justness of
this position. What *is* religion? Not merely a
round of acknowledgments that we sustain relations
to the Maker of all; not mere confessing of his greatness and goodness, that he is "the greatest and wisest
and best of beings;" not mere saying over prayers
and praises, in attestation of our sincerity, from our
books or our memories: but, as our text expresses it,
it is " serving the Lord," obeying his laws in every
purpose, effort, deed, and word. And is religion, so
understood, a matter that can be confined to the Sab-
bath; insulated in the church; contained, like precious cordials, in curious vessels,—in forms, however
fit and graceful? No: it must overflow all boundaries and reservoirs, and reach into the most private
recesses, — into the most public displays of human
conduct and intent. It is like the all-pervading
element of electricity, — a very little of it may be
insulated to good purpose, to increase our knowledge of its properties, and to subserve special
important ends; it may be enclosed in a vial, and
show its potent nature as it sparkles beautifully and
darts noisily from point to point, indicating its real
affinities; it may shoot a momentary shock through
our nerves, felt one moment, and gone the next;

it may write, in letters of fire, the news of an event many miles from the spot where it occurred: but the great fountain whence this brilliance is drawn spreads and circulates through all nature, and preserves the equilibrium of the globe. And so religion must not only refresh our frame with her special infusions of high truth and motive, as we lay aside our burdens at the week's end; she must not only on occasion do beautiful and striking things with her ritual, and her doctrine, and her eloquence; but the love of God and the fear to offend him, a conscience tender as the apple of an eye to all his precepts, and a flame of grateful, hourly rising devotion for his continued mercy, must extend to and compass about all our experience, keeping the holy poise of our souls within us undisturbed amid the strongest temptations and seductions of life. Or, else, our loudest devotions here at the altar are insignificant breath in the ear of the Most High; our songs are but an indolent whiling away of our time, with recumbent hearts in these seats; and our most serious ordinances but a poor semblance, with no solid reality; at best like the shadows cast from clouds that sail of a summer-day above us, almost as empty nothings as the shadows themselves.

What religious virtue can be named that should not be carried into business in the most direct and immediate manner? Shall we speak of that first cardinal excellence, — truth? Is not its presence needed in the market-place?—oh! where is it needed more? And is any exception to be made, in any

case, to its obligation? Is a false oath ever to be
taken? Does it in the least alter its nature, by being
sworn in a business-transaction, whether it be sworn
to a private man, or to the officers that represent the
nation? Tell me how much it differs from the lie
that was told by Ananias and Sapphira, when asked
whether they had sold the land for so much; and
make out the case how they lied to God and the
Holy Ghost, and the ordinary business-deceiver has
lied only to man! Let us understand the morality
by which false descriptions of goods and estates,
deliberate concealment of defects, studious vaunting
of unreal excellencies; or the saying by the buyer,
"It is naught; it is naught; but, when he is gone
his way, then he boasteth;"—let us understand the
morality by which these things are made to differ
from falsehood to a friend, or from deceit in a family.
I fear God reckons them upon one scale; and that he
does not keep, however man may, different sets of
balances to weigh things of the same quality.

Justice is another trait altogether religious, partaking of religion's essence. Is this a thing merely
to muse over in ideal contemplation, to adorn with
mock honors in our fancy's ingenious decorations,
and to hear sublime praises of in solemn courts, and
then to think its obligation fulfilled? Or is the
very place where alone this religion can be fully
practised, and surely tested, that of the serious avocations, the business of life? And if a man makes,
or is suffered by his church to make, any signing of
a creed, any minding of a form, any absoluteness

of humility in confessions of faith and submissions
to Christ, or any extent of partisan-services, to be a
substitute for this solid, living virtue ; if any man is
suffered to have the swing of his worldly practices
and desires, and, so long as he commits nothing
scandalous and abominable, have no inquisition made
into the habit of petty injustices, — then, I say, *that*
whole idea of religion is false and worthless, technical and unreal.   And the justice you are bound to
carry into business is not simply legal justice, what
you can be compelled to do to keep out of the fangs
of the criminal code, but moral and Christian justice.
The justice many do unchallenged is not like the
justice of God.   But your equity, religious business-
man, is to emulate his !

Once more : is not mercy, that lovely attribute of
religion, entitled to any entrance into the walks of
business ?   Have you all admitted the proverb to
be a sound and true one, that "there is no friendship in trade," — no legitimate exercise of a noble
and generous disposition, no fit room for the love
of man ?   It is a scene, I admit, for the exercise
of sagacity, for the reward of ability, for the accumulations of a strong and diligent and skilful hand.
I would never sound the trumpet for a fanatical cru-
sade against the very nature and directly proposed
objects of commerce, which I believe God himself
ordained.   But are there not many cases where a
true-minded, Christian man will show that holy
grace, whose "quality is not strained, which drop-
peth like the gentle rain from heaven upon the place
beneath."

A man in the humbler sphere of life came to a
wealthy leader, and said to him beseechingly,—
" Will you delay, for a day or two, the lifting of this
incumbrance from my land ? If the contract is urged
to the letter, I am a ruined man ; but very soon I
have the certainty of freeing myself. Will you delay
for a day or two ?"— " *Not for a day :* if the matter be not settled before another sun, it goes without remedy into the operation of the law." But, in
smaller things, — though I desire no man to be
cheated or to lose his wits in making a bargain, —
when I have seen an opulent person beating some
poor vender of herbs or vegetables down to the lowest point at which he or she would choose to sell,
rather than carry them back, the picture has not
been ludicrous, but altogether serious to my mind,
and I have felt an inexpressible disgust at the meanness, the want of all magnanimity and grandeur of
soul, that could exist in one moving in polished circles, showing many amiable dispositions, and capable perhaps of making, the next hour, a rich present
to a relation or friend, though he had no feeling for
a fellow-man !

I might even show, that there is no better place
for the exercise of piety, the ground of all religion,
than the busiest street in town through which you
walk. I can conceive of a prayer or a thanksgiving
rising as clear and as fervent from the path heaped
and clogged with rich imports from every clime
under heaven, as from the swept and garnished aisles
of the sanctuary. For who has arranged this won-

6*

derful process, for a universal exchange of the products of every season and soil; for the easy communication, every month almost, of ten thousand harbors; for the commanding, at any one civilized point on the earth's surface, of what every other point all over it can offer for comfort, convenience, and luxury; till a piece of ice from the frozen ponds of New England can be given for the delicious spice of the tropics? Who has arranged it to bring every fruit and herb and grain and root, and manufacture and medicine, within the reach of a single one of his weak, mortal children; piling the riches of all nature, through this medium of commerce, on a single table in a single house?

And shall the ministers, the priests, in this divine service, carrying out the great Creator's bountiful designs, transmitting the rich provisions of which they enjoy the best part themselves, — shall they be prayerless men, thoughtless of the rock from which they, with all their means and instrumentalities, are hewn? Shall they do anything inconsistent with prayer? Shall they say, "It is my ship, and my capital, and my own right arm that has done this, and not Almighty God"? Shall they not carry piety, a perpetual respect to the laws and attributes of the Almighty, to his truth, his justice, his mercy, into all their words and dealings? If they do not, how much of fancy or ingenuity will you say there is in intimating that they, too, sin against God and against the Holy Ghost?

Is anything lacking to make out the apostle's case

of carrying religion into business? And yet there is unquestionably, in the minds of some business-men, a lurking scepticism in this matter. Nay, it has been expressed repeatedly to ministers of the gospel, that Christian principles cannot *strictly* be applied to all the affairs of business, and that he who should attempt to apply them must fail. Business may be done on a wrong system; but, to do anything in it, one must stand upon the platform upon which it has universally settled down. A man must compromise somewhat the rigor of religious principles, or starve. I pronounce this plea calumnious. There are men, I am sure, who have succeeded, not at this expense of their principles. There are men now succeeding, *religiously* too! How nobly their foreheads, pale with toil, shine out from the dust and sweat of the shop or the office, on the crowded and noisy highway of life; more nobly, to my eye, than the fronts of brave warriors, through the smoke and din of the battle-field; for they are doing their duty to their God in the exposed and dangerous places of the great field of humanity.

"Honor to whom honor" is due! But, if it be true, as I will not say it never may be, that a man must cheat or starve, why, the case is a plain one, — the religious man will starve. A few authentic martyrdoms in the cause of honesty, if the world's custom will drive us to that, would do as much good, I verily believe, as ever the same number of martyrdoms in the cause of religion. Nay, in the cause of religion, I maintain they would be. A Polycarp,

a Latimer, a Servetus, burning bound at the stake,
because they would not recant their fidelity to God
and to Jesus, is clothed with no more honor, and
accomplishes, for aught I can see, no more good in
sensibly raising and purifying the world we live in,
than that man now, in whatever place or circumstances, of whom it could truly be said, " He perished, because he would not deceive. He embraced
poverty, because he would not commit fraud. He be-
queathed want to his children, because he would not,
even though he could without the least peril to his
good name, leave them gold stained with a secret rust
and canker." I know of no great expounder of moral
principle, I know of no eloquent teacher of divine
truth, who is more useful in God's world than a business-man that carries his religion into his business.

I ask your patience only to give in addition an
emblem, covering the whole ground of my subject.
As, now some years since, I walked the streets of
the most famous commercial city of this continent,
I found that I had insensibly approached into the
avenue on which the greatest operations of business
transpire. I admired the massive pillared structures,
thickly closing in together on either side, that
seemed built to endure with the world. I saw the
clustering gilded signs of every mode and shape of
negotiation, bond and mortgage, property and life
insurance, lending and borrowing ; the Briareus of
credit stretching his hundred arms into foreign
towns; the barterer of money offering every species
of value, anywhere current, at sale ; and the great

net of business, with all its golden links, spread out
and shining as I had never marked it before. I
noted the faces of the passers-by, and observed
what clear and sharp outlines these active pursuits
had given to every feature. There was pleasure
with anxiety, a sunbeam or a shadow, the gleam of
prosperity and the cloud of adversity chasing each
other along, or mingled together in the conversing
group. The white sails of ships that had arrived
from distant ports, or were hoisting canvas for
Europe or the Indies, opened and furled before my
eyes, at the foot of this magnificent passage.

Here, thought I, is the concentration of the powers
of this world; here the visible and mighty throne of
Mammon; here, all by itself, and too much given
up to itself, the spirit of gain, the love of riches, the
devotion of the human body and the human soul to
one earthly end. As I lifted my eye from the maze
of granite walls and marble columns, and hurrying
troops of men, I beheld at the head of the street a
broad and bold tower piercing the sky, on whose
then unfinished shaft recent blocks of stone had
been laid; and in *that* I saw the most costly and
splendid church of this country,—arches and Gothic
pinnacles, and curious alcoves, and carved ornaments,—as though the spirit of reverence, as though
the fear of God, the very genius of prayer, had built
a monument to swell above the wide roofs below,
to preside over every transaction on the worn pave-
ments beneath, and to gaze with searching aspect
into every face that appeared there, and the heart

under that face.   Such again, I thought, is the true
relation of religion with business, — to rise above
and command it, and be ever present before it, in
full, majestic sight.   Oh, my friends, that this could
be for us and for all a true emblem of the actual
connection of religion with business !   Then business would have a higher office than to provide for
this passing world.   It would educate us even for
heaven.   In our Saviour's own sublime language,
we should " make to ourselves friends of the Mammon of unrighteousness ; " so that when we failed,
as we must all and for ever fail on earth, " they
would receive us into everlasting habitations."

DISCOURSE II.

WORKING OUT OUR OWN SALVATION.

Phil. ii. 12, 13. — WORK OUT YOUR OWN SALVATION WITH FEAR AND
TREMBLING; FOR IT IS GOD WHICH WORKETH IN YOU TO WILL AND
TO DO OF HIS GOOD PLEASURE.

GOD is the author of salvation, and Christ is the way
of salvation ; but salvation never can be ours, unless
we work it out.   It is not a thing to be seized in
some happy moment, to be reached by a spasm of
exertion or a thrill of compunction.   It is not an
unconditional gift, or a mere mysterious influence,
or an instantaneous transformation, but a work.   But
it is very important that we take no narrow idea of
what this working is.   Some Scripture-passages, as
you know, contrast works with faith, declaring their
worthlessness without it ; but by works, in this connection, is commonly meant the ceremonies of the
Jewish law or the decencies of morality,   How can
these avail with God, without the living principle
of sincerity.

Again, other Scripture-passages set forth the worthlessness of faith unattended by works.   " The devils
believe, and tremble." — " Show me thy faith without thy works, and I will show thee my faith by my

works." But there is no contradiction. Here the
word is used in a higher sense, meaning the substantial deeds of justice and humanity, which must be
added to the forms of piety, to prove the reality of
the religious principle.

But *working*, even in this sense, does not seem to
answer the precise intention of the text. There is a
higher working than in outward observance, or even
visible conduct. It is a working which includes and
enlivens both, — unites both with the heart's faith ;
making religion neither mere formality, nor mere
morality, nor mere spirituality ; but binding spirit,
morals, and forms in one living whole. And it is
this sincere working of the soul, in which all its powers of thought are involved, to which all its energies
of will are devoted, — this inward, all-embracing,
ever-acting, and unconquerable resolution, that Paul
enjoins. But men have preferred any other method
of salvation to this divinely commanded one. They
have greatly preferred, for instance, to wait for a
miraculous renewal. In the fable, one hindered by
the way implores help of Hercules ; but the answer
is, that he must first try to help himself. And so, as
I read, does the true God teach us in that book which
is no fable, but the rule of our destiny.

Do we, then, make void the influence of the Holy
Spirit in man's conversion ? By no means. The
presence of this Spirit in the soul, offering salvation,
is set forth by the apostle as the very reason why
we should work our own salvation out : " *For* it is
God that worketh in you to will and to do of his

good pleasure." Far be it from me to disparage the work of grace within us! There is no prizing its help, its necessity, and its mercy ; for

> —— " Oars alone can ne'er prevail
> To reach the distant coast;
> The breath of heaven must swell the sail,
> Or all the toil is lost."

But the gale alone will not bear the ship to her destined port, without the mariner's toil ; so neither will the wind of the Spirit land us in the blessed haven above, unless we keep our own souls in its current. And, if I may carry the comparison still further, I believe the Spirit of God is as impartial as the breezes of the sky. It is no respecter of persons. There is no favoritism in the court of Heaven. The divine Spirit pleads with us all, and yet assures us, alike in the Bible and the soul, that we may resist it, quench it, or grieve it away.

As the sun and rain visit all nature, but it is only where the hand of cultivation has been that the precious grain is reaped, and yet all the labor in the world could not reap a kernel without the sun and rain ; so the divine Spirit folds all minds, but the growth is poor without inward industry, though all human struggles could bring forth not one germ of virtue without that Spirit. Is not Paul right, then, in making the influences of the Spirit the reason for human exertion, instead of a substitute for it, or an excuse for its slackness ?

We gain a further illustration from the operations of human genius and art. There are thoughts and

7

images flashing across the mind in its highest moods, to which we give the name of inspiration. But whom do we honor with this title of the inspired poet? Him who merely has these abstract momentary imaginations? No : we call him but a dreamer. It is only the man who can put his dream into shape ; who can bring forth these ghosts of the fancy finely embodied ; who can work out his sublimest thoughts in language, as in adamant.

So, in the business or arts of life, there are men forever forming magnificent plans of adventure or discovery, and prophesying wonderful improvements in human condition. But, if they never show any results worthy of their conceptions, they pass only for visionaries.

Even such dreamers and visionaries, perhaps the majority of the race are in regard to religion. For it is not to be doubted, that all men have moral ideas ever in the ascendant of their actual lives. They have, all above their own will or merit, spiritual promptings, conscientious monitions, impulses to purity, motives to humility, desires of fidelity, melting moods of forgiveness, and strong embraces of kindness ; the law of the mind soaring over the law of the members, the spirit shaming the excesses of the flesh, and, in short, a perpetual intimation as from a higher nature, " Thou art capable of something purer, nobler, infinitely better, than thou hast become." And what are these but the Spirit that must not be quenched, — the Divinity that should not be resisted ? Theologians dispute whether we can distinguish the influences of the Holy Spirit within us. But these things we can distinguish, and we know they are the glory of our being. We praise them in others ; we are excited, as by nothing else, by their more conspicuous displays. But are these things in themselves our salvation ? Nay, what are they but our condemnation and shame, if we allow them merely to glimmer, as heat-lightning, on the borders of the soul ; never incorporated into our principles, never wrought out in our lives ?

In fact, when we come from these lofty counsels of the breast to our practice, how often does some strange jugglery cheat us of what we thought was in our very hand, leaving but a spurious substitute of baseness and sin ! Alas ! self-interest, sensuality, passion, is the only magic needful to transform us out of our angelic nature into low self-indulgence and fraud. Our best purposes thus become like the busy sparks of the furnace, that for ever rise and crackle, but die, as they shine, in the cold air ; or like the meteor I saw the other night, blazing as a star of the first magnitude under the moon, but floating away into nothingness before I could determine its shape.

Is there any exhortation, then, so important as that in the text, "Work out your own salvation"? Arrest these flickering sparks, and nurse them into flames of generosity. Fix these flitting meteors of the mind, as guiding stars, in your soul's firmament. The question of every man's actual salvation lies just here, in his slighting or living up to these higher suggestions. As God's word is true, his working in us, though essential to our salvation, will not save, unless we work out what he works within.

Again, as salvation is a work which Scripture declares God will not do for us, so neither can man do it for us. Time has been when, like a muttered charm, the words of others, the mere salutations and benedictions of godly men, were thought to have a saving power; or when the administering of some sacred rite has been deemed the essence of salvation. Kings have requested to receive holy unction in dying moments, as though that could cleanse away crimes of ambition and adultery; and the priest himself has thought he might rescue a soul from endless despair, by arriving in time for a baptism.

Even now, that these gross ideas are with us for the most part done away, there are many who seem to think their salvation can be wrought out for them by others' preaching and visiting and pious conversation. They are ready to accept the most unworthy riddance of their own responsibility. They are willing to subscribe a creed at others' dictation; willing to undergo an experience by others' prescription; willing to adopt a covenant of others' construction. For all this, how easy to do, compared with working out their own salvation! Not that I would undervalue the means of religion, any more than the influences of the Spirit. Teaching and sympathy and sacred ordinances are important; but it is indispensable that we add to them our own exertion. For again speaks the holy word, "Let every man prove his own work; for every man shall bear his own burden." You cannot be transported into heaven : you must travel thither.

> " Must I be carried to the skies
>   On flowery beds of ease,
> While others fought to win the prize,
>   And sailed through bloody seas?"

In regard to foreign influence, the noblest that one man can exert on another is, not to impress his own image, but to stir up this personal energy. The best charity is confessedly that which enables the needy to help themselves. And thus to waken another's soul to self-help is a higher power, a grander ambition, than Cæsar's. Every one that does it is the true minister of Christ.

Our whole constitution is framed on this idea of our own working to be saved. God has dealt with us in the inner world of our souls, as in the outer world of nature. He has not made creation a garden of ever-produced and undecaying fruitage, but rough with the precipice and the torrent. He has written the solid granite and rude forest all over with the same sentence that is recorded in the Bible, — "In the sweat of thy face shalt thou eat bread."

So a like decree, stamped in the constitution of the soul, commands us to earn our spiritual food by our own labor. We are made, not holy, but to become holy. Various tendencies to good and evil struggle together in the human breast. *There* is a wilderness to be subdued and made fruitful, tempests of passion to be calmed, luxuriance of sensuality to be lopped. Only of those striving to do this

7*

does the prophet declare, " Their souls shall be as a watered garden." Here, I suppose, lies the truth in the dispute about native depravity, — not that the All-holy has given us a constitution that is depraved, but one by which we are tempted to depravity ; for thus only could our spiritual power be brought forth, and our highest glory consummated. He is great who has overcome evils and foes. God would have us to be great, and has therefore given us evils and foes to overcome.

Is not man a nobler being for having had the material world given to him ragged with mountain and ravine, foaming with gulfs and seas ; instead of a smooth table-land, sunny and rich in sensual delight, with mines of treasure on the surface, needing no subterranean search ? Is not man honored by the stirring precept in Genesis to "subdue the earth and have dominion over it "? And may he not be a nobler being also for the inward roughness of his own nature, for the very wildness of his passions, for the very hardness of that soil where his virtues are sown ? Oh ! yes : here is another region for labor more severe, and dominion more extensive. Here is the other world Alexander might have conquered, and spared his tears that there was no other to conquer. Here are chances for glory beyond all the dreams of ambition ; for " he that ruleth his spirit is better than he that taketh a city."

By no brief and intermitted exertion is this triumph to be achieved. As well, on the material globe, could the path of the railroad be run through rocks and hills in a freak of convulsive effort, as the soul's salvation be wrought out by a sudden start of the will, or one agony of remorse.

Once more: — I have said we cannot rely on other men or on the Holy Spirit to do *our* work in the business of salvation. So neither is it safe to rely on any natural goodness of our own disposition, which seems granted to some more than to others. This fine temperament of soul, like a good constitution of body, is easily ruined; while a poor constitution, taken in time, has been nursed into strength. In the soul, as in the body, exercise is the stern condition of health. A like analogy is seen in the richness of nature. The emigrant to the West, in that unbounded fertility where no hand of care has been, finds but coarse growth and poisonous decay in spots that might produce every luxury to the taste. So have I seen, in the moral world, faces cast in the mould of all honor and virtue, inlaid with the lines of beauty and capability, — brows on which they who judge of mind by outward marks would have staked their credit: yet indolence sat there as an incubus; power there ran to waste and to evil; and deformity there, slow but sure, stole through the frame and features; till in things spiritual, as sometimes in things material, the best became the worst by corruption.

"Work out your own salvation" is a law, then, from which there can be no exemption. Though the Holy Spirit inspire us, and human sympathy help us, and our own disposition prepare us for sal-

vation, salvation never can be ours, unless we
"work it out."

In spiritual as in worldly prosperity, men differ
mainly, I suspect, through the different degrees of
their industry.   It is related of the great Benjamin
Franklin, that he recorded his faults on a scale, and
set about their cure, as a matter of business, one by
one.   And, my friends, I have no great hope that
we shall any of us advance much, till we make
religion a matter of business.   I apprehend we are
not dealing in this matter, as some appear to fancy,
with a capricious Being, who comes and goes ; is
now ready, and again not ready ; — a Being who
lays down solemn laws, and then, in their despite,
holds a new miracle to correct each case of human
folly ; — but with a Being whose outstretched arms
wait for every prodigal, yet who strictly requires
that the prodigal himself should arise, and come to
his Father.

I know nothing of more mysterious and vast sublimity than the relation God fixes between himself
and man ; treating with him on terms as with an
equal, empowering him even to resist himself, but
inviting him to be a follower of himself as a dear
child ; even as a human parent says to his child,
on his assuming his own responsibilities, " I have
done for you all things in love, and still shall do.
But you are free: only by your own choice can you
become great and good.   The world is before you.
Go, work out your destiny."   So speaks God to us
all, and, sublimely veiling his Almightiness, retires

from overpowering our freedom; but still bends his unseen eyes upon our doings, and offers his invisible Spirit to our aid. And yet, though some of his children do what is well-pleasing in his sight, — of others, as the prophet declares, the Divine no less than the human parent must say, " I have nourished and brought up children, and they have rebelled against me."

So let us not do, my friends. Let us do the work of salvation which God has appointed, and in which God helps. It may be hard at first; but it is not so hard as the woe from which it saves us. And is there not a thrilling joy in casting off the prejudices we see so many allowing to hang upon them year after year, and subduing the passions which in so many are ever on the point of conflagration; with a still more uplifting satisfaction in fixing the rock of principle where prejudice was removed, and kindling divine affections where human passions have been quenched? As the work proceeds, we grow unconscious of its difficulties, and more glad in its success. The soldier feels the weight as he puts on his armor, but not in the thicket of the battle.

Then, too, character is no dead capital: it bears interest. Like the pound in the parable, it gains ten pounds. As it multiplies more, like an immense property, it makes incalculable increase. And the end is salvation; not mere deliverance from an outward hell, a rescue from officers of justice, but a redeeming of the soul itself, the abolition of all slavery there, the cure of all intemperance there, the ceasing of all war there; while deep peace and soberness and freedom flow through every channel of the mind, keeping it in calm strength and silent joy; "strong, without rage; without o'erflowing, full;" beginning in it heaven below, fitting it for heaven above.

I invite you, then, as to your highest good and joy, to this inward work of the soul. Those engaged in it are the workmen that need not be ashamed. They imitate God himself, who not only thinks and loves and wills, but, as Christ declared, "worketh hitherto;" filling the universe with new forms of being, fresh manifestations of goodness, and preparing to render "to them who, by patient continuance in well-doing, seek for glory, honor, and immortality, eternal life."

DISCOURSE III.

NOMINAL AND REAL CHRISTIANITY.

Luke xiii. 26, 27. — THEN SHALL YE BEGIN TO SAY, WE HAVE EATEN
AND DRUNK IN THY PRESENCE, AND THOU HAST TAUGHT IN OUR
STREETS. BUT HE SHALL SAY, I TELL YOU, I KNOW YOU NOT
WHENCE YE ARE.

In the passage containing these words, the kingdom
of God is represented under the figure of a social
festival, to which the master of the house has
invited his chosen friends. When he finds that all
are assembled, he rises up, and shuts to the door.
Afterwards, other persons arrive, and solicit admission. He answers that they are strangers to him,
and he cannot open to them. But they remonstrate,
that they have been on terms of familiarity with him;
they had eaten and drunk in his presence, and he
had taught in their streets. Yet he rejoins only with
the solemn asseveration, "I know you not whence
ye are. Depart from me, all ye workers of iniquity."

The application is obvious. Much has been said
about what is transient and what is permanent in
Christianity. But a far more important distinction
is what is nominal and what is real in Christianity,
as it respects personal character. The persons re-

ferred to in the text were the first nominal Christians. They were those who had gathered round
Jesus in the crowd, had listened readily to his words,
had joined in his retinue through the streets of Jerusalem, had wondered at his miracles, and had crossed
the lake or gone into the wilderness after him, to
renew the pleasing astonishment. They had probably never taken any active part against him,—never
been forward to accuse him,—never been busy in
exciting the tumults which endangered him,—never
lent or would lend their voices to the cry, "Crucify
him, crucify him." And so they hoped to be reckoned among his true disciples. But he did not
know them: they were nominal Christians only.

It is to be feared that the text has rather gained
than lost emphasis by the lapse of time, and that the
reality of our religion falls now more short of being
co-extensive with its name. The external and appa-
rent triumphs of the gospel are great. Its banner
stretches over hundreds of millions of mankind. No
sea that its missionaries have not crossed,— no shore
or discovered island, on which its professors have
not landed. The whole globe is so woven in, as
with magnetic wires, in every direction, with an unbroken chain of Christian institutions, that, if every
link in every heart in Christendom were sound, the
world would be inundated with the Christian faith
and spirit, and the millennium soon be no fanatic
dream, but a fulfilled prediction.

There is outward honor enough paid to Christianity. See it in the annual celebration, so wide over

the earth, of our Lord's resurrection from the dead.
From Greek and Roman cathedrals, as the day
returns, all along to the village churches of this
Western continent, even as the sun rises over the
earth, the public rejoicing over that greatest of all
earthly events spreads. On some little station, like a
fort amid the Pacific Seas, the Easter song is sung.
On the vessel's deck, in the Atlantic Main, as she
tosses up against the gale, the mariner turns over
his almanac to fix the date ; and the excitement that
swells the multitudes in populous cities, by invisible
chords of sympathy, reaches and electrifies his
breast. But are all these myriads, according to the
intent of what they celebrate, living as immortal
beings ? Are they all actually looking upon the
grave as but a low-arched portal, into which men
pass after the great Forerunner, only to rise and
move on at the other side ? Are they clothed, in
their conduct, with the dignity and purity which
become those upon whom the light has streamed
from the land of spirits ? What proportion of them
are so doing ? What proportion of us are so doing ?
Who has asked himself, "Am I, by faith and my
conversation in the world, risen with Christ, and
seeking those things which are above, where Christ
sitteth on the right hand of God ? " Or who must
confess that the event which has fixed the day of
Christian worship for all ages, and, in the long reach
of its influence, assembles the weekly worshippers
of a myriad of congregations, has not yet carried

8

his thoughts and motives beyond the narrow horizon
of earthly interests and plans?

Alas! these exultations over any of the great circumstances of our Lord's history become somewhat
sad to the soul, when we ask that searching question,
how far they are a formal and nominal, and how
far a real and spiritual, thing. The green bough,
taken as the symbol of the rejoicings over Christ's
birth, not only gladdens but grieves me, when I see
it hanging at the window of a worldly, self-seeking
man, who appears to be no less worldly and self-
seeking that he has hung it there. And the observance of the set time of lamentation over Christ's
cross, lamentation for the sins and passions of the
human heart, (for what else in that wonderful scene
of Christ's moral and spiritual glory was there to
lament over?) that lifted up that innocent form, and
nailed those hands and feet strong and swift only for
errands of mercy, — the observance itself becomes
an unspeakable sorrow and a bitter shame, if our
human passions and our unforsaken sins go on all
the same before that unparalleled spectacle at which
the sun in heaven veiled his face, and the earth
beneath was shaken.

Nay, the distinction in the question is more close
than these occasional reminiscences suggest. How
far are we nominal and how far real worshippers in
the regular service from Sunday to Sunday in God's
house? In the consecrated temple you have secured
your place; you pay your part to support the order
of its ministrations; you attend upon the service;

you enjoy intellectually its thoughts and devotional sentiments. Christ himself is a being altogether spotless and lovely to your imagination. But how far is this a nominal and customary performance, and how far the very substance and hope of your heart?

I would not make what is to justify the Christian name a hard and severe exaction. I would not use any overstrained language. I know that our religion proposes a lofty attainment, which rises before our steps like successive height over height to the mountain-traveller. It is not required that a man shall be already perfect, in order to be a true Christian. But it is required that he should be a sincere seeker after perfection. It is required that he should be moving forward, and advancing up the straight and narrow way of life. And to this point our questioning may well and soberly come. Is God's word a fire burning away what is evil in our appetites? Is it a hammer that breaks in pieces the rock of our prejudice, or the idol of our lust? Does every stroke of it, as you hear, echo along the chambers of your soul? Is every line of it, as you read, written on the fleshly tables of your heart? Does the sharp edge of truth chisel out, in the deep quarry of your bosom, the very image of your Saviour? Does the eternal commandment of duty sink into your living affections, and shape them after the pattern of a divine rectitude? Do you suffer the sword of God's law to cut off the right hand of every darling propensity, of which you are con-

scious, which would seize the forbidden fruit?
Then you are not a nominal Christian only, but a
real disciple of your professed Master.

But he with whom this worship here is a matter
of the passing gratification of the hour, or, it may
be, of the dissatisfaction or indifference of the hour,
and who does not accustom himself to think that
consequences high as heaven, deep as hell, depend
on his decision respecting it, — he is a nominal
Christian merely; and verities, sublime as the character of God and the immortality of the soul, pass
smoothly and superficially over him, and leave no
mark, as from the keel no furrow in the wave, no
trace behind the arrow through the air.

We do not, it is to be feared, give to our religion the peculiar and separate importance which it
deserves. We mix and dilute it too much with
other influences, — make it part and parcel of the
common round of business, amusement, and festiv-
ity, which it should rather preside over, control, and
purify. As the pagan temples, by receiving a few
superficial additions, were made into Christian sanctuaries; and as the heathen philosophy, a little modi-
fied, was substituted for the Christian doctrine; so we
think that a few circumstantial changes will make a
worldly life Christian, and that the fashion of the day
need only be clothed with the external rites of religion to meet the solemn requirements of Heaven.
Whereas the true operation of our religion is to
regenerate the soul, to rebuild the life, to alter the
essentials, to put a new spirit into the man, and

make a new creature of him; if the love of gain
and ease and human approbation have been hitherto
his controlling motives, setting in place of them the
love of God, self-sacrifice, and for the desire of
man's poor flattery the superior aim at his moral
salvation. And who that reads one page of the
Bible can regard the effect as any less signal and
important ?

Are you nominal Christians or real Christians ?
We are all one or the other. Suppose the angel of
God should descend, and, breaking up the decent
and orderly ranks as they now appear, classify us;
how many would be on the one side, and how many
on the other ? — on your conscience, my friend,
where would *you* be ? It is said that there are in
Boston more than twelve thousand communicants
professing their love for Christ in the ordinance of
his supper? Are they all real Christians? They
would shake this city from the centre to the circumference, if they were. Not a sin, public or private,
could dare long to stand unabashed before their
searching gaze and spotless example. For virtue,
religious character, is influential. It is not to be
altogether withstood, any more than gravitation or
the tides. A healing and reforming power will go
out of it (for this is God's ordination) wherever it
moves. We talk of reform and reformers. A good,
virtuous, Christian character is the only real, effectual, lasting reformer in the world. And before
twelve thousand real Christians, these vile deceptions
in trade, — these social pollutions, the horror of

8*

which we are just beginning to see, — these evil customs, that exist only by compliance and sufferance, — these traps and temptations, now set without a blush to take captive men's honor and virtue, would flee away with a brand of intolerable ignominy from our sight. The existence of bad habit and bold iniquity is, rightly viewed, a reproach to the church; for, were the church really what it is in name, the habit and the iniquity could not so quietly endure. I think every disciple of Christ, who has sensibility, feels a little ashamed, when he hears of any startling crime or moral disgrace occurring near him. For he feels, that, if he and his companions were what they should be, and acted on their fellow-creatures as they should act, the neighborhood and the community would be lifted above such conduct. Yes: an influence goes out from pre-eminent goodness that cannot be altogether resisted, and never dies, but works on immortal in the earth, even after its translation to the heavens. I passed by the spot where one of the truly excellent of God's children had lived, and saw that they had levelled the old mansion to the ground; but that departed Christian soul was as near to me and moved me as though I had expected her wonted greeting at the door.

It is very melancholy to see that the chief disputes in the church at present are about the nominal and external in religion; Christian men and ministers alienated from each other by petty questions respecting forms of procedure, orders of service, and modes of prayer; the weightier matters sacrificed to this

"mint, anise, and cummin ; " the spirit of evil raging
in the world, and gaining new triumphs while this
miserable internal strife goes on ; and Jesus Christ
solemnly, from his throne in the heavens, looking
down for the pith and core of his gospel, while his
followers thus clutch the dead stalk and husk, and
impose it for the bread of life ; the outward methods,
which in their simplicity tend to promote the inward spiritual growth, made, like lifeless, curiously
wrought petrifactions, actually to stand in the way.

We are amazed when we hear of the superstitious
multitudes in a foreign town flocking, from the cir-
cuit of a thousand miles, in crowds, one endless
procession, to see an ancient coat exhibited under
the pretence of its being actually the garment once
worn by Christ.   But, if we trust in any way to
external services and ceremonies, or to our peculiarity of these alone, for our salvation, our amazement
had better be turned to ourselves.

It cheers us to see that noble enterprise in which
some of the larger bodies of believers are going forth
to Christianize by missions the heathen world ; but
there is one previous question to be put, namely, how
we shall Christianize Christendom.   It was asked of
old respecting the Roman guards of the imperial
throne, " But who shall guard those very guards ? "
a pertinent query, as it proved.   And who shall
make the nominal to be real Christians, — make
them to be true soldiers of the Prince of peace ?
Missionaries go forth from nominal Christendom
into Heathendom in every distant-bound ship and

far-journeying company ; — missionaries who exert
an influence for or against the Christianity they profess, without being sent by any missionary establishment.   Every large religious society is continually
representing itself somehow to hinder or advance the
gospel of Christ in every quarter of the globe ; —
a representation none the less real, and it may be
in some respects more effectual, because it is infor-
mal.   Our sons or brothers go from us, and tread
the busy walks of Paris or London.   They mingle
in with the sallow swarms that pour through the
streets of Calcutta and Smyrna.   They land on
the islands in the gulf, or sail from point to point
along the farthest South American shores ; and,
wherever they go, they carry an influence for or
against the Christianity in which they have been
born and baptized.   Members of a Christian church
now reside on a little island in the midst of the
Atlantic Sea.   Beyond the lakes and mountains of
the West may be those who have come up to the
house of God in your company ; for there are those
who have gone up in mine.   " What impression did
he leave ? "   I asked of one who had followed in
the track of a friend, in his travels in the far East.
" Everywhere," the answer was, " where he had
been, was the mark of the Christian : in Syria and
Egypt, among the Mahometans and the Jews, with
whomsoever he held converse, still the mark of the
Christian."   Christian character is a thing that
always leaves its mark.

What do such things teach us ?   Be a Christian

where you are, and you will exert a Christian influence widely over the world. Be not a nominal but a real Christian, and virtue will go out of you over parallels of latitude and across meridians of longitude where your feet never stood, and your voice will never be heard. Be a Christian society in fact as well as in form, and you will do more to convert mankind, ay, even in heathen lands, than by the mere expenditure of hundreds and thousands in silver and gold. Be a Christian in your disposition and life, as well as appearance and profession ; or, as the word of the Son of God shall prove true, you can have no greeting for yourself from him at last but — "I never knew you. You worshipped, in the outward form, in my Father's house. You sat at my table. You fondly thought yourself a Christian, and you passed for a Christian in the world. But I never knew you. There was never any real sympathy between your spirit and mine. Your thoughts and motives were not mine. You did not love God and man with an affection like mine. I never knew you : depart from me, all ye that work iniquity !" God, in his infinite mercy through Jesus Christ, grant us a better salutation in the hour of our great and extreme need !

DISCOURSE IV.

THE WIDOW'S MITES.

Mark xii. 43. — THIS POOR WIDOW HATH CAST MORE IN THAN ALL
THEY WHICH HAVE CAST INTO THE TREASURY.

THE Treasury was a part of the Jewish Temple,
devoted to the reception of gifts consecrated for religious purposes. At the time to which the text
refers, the Saviour had been sitting near it, answer-
ing the cavils of the Scribes and Sadducees, till they
were completely silenced. Then, the conversation
ceasing, he looked up, and beheld the people casting money into the treasury ; and many that were
rich cast in much. "And there came a certain
poor widow, and she threw in two mites, which
make a farthing."

At once the Saviour's mind, ever alive to the impression of moral beauty, was excited. He cared
nothing about the greatness or smallness of outward
deeds, but observed only the grandeur or meanness
of the soul. Thus the humble gift moved him
more than all the splendid donations ; and he even
called his disciples to him, that he might express to
them his solemn approbation of the woman's disinterested charity.

"This poor widow hath cast more in than they all." There is a seeming paradox in this declaration; but, on considering, we may find a greater propriety in it than we might at first suppose. In some important respects, the widow had cast in "more than they all,"—not, indeed, in absolute amount; for her charity could even be distinguished only by the most insignificant term of value. But, it is important to be observed, the greatness of a gift cannot be determined by its absolute amount : it can be truly ascertained only by a moral standard.

The first index on this moral standard points to the ability to bestow. The widow had given more than the wealthy, in proportion to her ability ; for, while they contributed of their abundance, she had given in her penury. With no rich fund on which to draw, but only the slender resources provided for the present necessity,— the stay of her life removed from her side, and she left alone in the world dependent for daily food on daily labor,— still she so reverenced sacred institutions, she could not refrain from yielding her contribution to their support. And she gave the whole treasure she could at the time command ; for, though it was but "two mites," we are informed it was "all her living." She was willing to go without even her plain fare, and fast for a time, trusting to Providence for future supplies, that she might help the service of the house of God.

How far, then, did the benefactions of those wealthy ones fall below her offering ! All they gave, much as it was, never caused them to sit at a less sumptuous table, or repose on a couch less costly, or wear less precious raiment. Their contributions were as much less than their living, as the widow's mites, which were " all her living," were less than their gifts of gold. And, even while they stood at the Temple, their servants were busy in their rich dwellings, preparing savory viands against their masters' return. But the widow's habitation was desolate in her absence; the fire had gone out upon her hearth; and she must return, not to a luxurious feast, but to an empty board. In such circumstances, abundant, indeed, was her contribution. To have equalled her generosity, they must have coined their fields and cattle into silver and gold, and filled the treasury to overflowing with the price of their whole estates. Truly, the poor widow gave more than they all ; for the true measure of a gift is determined, not by its absolute amount, but according to a moral standard. And one index of this standard points to the ability to bestow.

But a second mark upon this standard indicates the disposition that prompts the gift. May it not be laid down as a principle, that the greatness of a gift depends, not only on the ability to bestow it, but on the feelings with which it is bestowed ? There may be no generosity in the most magnificent bequest ; while a soul overflowing with love may accompany the humblest present. You may remember that you have often been most grateful for the simplest tokens of regard, while the glitter of jewels and richly wrought robes has fallen coldly on your eye. Indeed, we may even say that strong love is disposed to make use of unpretending symbols. It shrinks from display. It knows that no price of pearls and gold can equal its own richness. And it would make its own richness felt, not convey a certain exchangeable value. Thus more affection has been expressed by a flower, or a lock of hair, or some simple article of household convenience, than by diamonds and rubies.

Many of those Pharisees who gave most abundantly to the treasury were doubtless moved, not by a feeling of love at all, but by a spirit of pride and ostentation. Having no reverence for sacred institutions, they thought perhaps that they were not so much discharging a debt to their Maker as conferring a favor on his servants. They would be praised for their generosity, and therefore rendered their gifts, not with modest concealment, but with conspicuous display. Oh! how often is this virtue of charity thus prostituted to base ends! Men take to themselves great merit for alms-giving, when all their benevolence abridges no personal comfort, perhaps no sensual indulgence. They may use their charities to gratify the pride of appearance, or to gain improper sway over other minds ; or they may consider their generosity an atonement for their sins, as if an apparently good deed could sanctify a really bad motive. Such impulses have swayed many in all ages, degrading charity from a high virtue to a fair-seeming vice; and they may have actuated those of whom Christ spoke.

9

How different the motives of the poor widow!
and how do they exalt her deed above theirs ! How
far removed from ostentation her spirit, when she
could go up in the midst of the proud company, and
humbly place her little sum by the side of their
splendid offerings, where she knew it would be compared by the assembled gazing throng to so great
disadvantage ; unconscious that one eye was looking
on, able to discern it in its real superiority ! How
genuine and pure her benevolence, when she was
willing personally to suffer, if only she might give!
But, though her offering was so slight, what a joyful
consciousness must she have had within, entirely
unknown to the haughty ones about her,—the consciousness of doing all she could from a pure and
disinterested affection ! Here, indeed, is a sense
in which her offering was greater than those of
the worldlings. It was greater in her own soul.
Small, indeed, was their gift in the estimation
of their own secret thought. Inferior was its
weight in the scales of conscience ; but great and
glorious the integrity and joyfulness of the widow's
spirit. The widow's gift was greater, then, because
it came from greater love.

There is still another index on this moral standard, which determines the greatness of a gift. This
index points to the good effect resulting from the
gift. The importance of any action is to be esti-
mated, not merely by its present character, but by
its ultimate influence ; and in this view also it might
be said, that the widow cast more into the treasury.

It is not the deed we perform, but the spirit we display, that exerts an abiding influence. It is the generous motive that inflames the world, and excites men of after-generations to follow in the course of well-doing, which has been already nobly trod. And how many hearts has this lofty spirit of the poor widow, thus celebrated by Christ, inspired with the same self-forgetful love, and impelled to the same noble conduct! Little was it thought, when these events were passing, that the knowledge of them would be so widely spread, and that the little group that day gathered at the Temple would be fixed in a moral picture to be gazed at by the eyes of men in all time. Little did those rich ones suppose, that the widow's gift would become famous through the wide world, and judged as so much more worthy than their own; and she herself, though standing in that lowly figure, be for every coming age the noblest of all illustrations of a disinterested spirit.

Viewed in its ultimate influence, then, her gift was greater than theirs; and, thus regarded, we may even say it was absolutely greater. For, if we consider all the effects of her example in cherishing a true benevolence, and leading others to be bountiful, even the sum of the rich men's benefactions would dwindle and fade into nothing before the greatness and splendor of offerings devoted to the cause of religion, which have grown, as an immense harvest from invisible seed, out of the widow's mites. Truly, these mites, cast into the treasury, did not retain their original form, but swelled into a value vast and unmeasured. She gave, not only to the Temple at Jerusalem, but to every Christian temple under the heaven, whose foundations have since been laid. By a single act of self-denial, she has been charitable to the whole world; and for what she did, in humility and sorrow that she could do no more, the whole world will confess itself under obligations, and be grateful. " Of a truth, this poor widow hath cast in more than they all."

The subject we have been considering naturally suggests an absolute truth, apart from the particular case presented in the text. " She hath cast in more than they all." We may say, generally, it is not great but small things, not imposing but humble deeds, that make up the great sum of good influence. The mites and farthings are more than the shekels and talents. It is not a few splendid gifts, but countless small ones, which keep the virtue of charity alive, supply the needs of a million sufferers, and give ample support to all good institutions. A deluge does not water the earth; but the tender roots spring under the fine drops of the universal rain, Look at all the great associations for the support of government, education, philanthropy, religion. How are they kept in being ? Not chiefly by costly gifts, but by humble offerings. It is not the talents, but the mites, by which they are nourished. The great structures of science and art are built by the ceaseless contributions of millions, as the little insects of the sea toil on without rest, till a new continent breaks through its waters.

But the principle I am endeavoring to illustrate has a yet more extended bearing. In regard to our own characters, we may say the mites are more than the talents. It is not what we think and feel and do on extraordinary occasions that makes the bulk of character, but the silent and steady accumulation of our every-day desires and motives and habits of life. Religion consists, not in spasmodic efforts, but persevering industry; not in doing much at one time, ·but all we can at all times. Think not thy little, if it be all thou canst, will be despised : think not thy much, if it be less than thy ability, will be accepted.

Measure not your religion by its visible appearance. Its slightest manifestations may indicate more than its most noisy displays. It is the spirit of the deed that determines its character, whatever be the modesty and whatever the greatness of the deed itself. You may dazzle men's eyes with large enterprises in philanthropy, but possess nothing of the philanthropic spirit; and so you may do nothing wonderful in your whole life, yet, from your constant inward striving after holiness, the temple of God may at length stand in all its beauty in your heart. The mighty floods you see holden in mid air went not up with great commotion and fearful display; but ascended in invisible drops upon the sunbeams; and it is but a slow perspiring from the hills that supplies the earth's exhaustless fountains.

Character, happiness, salvation, depend not on the amount of what we do, but upon the dispositions and motives that prompt our conduct; and these

9*

appear in our most insignificant acts, as well as in
our most imposing undertakings. A pure motive,
a noble disposition, can be expressed as forcibly in
giving a cup of cold water as in the conveyance of
a rich estate. It can be shown forth as truly in a
word of kind counsel as in the publication of volumes
of wisdom. It can be illustrated as strongly in de-
fending the right in a small neighborhood as in ad-
vocating a holy cause in the counsels of the nation.
To the eye of the Infinite One, it may seem clothed
even more beautifully in a quiet, unnoticed deed,
whose performance by a right hand is not known
by the left, than in a proud achievement, whose
praise rings the world over.

Remember, then, that the most solemn interests
and fearful issues of life depend on things in themselves slight. The greatest man that ever lived was
dependent for character and happiness far more upon
his little acts than upon his great achievements. Of
how small consequence to him that particular date
when the battle was won or the bill carried, though
it have made the calendar illustrious, when compared with all the other days of the year! If these
be all days of vicious indulgence or vexing care,
what matters it in the comparison that on a single
day there is a festival and a show, and eyes of admiration are turned upon him, and words of praise
spoken? Do you, then, aim at great results? be
careful of your small actions. Would you gain the
joy of pure affection? it will not, at your wish, come
out full-formed in your soul. Nor will men yield it

to you on a sudden demand, or allow their hearts to
be carried as by storm. It is by many particular
acts and unfailing tokens of regard that you will
succeed : it is by the contribution of mites.

Would you secure a fair reputation ? The wise
and good, whose esteem alone is precious, will not
judge of you by the few shining deeds of philanthropy and honesty which you put boldly forth for
the inspection of the world, but by your constant
habits in business, your daily walk, your most private treatment of the humblest man in your service,
in short, by your contribution of mites to individual
happiness and the public good.

Above all, would you be truly religious, and secure the favor of an almighty Friend ? His eye
resteth ever on the soul ; and, to its infallible vision,
great deeds dwindle, or small ones are exalted, according to the temper from which they flow. Splendid pretences of generosity appear in all their
hollowness, and true habitual kindness alone is accepted. Forms and flatteries, sacrifices and prostra-
tions, are all vain without a constant piety. Selfish
thanks for sudden prosperity, and selfish cries for
help in sudden danger, mount not to his throne like
the grateful incense of "prayer without ceasing."

Wait not, then, for extraordinary occasions. The
present moment, and the mite you can contribute as
it passes, are your all. For, rightly viewed, what
is the present moment but the index on the dial-plate,
for ever moving till it makes up your whole life ?
And what is the mite you now contribute but that

exertion of your whole strength to meet the present
demand, without which, in the longest life, nothing
is accomplished? The whole of religion, then, is
comprised in one simple direction: Do all you can
from a pure motive *now*. Thus, small as your
actions may appear to men, like the widow's mites
they will be great in the eye of Heaven; and
though they attract not the admiration of the world,
they will secure your eternal peace.

DISCOURSE V.

FORBEARANCE.

Col. iii. 13. — FORBEARING ONE ANOTHER.

So writes Paul to the Ephesians also. It is an exhortation very simple, yet important. You whose lot unites you in the same local habitation and name, — you who are leagued in friendship or business, in the changes of sympathy and the chances of collision, "forbear one another." The matter is too plain for explanation, and yet the joy and woe of human life hang upon it. What is the great evil in our lot of mortality? Is it sickness, death, sorrow? No: it is misunderstanding, disagreement, alienation, — the passions of men, a thousand-fold more afflictive than the ordinations of God. In our providential griefs, fountains of tears refresh us; sweet memories console, and mysterious hopes beckon; but what consolation for our distrust and scorn and altercation?

Such a confession may not be made aloud. Aloud we may lament only the outward distresses. As men hide the infirmities and diseases of the body, so we cloak and bandage over the heart the real troubles, deeper than all the ills that "flesh is heir to." How shall we cure these? A sure remedy is named in the text, — "forbearing one another." And what is it to forbear? It is to endure injury meekly, for the injurious person's sake, when in a rigid account we might seem justified in resistance or complaint. And to be unforbearing is to fire at insult, burning to be proudly even with the insulter, like the literal Jew, saying, "An eye for an eye, and a tooth for a tooth." Forbearance is yielding something we might claim, pardoning when we might punish, sacrificing a legal or customary right to a moral affection, foregoing a desire we might urge from a willingness, like our Master's, not to please ourselves. In the domestic circle, to forbear is to curb our imperiousness, repress impatience, pause in the burst of another's feeling, and from our bosom pour oil on the billows, instead of adding to the swelling tide.

Now, I am aware this is a virtue few appreciate. It seems no great and splendid thing, in some daily issue of feeling or opinion, to withhold a little, to tighten the rein upon headlong propensity, and await a calm for fair adjustment. It is a very unambitious, undisplaying virtue, not so likely to be marked and praised as smartness and spirit, and readiness for an encounter. Its symptoms are not to most persons striking; being a quiet attitude and lips, that, like Christ's when he was accused, answer nothing. And this, the undiscerning may mistake for dulness, or want of becoming chivalry. But to the all-seeing God there is a beauty in such repose, beyond the exploits of strength and bravery. In the finest statues of ancient art, the last perfection is a calmness of posture, seeming to embosom unbounded power.

This virtue of forbearance, from Gospel to Epistle, runs along the whole foundation of Christianity. Indeed I must consider it a mark of Christ's divinity, that he should make a self-restraining meekness so crowning a virtue of his religion, in an age which had little to remember but universal violence and bloodshed. The whole idea of virtue under the Roman sway was active courage. Nay, the very name *virtue* meant martial valor, the strength of the sword-arm, and the achievements of battle. It was speaking against the customs of ages, alike the passions of barbarians and the virtues of civilization, when Christ said, "Resist not evil: when one cheek is smitten, turn the other." Men had not thought that it required more power to let go the sword than to wield it, to drop the hand than to clench it. Nor have many of us even yet entered into the full sublimity of his words to Peter, after he had smitten the high priest's servant, "Put up thy sword into the sheath."

Not that Christ would replace the Roman valor with a weak pusillanimity. Forbearance is not cowardice or want of feeling, pale apprehension trembling in the breast; but, when the blood of passion redly mounts, it is that victory over one's self grander than over a city; and, so viewed, I maintain it to be a trait of perpetual and vast consequence. Made universal, it would strike off half the catalogue of human woes. Do you ask me where are the most discouraging triumphs of sin? I will not point you to a few battle-fields, smoke-wreathed and reek-

ing, those volcanoes of the human heart that loose
its pent-up vapor and fire. War is a great evil in the
world, but want of temper is a greater. I intend no
paradox : soberly I believe the fretfulness of human
life is a greater evil, and destroys more happiness,
than all the tramplings of invasion and conquest.
There is excitement of thought as well as passion in
war. Mighty ideas of right may mingle in its motives, heroic endurance of every hardship attends its
progress, and saving the sacred palladium of freedom is sometimes its result. But the excitable
peevishness that kindles at trifles, that roughens the
daily experience of a million families, that scatters its
little stings at the table and by the hearth-stone, that
introduces a prickle into the whole clothing and
movement of life, what does this but unmixed harm?
What ingredient does it furnish but of gall? Its
fine wounding may be of petty consequence in any
given case, and its tiny darts easily extracted ; but,
when habitually carried into the whole texture of
life, it destroys more peace than plague and famine
and the sword. It is a deeper anguish than grief
or the gasp of death ; it is a sharper pang than the
afflicted moan with ; it is a heavier pressure from
human hands than all you feel when the Almighty
"hath touched you." Save, then, I beseech you,
this broad deduction from your comfort and immense
addition to your suffering, by heeding the apostle's
injunction, — by bearing with one another's foibles
and excitements, and forgiving one another's offences
or neglects.

What a genial companion in the house is he or she that does this! And, on the other hand, how many persons, perhaps of fine abilities and magnanimous virtues, we one and all say we would not wish to live with, because they are nervous and captious, and carry a tinder with them that catches at every spark! Would you make yourself dear to every domestic scene you enter, form the habit of forbearance, and all your kindred will bless your face for its own benediction. Your very coming-in at the door shall be as a balm; and that comfort is not insignificant which is repeated, a drop of sweetness in every draught, a thousand and a million times. While the effect of forbearance will be, not only to make you comfortable to others, but to deepen the power and harmonize the development of your own soul. On the contrary, have you not observed that an acrid disposition is a vitriol that eats into all it touches, and leaves a sore at every spot, and a stain on every thread of existence? Have you not found that an unpleasant temper, though corrected from outbreaks and not possessing the nerves, does yet, like a slow, silent moth with invisible teeth, sharply bite into the splendor of the social fabric, and consume away the beauty from all affection's form and drapery? And is it not a simple remedy for all this anguish? Forbear; give up a little; take less than belongs to you; endure more than should be put upon you. Make allowance for another's judgment of the case: differing in constitution, circumstances, and interests, we shall often decide differently about

the justice and integrity of things ; and mutual concessions alone can heal the breaches, and bridge over
the chasms between us.   While quick resentment
and stiff maintenance of our position will breed endless dispute and bitterness.

The strain of remark I have been pursuing, applies,
of course, peculiarly to matters of personal concern.
There are occasions, involving first principles, when
we must by no means bend or waver.   We must
never compromise men's solemn rights, or desert the
cause of God, to please the whims of the capricious,
or feed the avarice of the unjust ; though even here
we need not, like angry zealots in what they imagine
their holy displeasure, pour out seven vials of wrath
as a sacred libation.   Still we are never to quit the
post of religious sincerity and Christian magnanimity,
whatever insults or opposition we may meet.   This
distinction is made—how beautifully !—by our great
Teacher and Pattern.   Blasphemy against himself
he could bear silently, though not blasphemy against
the Holy Ghost.   He forbade any resistance to the
soldiers sent to take him, saying that a prayer to his
Father would bring more than twelve legions of
angels for his guard.   Oh ! yes: had it been his object to be guarded, the troops of heaven would have
mustered innumerable on the earth.   But he would
guard only the principles of truth and the glory of
God ; and their everlasting defence was in his unop-
posing submission.   Their weapon was a wound
unresisted ; their eloquence was scorn calmly accepted ; their sign of universal victory was not the

Roman legionary's spear, but the cross which flamed in the sky to the vision of Constantine, and must flame mildly on as the standard of Christ's soldiers till it conquers the world.

When John, in the Apocalypse, looked for the lion of the tribe of Judah, he beheld a lamb as it had been slain. This touches the heart of the Saviour's excellence ; and what is the language of his cross, all in one word, but *forbear?* A seemingly trifling work to do for once ; yet accomplish it every day, and every hour, in your family, with your friend, your companion, among all you deal with in the commerce of life, and, in addition to showing a Christian spirit, you will bring about great results. You will shut out a flood of misery, you will accumulate a fountain of refreshment, you will send forth a perennial stream of gladness ; for this mere trifling circumstance of feeling about life's little concerns, everywhere repeated and multiplied, makes the bulk of life's experience. One thread running many ways composes all the loom has ever woven. So a little matter of temper that may seem even ludicrous, yet in which the main wish is to right and justify one's self, to be up with an antagonist, to get one's dues according to one's notion of them, — even this trifle of temper is the small grain of mustard-seed, from which grows the majority of alienated friendships, divided houses, unhappy homes, and wide-blazing wars, that have saddened the earth. The original cause of grievous offence, like the ultimate particles of matter, is often invisible, save to the microscopic eye of jealousy. But " by long forbearing," says the wise man, " is a prince persuaded ; and a soft tongue breaketh the bone." The most ingenious of fabulists, whose principle is to picture human traits by the dispositions of animals, describes a swan who saves his neck from being cloven, by the music of his voice. Is it not a true emblem ? How many a life, how many a soul of man, has been saved by like music, struck from the living lyre of an amiable heart !

Do you finally ask how you shall learn to forbear? This virtue particularly needs industrious culture. It may not be produced by occasional strong efforts, by struggles severe, and not repeated ; but, on the contrary, by improving every little occasion to quench strife and fan concord, till a constant sweetness smooths the face of domestic life, and kindness and tenderness become the very expression of the countenance. Forbearance must grow, indeed, just as irritability does, by degrees. The old man who would teach his sons the benefits of harmony showed them a bundle of rods, united how strong, but separate how weak. The form and application of the story may be varied. The little twig you cast into the flame of controversy is no great thing, though it crackle for a while ; but, thrown repeatedly on the one side or on the other, it becomes a bundle of fagots for the burning which wraps the peaceful house in conflagration. " Behold, how great a matter a little fire kindleth ! " Word succeeding word, answers more and more warm, till they wax into vile accusations, to end in blows and bloodshed; while the quarrels of children are a too faithful miniature of the battles of nations. So let successive words and deeds of charity cultivate the virtue that is opposed to this vice.

Again, practise forecast. Are you tempted to irritable, censorious speech, or violent deeds, think not of the present only, but of the future? At leisure, how often have men repented of what they did in haste! How often have they recoiled, in mortification and bitter distress, from the opponents they had prostrated! How often has the cold corpse of a human being taught them too late that compassion which his living presence could not. How eloquent are the remorseful teachings of the grave, in which we sometimes hear men say they have buried their enmities! Alas if they have no other offering to the grave of a fellow-creature! Oh! yes: cold death teaches lessons which hasty life skips. Marble lips speak louder than living tones. Abel's blood, that cries to Heaven, is not unheard in the ear of Cain. There is a resurrection, not for the dead only, but for the injuries you fixed in their hearts, — in the hearts, it may be, of those bound to your own, to whom you owed but all offices of gentleness.

> " Feebly must they have felt
> Who in old time attired with snakes and whips
> The vengeful Furies. Beautiful regards
> Were turned on me; the face of her I loved,
> The wife and mother, pitifully fixing
> Tender reproaches insupportable."

10*

Oh! my friends, avoid these fatal shafts shot from eternity! Now so forbear and forgive, that you may see looking at you, through the mists of the grave, only the faces which, before they went, you clothed in smiles; that you may behold in your dreams only loving features and beckoning hands. Guard yourselves in the armor of forbearance, even the panoply of your own mercy, against the condemnations of the great Divine tribunal. For the Bible, passage after passage, makes God's forgiveness of us fearfully to hang on our forgiveness of each other: "He shall have judgment without mercy that hath showed no mercy." A ruffian having once struck a certain Mussulman, he thus addressed him: "If I were revengeful, I should render you outrage for outrage. If I were an informer, I should accuse you to the caliph; but I love better to pray God, that, at the day of judgment, we may both be received into heaven together!" And do we Christians need to be reminded, that "forgive as we forgive" is our only allowable supplication? If we need not, and expect never to beg, the mercy of God to ourselves, we may withhold our mercy from our fellows. If we have not the ten thousand talents to be forgiven, we may refuse, like the base servant, to forgive the hundred pence. It has been a custom with some, when the temptation to anger overtook them, to wait till they could repeat the Lord's prayer; — a good expedient, if we repeat it till we have truly learned it by heart!

DISCOURSE VI.

SPIRITUAL PEACE.

John xiv. 27. — PEACE I LEAVE WITH YOU : MY PEACE I GIVE
UNTO YOU.

THERE are few whose idea of happiness does not include peace as essential. Most men have been so tempest-tost, and not comforted, that they long for a closing of all excitements at last in peace. Hence the images of the haven receiving the shattered bark, of the rural vale remote from the noise of towns, have always been dear to human fancy. Hence, too, the decline of life away from severe toil, rapid motion, and passionate action, has often a charm even beyond the kindling enterprise of youth. The cold grave itself repels not altogether, but somewhat allures, the imagination.

> " How still and peaceful is the grave !
> .   .   .   .   .   .
> There passions rage no more,
> And there the weary pilgrim rests
> From all the toils he bore."

Especially has heaven risen to the religious mind in this complexion of tranquillity. We cannot con-

ceive of it but as free from all disturbance, broken
by not a sound save of harmonious anthems, which,
like murmuring waters, give deeper peace than
could be found in silence. It is the voice of the
Christian enthusiast : —

> " There shall I bathe my weary soul
>   In everlasting rest,
>   And not a wave of trouble roll
>   Across my peaceful breast."

But man so longs for the blessing of peace, that
he not only soothes himself with these images from
afar, but hopes to foretaste their substance. And
what are his views to this end ? He means to retire from business to some spot where he can calmly
enjoy what he has in vain panted after in the chase
of life. Perhaps he tries the experiment, but finds
himself restless still, and learns the great lesson at
last, that peace is not in the landscape, but only in
the soul ; and that the calm sky, the horizon's
circle, the steady stars, are only its language, not
itself.

Perhaps he seeks peace in his home. Every thing
there is made soft to the feet ; each chair and couch
receives him gently ; agreeable sounds, odors, viands, regale every sense ; and illuminated chambers
richly replace for him at night the splendor of the
sun. But here again he is at fault. Peace comes
not to him, though some angel seems to have made
his varied apparatus for producing it. He may be
outshone by a neighbor ; his high estate may draw
envy and ill-will ; these " precious " senses them-

selves may refuse the proffered bliss, and ache with
disease.   Peace is not in outward comforts, which
the constitution sharply limits; which pass with
time, or pall upon the taste.   The human mind is
too great a thing to be pleased with mere blandish-
ments; to smile, like an infant, at whatever glitters.

> " Man has a soul of vast desires :
> He burns within with restless fires."

And the solemn truth will come home irrisistibly, at
times, even to the easy epicure.   Something is
wanting still.   There is more of pain than peace in
the remnants of feasting, and the exhausted rounds
of pleasure.

Man has sometimes sought peace in yet another
way.   Abjuring all sensual delights, he has gone
into the desert to scourge the body, to live on roots
and water, and be absorbed in pious raptures ; and
often has he thus succeeded, better than do the
hunters of pleasure.   But unrest mingles with his
tranquillity.   His innocent, active powers resist this
crucifixion.   The distant world rolls to his ear the
voices of suffering fellow-men ; and even his devotions, all lonely, become selfish and unhappy.

How, then, my friends, shall we gain this peace
so longed for, but in vain ?   There is one being
who, we believe, enjoyed it, and promised it to his
friends.   He was neither voluptuary nor hermit.
His life was a holy hermitage in the midst of
worldly excitements.   And this peace of his he did
not for others postpone to a distant day, or shut up

altogether in heaven, but left to his disciples on the earth.   What, then, was the peace of Christ?

The sufferings of Christ have had so prominent a place in the speculations of theology as to hide his inward spirit.   But poverty, wanderings, persecutions, desertions, disgrace, and death were to him but as an outer garment concealing unknown riches. " Man of sorrows, and acquainted with grief," as he was, by his own word there was a great deep of glad and peaceful life beneath, where grief could never come.   " My joy is fulfilled," — " That my joy might remain in you," — " My peace I leave with you ; " — such under-tones from his inmost spirit rose to his disciples' ears.   Let his character, then, teach his meaning.

And first, if he had peace, peace is not inactivity ; and they mistake who give a material sense to the images of heaven as a state of rest.   If Christ's life represented heaven, its peace is not slothful ease, but intense exertion.   How he labored in word and deed of virtue, so that often his prayer must fill up the night, or be deferred to a place of loneliness !   He raised no grand tribunal, as a ruler's throne or a high priest's chair, for men to bow to indolent authority.   But he walked in coarse raiment from town to desert, from city to city, to the waves of the sea. His ministry was toil from the day of his baptism to the scene upon Calvary.   And was all this fatiguing and unsatisfactory to him?   Not so, but his life and peace.   He expressed no wish to retire to an unoccupied ease : that would have wearied him indeed !

They mistake who look with pity on the Saviour, because of his absorption in endless tasks of duty. This was his joy. He was so peaceful, because so engaged. Utterances of wisdom, prayers to Almighty Power, submissions to duty, and visions of faith, — all conspiring to the unspeakable exaltation of his spirit, — were the very element of divine tranquillity.

And so earnest must we be, if we would bathe in this element. I appeal to you. When have you had most calmness and peace? When you had least to do; and mornings came and went, and suns circled, and seasons rolled, and brought no serious business? Do you not yourself confess, that time then has been a burthen; existence, a weariness; and this hungry soul, which craves some outward nourishment, has fallen back to prey upon itself?

I have seen the young man relieved from the excitements of hardy effort, the girdle of duty loosed; but discontent sat side by side with idleness in his face, his body drooped more beneath its own pressure than under the weights for which bracing struggles had given it nerve, till disgust, too great to be borne, drove him back to the activity whose bonds he had broken. I have known the young woman pass restless from place to place, because exempt from the necessity of industry, till vanity and envy, growing rank in her vacant mind, made her far more an object of compassion than those who work hardest for a living. Oh! no: you have not been most peaceful when unemployed. The laborer has peace who wipes the sweat from his brow at the closing day ; the careful mother, whose hands have been in a thousand places for repair or supply in household convenience ; the scholar who has searched through heavy tomes after references for his essay or history ; the lawyer who has exhausted the last drop of informations and legal precedents in his case ; the man of business, after honest fidelity to every claim ; the lover of men, from his long circumnavigations of charity ; the dying man, who looks back on days spent in noble action, — these have deeper peace than any idler that ever lived. True, they may think, at the pauses of severe toil, how sweet would those pauses be, if prolonged into wide intervals of rest. But let them not deceive themselves. It is the toil itself that has made the pauses pleasant. The same time would be changed into unresting ennui, were the nerves of labor relaxed. Twilight would lose its gratefulness, and sleep its delicious boon, and days of occasional liberty their rapture, at the first concessions to indolence. Perfect peace will be found here or hereafter, not when we sink down into torpor, but only when the soul is so wrought into high action as to find in it the breath of life.

But, besides his spiritual activity, another element of the Saviour's peace was his sinlessness. Nothing has so much disturbed tranquillity as conscious guilt, or the memory of wrong-doing. Slander, persecution, revenge, may have had a savage gladness in their greedy satisfactions ; but the soul never reflected on them but with pain. In the heat of conflict, when passion had the lists to itself, Napoleon exulted to see ranks on ranks hewn by the sabre, or swept by the cannon-ball ; but, the historian tells us, passing after the strife over the silent battle-plain, he was overcome by a dog crying at his master's corpse.

And such is the law. Play the game of passion while the blood is up, speak the word that envy urges, trample down modest worth in an ambitious career, and the excited hour thrills with demoniac delight. But, in the coolness of the veins, let lonely thought look back at the picture of broken hearts made by your falseness, injustice, cruelty, and the thrill turns into shuddering. So, whatever the sin you propose, remember peace shall be the payment.

But the Saviour kept his peace by being sinless. Sinned against all his life, and sold for silver, *he* never sinned, nor bartered his peace. We have no complete record of his early youth. But what touching interest, what heavenly beauty, would be in a true picture of that one young heart, keeping the pearl of infant-purity which all mankind have had, but lost, spotless unto manhood ; — guarding the holy bulwarks of his virtue unsurmounted by a single foe, while thousands circled them about, till that angelic holiness inspired him to teach gray doctors in his childish years, and, finishing the long experiment with triumph over the diabolic foes in the desert, the only sinless being the world had seen became the commissioned Son of God, — miracles in his hands, heaven and immortality upon his lips !

11

And, beneath the scorn and inflictions of men, must not the Saviour have had, in this sinlessness, a fountain of peace, proof against all the heats of malignant rage ? Oh ! yes : to remember that he had never sinned, never injured, never envied, never deceived, — must it not have made his whole life as one channel of glad emotions, which no man could turn from the memory of his mind ? Human malice may circumvent to blot the present hour ; but what hand shall tear out the colors of the past? And how swift, my friends, flows the present into the past, adding ever more to those pages stereotyped for our souls' eternal reading ! Will we trust our peace with angry words, with envious looks, unkind and selfish deeds, for that printing ? Or shall we, like Jesus, keep our life sinless, that our reflection upon it may be sweet ?

But there was one more element in the Saviour's peace, — not only his sinlessness, but his moral harmony. His was not mere innocence, but clothed in the charms of ever-growing beauty. As the white sprout of the seed, rising, takes the richest colors from every element, earth and air, wide ocean and the distant sun, so did his pure spirit add strength and glory to its innocence as it grew. There is a spiritual proportion, where every power does its work, every feeling fills its measure ; all knowledge, desire, and will, playing gently into each other, make a common current to bear the soul along to ever-new freedom and joy. The peaceful heart is quiet, not because inactive, but through intense harmonious working. The peaceful land rivals not the noise of that quaking under the shock of arms. Yet the waving grain, the spreading sail, rising cities, and the factory's low hum, bespeak more toil than burning towns, and sinking ships, and smoking fields. So the same measure of sound, which, harshly given, stuns the ear, shall but gladden when expressed in melodious concord.

But the fruits of industry, the harmonies of music, are the faintest emblems of this sublimer peace of the soul. There are times — they only can understand who have known them — when passion is dumb, and purest love maintains her whole dominion; when God is not cried to, but felt in holy influence, speaking to us more than we to him; the home-sick wanderer is happy in his Father's house; from the deep gladness, a forgiving wish flows forth to every wrong a fellow-man has done us; sighing winds and sweeping storms but strike some new string of the surpassing joy; calmly rise up the faces of our dear departed, no more to unseal the blinding tears, but for invisible embracings; and the soul, showing itself substantial amid all these earthly shadows, looks unfearing into the grave of the body. What are words to us now, — present and future, mortal and immortal? We live, — how should we ever die?

Only in such seasons of our own experience can we know something of the Saviour's peace, which, passing understanding, refuses to be described. Alas that our own moral discords should so hide from us the blessed vision! These inward discords are the great woe of life. There are those who are grieved by nothing so much as the scenes of battle still burning on the earth. They bend every energy to extinguish these dreadful flames, and long for nothing as for the accomplished prediction of peace on earth; and it is well. But this sounding pageantry, marching in its fit coloring of blood, melancholy as it indeed is, is but a sign of the real evil within. The clash of armor is but an echo of collision in the soul; and could you still at a wish the cannon's roar, the end would not be reached, without subduing too the conflicts there. It is not the results that are so mournful, but the cause. Outward suffering is the lot of human nature; and it is cheering to see it bravely borne even on the battle-field. The groans from the soldier's hospital are but a small part of the general groan of humanity. But, ah! those " groanings that cannot be uttered "—in the deep heart,— these ask our tears, and these our toils. Of these it is that war and slavery, rapine and murder, are but the hollow, earthly reverberations.

Hail to the lovers of peace and of freedom! But aim not merely at the surface. Cure the human mind by making your effort conduce to its cleansing from sin and its moral harmony. Touch your work with clean hands. Your passion but puts weapons into the hands of hostile passion: violence can propagate nothing but itself. The harmonious and peaceful soul, too, will multiply its image in deep engraving.

For human good, then, as for private joy, let us seek to receive the peace of Jesus, by being, like him, active, sinless, and holy. The heavenly proportion of his spirit, a harmony in itself, was alive in gladness to every touch of the Divinity, and made his life loving to all mankind. All nature, too, as it were conscious of his secret, changed her forms, stilled her waves, gave up her dead, at his voice; yielding herself his mighty witness, that he came from God and abode with him. And, though we may not have his power (the seal of a peculiar mission), he has left to every sincere follower a richer possession in his peace. Said he not to the seventy, whom he sent forth awhile entrusted with that seal, "In this rejoice not, that the spirits are subject unto you; but rather rejoice, because your names are written in heaven"?

11*

DISCOURSE VII.

THE SPIRITUAL MIND.

Rom. viii. 6. — TO BE SPIRITUALLY MINDED IS LIFE AND PEACE.

WE often hear it said of one or another individual, "He is a very spiritual person," or "He is very unspiritual." What is meant by these expressions? What is it to be spiritual, or, as our text says, "spiritually minded"? In the first place, the passage containing our text informs us that "to be spiritually minded" is opposed to being "carnally minded." The sensual thought, the eyes that rove after, the imagination that shapes, the soul that hankers for, forbidden pleasure, are anti-spiritual.

Again, while the spiritual is opposed to the carnal mind, we learn from other passages of Scripture it is more than what we commonly signify by morality. A man may be honest in his worldly affairs, just in every business-transaction, blameless in every earthly relation, without being truly spiritual; for, besides the earthly and human relations in which we stand, we sustain relations heavenly and divine. God and immortality have a holy claim upon us. We owe special duties, in the upward way, of prayer, meditation, self-surrender, and devotion ; nor are we spiritually minded, unless we inwardly use ourselves to these motions of heart and soul, which run into no material or sublunary channel, but tend aloft beyond the sphere of the earth and the sun. A supreme, uncreated excellence and glory must haunt, elevate, sanctify, and draw us on to another citizenship than that we hold amid these clay-built abodes, before the spiritual mind, with its "life and peace," can be unfolded within us. We must not only find motives in God and the spiritual world to propel the current of moral duty from our hearts through the earth, but still more discover in the infinite majesty and holiness mighty attractions, towards which another stream of revering, obedient tributes shall constantly swell from the heights of inward homage, self-denial, and pure consecration.

Once more : " to be spiritually minded," while standing in opposition to what is " carnal," and completing what is "moral," is also the signification of what is "formal." The outward observances and institutions of our religion have no sense but to express and awaken the exercises of our spiritual nature. They must, of course, be dull and naught to those who lack interest in spiritual things. They are dead forms, empty vessels, unless filled and enlivened by this holy element of regard for what is invisible and everlasting ; but, as conductors and quickeners of this element, they have life and meaning. Were our religion a mere system of ethics, it could be written down in abstract propositions upon the page, or enforced in a style of purely didactic address; but, being a religion which would introduce and bring us into contact with vast and immeasurable realities that stretch off from this shore of existence into an eternal state, it must have sacred symbols as well as moral instructions,— it must have solemn exercises of spiritual feeling and affection, as the shadows and beginnings of that coming life and holy experience, from which the shapes of earthly business, the grosser ties of human relationships, and the occasions of the lesser moralities in mere worldly dealings, will finally be swept clean away. And, according as we go through these punctual rites of prayer and praise, communion and consecration, with a wordly or a spiritual mind, they will be a mechanical and unmeaning mockery to us, or the very glimmerings and reflections of the gates of heaven.

But the spiritual mind, while opposed to what is carnal, completing what is moral, and discerning the significance of what is formal, has, of course, a positive and intrinsic quality of its own, which we must go beyond all terms of negation and comparison to set forth. To be spiritually minded, then, is to have a sense, a conviction, and inward knowledge of the reality, solidity, and permanent security of spiritual things. It is to believe and see that there is something more in God's universe than outwardly appears ; something more than this richly compounded order of material elements, with all its beauty and lustre ; something beyond the sharply defined glittering objects that crowd the landscape. It is to understand that day and night, seed-time and harvest, summer and winter, are not the only facts possibly subject to the notice of the undying soul. It is to be aware that even the broad streets and mighty pathways which the astronomer descries, laid out from globe to globe, do not embrace the whole or highest survey of God's creation. But beyond, within, or above all, there verily is a scene, a society of lofty, intelligent existence, where are brighter displays of God's nearness and love ; a company of immortals, escaped from this empire of change ; a circle of children in harmonious ranks about the infinite Father, on whose forms, " vital in every part," death comes not to lay his finger, and whose feet, no sorrow or disappointment can clog or trip, as they run in endless pursuit of truth and goodness.

The spiritual mind not only sees, as in cold vision, this inner or upper world gloriously triumphing in its stability over the passing kingdom of earth and sense, but enters into relation with it, feels surrounded by it, bows to it, and realizes an inspection from the living firmament of its power. It repeats, indeed, in the chambers of its own hidden life, the experience of the great spiritually-minded writer to the Hebrews, when, after enumerating a long list of ancient worthies, who had died in the faith many centuries before, their names rising up like ranges of mountains on the horizon of history, he represents them as actually present, like the amphitheatre of witnesses at the Grecian stadium, and says to his fellow-believers,

" Wherefore, seeing we are compassed about by so great a cloud of witnesses, let us lay aside every weight, and the sin which doth so easily beset us, and let us run with patience the race that is set before us, looking unto Jesus, the author and finisher of our faith; " a passage of stirring power, which no literature out of the Bible can match. And even such a holy, unseen environment the spiritually-minded man walks in the midst of, or, with a forthrunning and believing imagination, draws around him, and feels its potent virtue. He beholds vividly beside him their bright examples; for they have finished the race before him. He hears them, from their seats of bliss, with united cry cheer him on; and his feet gain swiftness in the way of all honor and well-doing. The rays from their crowns of glory are concentrated from the whole canopy of heaven into the little earthly space over which he speeds to do God's bidding; and he heeds not the ephemeral allurements of earthly pleasure, or the side-lights of human fame.

With the elder successful combatants in the solemn game and trial of life, who gather with their brave words and heroic deeds around him, come the later winners of the heavenly prize, those perchance he has known in the flesh, now with their white robes of purity, and palms of victory ; and voices of children, who struggled for a moment patiently, and spotless died, are added to the great chorus of encouragement and admonition, with their tender accents (it may be) sending a keener thrill to the resolving soul than comes even from the great archangel's mighty tone. All this actual, translated, ever-living loveliness and righteous honor of the sons of God, abashing and casting into the shade the vice, the mean corruption, the forsworn recreancy of this world, stimulates the spiritually-minded man to renewed endeavor for the truth and the right, which, however here abandoned, have been so nobly illustrated and maintained. More are for him than are against him. No faint heart can come, or failing courage have access to him. He is borne on by a mighty pressure from above, like a ship under the whole weight and motion of the atmosphere.

The spiritually-minded man stops not, indeed, with this encircling crowd of created and inspired existences: his worship runs along over their living lines to rest on the Creator, Inspirer. But they are the electric chain, through which additional supplies of the central fire reach him to augment what directly penetrates his soul. They are lesser mediators, adding new sparkles of light and heat to that which comes in a flood through the great Mediator and Intercessor, Jesus Christ; their virtues radiating from his crown, and forming a halo about his pre-eminent head. And, though the spiritually-quickened mortal may not, in the wide usage of the church, invoke aloud these saints in light, he will hear their spirits in the name of all blessed goodness, which they have tasted or reached, speaking to him with a prevailing exhortation to fidelity and Christian zeal. He will think of the steps he must take in this world, in order that his last footstep through the grave may but carry him right on in the path they are treading. The memory will affectingly come back to him of those with whom he may have sojourned; who really seemed in their exit, only to move forward, the line of their earthly march running into that of their heavenly career. For what had a Channing, and what had a Follen, — and I might call less famous, but equally noble names, — what had they to do but move forward on the same track they had been holding; keeping pace with angels as they had with good men, and conversing with the first-met inhabitants of heaven just as they did with the last-seen dwellers upon earth?

But this prepared condition of the spiritual man for an upper abode will not unfit him for his present mansion of earth and flesh, or for any of the duties natural and becoming in his most familiar and homely ties. His spirituality is life and peace, an animating no less than tranquillizing power. The spiritual world, in which God presides, and Christ intercedes, and bands of elder and younger angels minister, is no picture painted in the vault of heaven for him to gaze at with his mind's eye in idle contemplation, but a living, moving, admonishing force. From the shadowy host sounds forth in his ear the trump of duty, whose alarming blast, with incessant repetition, startles him from the slumber of indolence, rouses him from mystical reverie, spurs him to noble enterprise after the example of such pioneers and leaders. It has been said, "This is a world where none, save

God and angels, can afford to be spectators." But they are not spectators only, but workers also. "My Father worketh hitherto, and I work." They are workers, with whom the recluse, dreamy, mystical soul is not in sympathy, but only the soul that applies and busily works out in a daily task its brightest ideal. The truly spiritual man finds in the unseen region of the heavenly existence a source of motive-power, a vast auxiliary, an inexhaustible reserve of strength, coming in aid of natural conscience, which alone is insufficient to direct or reclaim us; but which, reinforced from these divine ranks, irresistibly triumphs with ever-fresh moral victory. Or is this dependence, which we would fain seek, inconsistently forgotten, as, fool-hardy and single-handed venturing into the fight with temptation, we fall under the power of sin? The stinging, degrading sentence of reproach from the spiritual world, with which we are in connection, seconds the upbraidings of our own heart, and recalls us by all the claim and value of that holy approbation we have forfeited, but cannot relinquish while repentance and will are left. Then comes back the Holy Spirit of God, with the escort of his pure and faithful ones, to blow the old peal of duty again into the listening soul; and we spring forth burning to retrieve our reputation of a celestial favor.

Mortal creature, spirit of Almighty inspiration, clothed in flesh! dost thou see the holy company, "part" of the army that "have crossed the flood," and hear the monitory strain? Living soul, ghost in clay, apparition in time! believest thou only in what

12

comes to thee through these five windows of the senses, so advantageously placed to let in the notices of material things; or wilt thou credit that thy Maker also fashioned thy heart to yield for the entrance of himself, and retinue of attending spirits? Breather of earthly air, yet partaker of a heavenly privilege; birth of yesterday, yet heir of immortality; mystery to thyself, definite figure, illimitable being! thy feet do not more surely gravitate to the earth than thy inward nature holds of a loftier sphere. Awake to thy spiritual relations; live up to their solemn dignity. Bind their sanctifying bonds around all the details of earthly pursuit. Insert them, fast and clinging, into every thought and purpose, that, when lower ties part, they may majestically lift thee up.

DISCOURSE VIII.

RELIGIOUS TRAINING.

Prov. xxii. 6. — TRAIN UP A CHILD IN THE WAY HE SHOULD GO ; AND,
WHEN HE IS OLD, HE WILL NOT DEPART FROM IT.

My purpose is not to give here a general discourse
on the common subject of religious instruction, but
rather to unfold the principle or method of education,
which is stated, though perhaps ordinarily over-
looked, in these so familiar and often-quoted words,
" Train up a child in the way he should go." I
would speak of the nature of training, or the difference between teaching and training, and the necessity of training as well as teaching.

A child may be said to be taught, when in words
we clearly convey to his mind any truth, or enjoin
upon his conscience any precept. He is trained,
when we ourselves so pass before him, in practical
illustration of the truth and precept, that he is drawn
along after us in the same way. This principle applies peculiarly to moral and religious instruction.
All that is wanted to perfect a child in many intellectual branches is to communicate to him in language clear ideas ; the end in view being either literal
information of certain facts, or the perception of

some scientific doctrine. But, in morals and religion, it is never information or intellectual perception that is the end; they are but means; action, character, is the end; and to give the child the mere means without the end is to mock him with a half-way and barren education, to show him that the holiest words are empty, and the very seed we are sowing in his heart fruitless. Teach morals and religion by all means; but, beyond this fail, not to train also.

Suppose you wish to instruct a child in benevolence or charity. You use the customary language on the subject to describe this crowning virtue. You tell him what it inclines one to do for the needy and suffering; you go on to dilate upon the beautiful sentiments which the exercise of it incites in one's own breast; you refer to distinguished examples of it that have blessed the world; you go up to the highest example, point to the loving Saviour, and read passages from his life in illustration. All this is teaching, and very good teaching. But now, again, you take your child by the hand, and lead him with you into some abode of poverty and want; you let him see with you the necessitous situation of the inmates of that cold and ill-provided dwelling; he marks the yearning of your heart towards them, and his heart swells in sympathy; he hears your friendly and sympathizing words, as, in the equality wherewith Christ hath made us free, you converse with your poor brother or sister; the tear that rises to your eye moistens his also; the satisfaction that exhilarates your soul he shares, as you freely give the needed aid; he witnesses the whole reciprocal action of a living bounty on your part, and a returning gratitude on the spot. And this is training. Is it not an addition indeed to mere teaching, proceeding from words to things, — an addition as great as when one, from nicely tracing the boundaries of the earth accurately drawn on a little paper-map, should go to traversing the seas and continents of the world ; or as when he should look from the minute starry tracery of a small globe, into the real glory and vastness and endless splendor of the heavens ? One such scene will avail more than many lectures to make your child charitable.

Or suppose, again, you would instruct your child in devotion, prayer to God. You speak of the nature of prayer; you speak of that relation to our Maker which makes it reasonable and due ; you speak of the happy effects it produces on our own minds, or of the futility of any objections to it; and you earnestly exhort the child to say its prayers morning and night to the great Father and Protector. But to what purpose, if the child is not moreover trained to pray ? — to what purpose, if the very house he lives in is a prayerless house, — a house without an altar of praise and supplication ; among all the sounds there that he hears pass and repass between mortal ears, none heard going up to heaven ; among all the references made there to human doings, none to an Almighty Will ? So far as mere teaching goes, the child must think life ought to turn on the principle of acknowledging and bowing to the Infinite Power and Providence. Yet, in reality, prayer turns out to be a mere

12*

topic of discourse.   But bridge over this chasm between the lesson and the fact; bend yourself before the Majesty of heaven and earth; let your child see your spirit mount on the wings of devotion; let "each revolving day and night witness your visits to the skies," and he will then follow; he will be trained to pray, and will learn more what devotion is from one fervent outpouring of the heart than from many long discussions.   The little bird, without speech or language, trains her young to fly.   She hovers over them, flies before them, makes the motions of her own wings distinct, slow, and gentle as she can, returns to induce them to follow,

> " Reproves each dull delay,
> Allures to brighter worlds, and leads the way."

So, in every virtue, the young are to be not only taught, but trained.   The gardener's training hand must first move before, wherever he would have the tender plant to follow after.   So only can the heart of childhood be directed in the way of religious growth.

Would you instruct your children in that cardinal excellence of truth?   You insist often, in words, on its importance.   It is well.   Teach it to tell the truth. But, more than this, train it to do so.   You rebuke deception.   It is well.   But practise not in any way what you rebuke.   Nothing is sharper, more curious and inquisitive, than the eye of a child.   It sees more than we are aware; it sees, and says perhaps nothing; it sees, and shapes its own course by what it sees. If you promise, perform. If you threaten, perform. If you state any thing, state accurately. Let it never detect you in a deviation from the fact. Be regular before it as the sun, and then you will train as well as teach. If, in this familiar reasoning, I may take a particular case, do you receive one with smiles and large demonstrations of favor, and then disparage him when he is gone? The child is noting all this. He marks the change in your countenance. He sees that your former face was a mask. He has an acute ear, too. The senses of childhood are quick. He observes that transition from sweet flattery to harshness, from the respectful to the scornful, in the tones of your voice. He sees that your former voice was affectation and a lie. You are making a hypocrite of him. You are training him to falsehood. A child upon frankly informing an unwelcome but flattered visitor that really no affection was felt towards her, was violently contradicted by the family, and subjected to a severe punishment for telling what she and they knew to be true. To what was she trained? Oh! that old maxim of Roman wisdom is just, that "the greatest reverence is due to the young,"—reverence to their capacities, to their power of appreciation, to every moral sensibility and affection they possess.

To take a single other example. Would we instruct our children to be kind and gentle? How? by a command? Not so only, but more powerfully by the affectionate and pleasant bearing and tone of our own speech and person. "With my children," said a friend once to me, "I am careful even to modulate my voice to the softest utterance, that no unamiable expression before them may ever escape me." A wise rule; for every thing is contagious with the young, and our sweetness or bitterness is speedily reproduced in their tender breasts and upon their so ready tongues. How, with upturned faces, they watch at our side, and drink in the spirit of all that we say or do!

May we not repeat now, with peculiar emphasis, our text, "Train up a child in the way he should go; and, when he is old, he will not depart from it?"

The doctrine of this discourse explains much that has been thought dark and inexplicable in the differing destinies of men. Parents and friends often wonder that, after all the pains taken with children, the frequent counsels and admonitions, they should yet afterwards go astray. But was the child, who has disappointed you, trained as well as taught? Did you uniformly go before to beckon and lead him after in the way you first pointed out? Some, no doubt there are, who grossly belie even their training; for, after all, their freedom of choice remains. Some angels, we are told, kept not their first estate; so some sons of men spurn all their privileges from a good Providence, and leap madly down from the noble summit of honor and virtue to which they were led up. But, in the majority of cases, the rule will hold good: your child will keep on as he has been trained. The strength of habit, the bonds of affection, the desire of a good reputation, will confirm the principles in whose actual exercise, by your own procedure, he has once been established. Few indeed are there who do not keep on in the way in which they have once decidedly set forth. The soldier in his age might as soon forget the drill of his early discipline, or the sailor the first calculations by which, under the rolling planets, he made his way over the uncertain waves, as your child the practical guidance to which you have actually used him through a series of years. He will keep on, if you have been his leader and forerunner, when your feet stumble on the dark mountains, and will run the race after, very much as you have run it before. The impulse you gave him shall not be exhausted with your earthly life. The teaching he may forget; the training, never: but, if it have been generous, he will, by his continual advances therein, do honor to your gray hairs; he will hold back awhile, in the land of the living, your steps as they begin to slide towards the tomb; he will make your memory honorable when your eyes are for ever closed, and find you again somewhere on the endless road of immortality.

But, if you train your child to an irreligious worldly career, as you must if you be an irreligious, worldly man or woman, you strike a blow, beneath the body you so tenderly cherish, into the finer and only enduring part. The iron enters the soul. Your own virtue is the only sure pledge and promise of your child's. You may lavish the attentions of teachers upon him, make him shine with accom-

plishments, lead him through the whole circle of
the sciences, and give him a good and liberal education, as it is called ; but it is not a good or liberal
education, if his conscience and his heart be left out ;
and these cannot be educated by words alone, but
must be trained by deeds.   If you have omitted this,
and the time ever comes for those words to pass
through your mind, " How sharper than a serpent's
tooth it is to have a thankless child ! " then you may
have to reflect (O God ! will it not be too bitter to
reflect), " It is my own fault, this very ingratitude."
As I think of such things, I cannot see a young
child by its parent's side, without trembling before
the future, whose veil I cannot lift.   Pass a few
years, and the deep channel of moral consequences
shall mark what the training has been.   Shall it
mark it as the green course of the fruitful river, or
as the barren gulley, where the devastating torrent
fell ?   The chief significance of the grave where
you lie down will be to fix the direction in which
you trained, and the point at which you left, your
child.   Your bark will disappear as it sails on over
the misty horizon ; but his bark shall hold the same
course.   Whither, whither shall it be ?

DISCOURSE IX.

RELIGIOUS EDUCATION.

Deut. vi. 6, 7. — AND THESE WORDS, WHICH I COMMAND THEE THIS DAY,
SHALL BE IN THINE HEART; AND THOU SHALT TEACH THEM DILIGENTLY
UNTO THY CHILDREN, AND SHALT TALK OF THEM WHEN THOU SITTEST
IN THINE HOUSE, AND WHEN THOU WALKEST BY THE WAY, AND WHEN
THOU LIEST DOWN, AND WHEN THOU RISEST UP.

RELIGIOUS education is a subject which not only interests professed teachers, as in the Sunday-school,
but is of still deeper concern to parents. To all
elders, employers, guardians, and whoever has any
superiority of wisdom, experience, or authority to
influence any child, it presents claims too momentous and strictly binding to be set aside without
aggravated guilt. We seem able in this day, more
than ever before, to entertain clear and encouraging
views of what can be done by education. A distinguished man, whose services to the general cause of
education can never be forgotten in this Commonwealth, after making extensive inquiries of persons
holding high offices in the business of teaching, as to
what proportion of the young could, by the power of
instruction rightly directed, be trained up into a good
and useful life, draws, from their united replies, the

no less cheering than surprising conclusion, that not more than one or two, if as many, out of a hundred, would fail of so desirable a result. Even the poor idiot's mind is now taking fire with the communicated spark of knowledge; his dormant susceptibilities of intelligence and virtue are waking up; and we are thus discovering new illustrations of the wondrous capacity of the human soul for development here, and endless development hereafter. We are on all sides admonished to purify ourselves for this work; for as Fenelon, that remarkable " discerner of spirits," says, " It is our own faults that make us impatient of the faults of others ; " so it is only our own good qualities that we can plant, and make to take root, in other minds.

In the confidence that this topic, especially of the religious instruction of children, engages already the regard of all, let me speak to you of the object at which you aim, its nature and difficulty, and the means of its accomplishment. And, first, of your object.

In all undertakings, a clear and definite idea of what should be done is pre-requisite ; and, obvious as this proposition may seem, it nevertheless indicates the point where many parents and teachers fail, by having only a vague and formal notion of their office. To have an idea and be inspired by it, to have the earnestness, enthusiasm, perseverance, it kindles, should be our primary care. The cultivator of the ground, the architect, the artist, the financier, the philosopher, the statesman, have each, and must have in starting, their idea of what they would accomplish; and the idea is to them an unfailing fountain of strength and encouragement. It is guidance to their steps, motive to industry, defence against despondency, breath of life. Our Saviour had his idea, and, having it, must be about his Father's business.

What, then, is the true idea in the religious instruction of the young? It is that they have in them a moral and spiritual nature to be unfolded, or, in other words, an original capacity for religious thought, feeling, faith, and affection. Here, however, it is necessary to observe a distinction, too much lost sight of, between being capable of religion and actually religious. Volumes have been written to prove man naturally, though in manifold forms, a religious being; made such, just as he is made with outward senses and powers to see and hear and walk. But there is this great difference: he instinctively or necessarily exercises these outward faculties, while the inward senses may lie mostly asleep and inactive to the end of his days. It might be said, in the same way, man is naturally a poetical, musical, or scientific being; yet poetry, music, and science are only the highest attainments of culture, the ever-improving results of patient study. So religion is not a thing which we find ready formed in the infant soul, as we find gold and diamonds in the mine; but it is a susceptibility which we must, with all pains-taking, develop from the feeblest germs into ever-increasing beauty and fruit.

It is probably this shallow or misconceived idea of

13

man as constitutionally religious, rather than capable of religion, which has suggested to some the conclusion, that little children are already divinely exercised in their souls, spiritually full-blown, before we lay our hands upon them ; and that our chief solicitude should be to keep them as they are, to preserve them from injury or alteration ; the only danger being that we shall harm them, that they will wander from God, or be misled by the world, and human life be to them a backward, not a forward course. And much has been said and written, implying that the common fact of our growth from childhood is such a loss and degradation ; all of earthly existence, one long failure. As a favorite poet has declared, " Heaven lies about us in our infancy, — shades of the prison-house begin to close upon the growing boy," till at last " the splendid vision " of transcendent " light " in " manhood fades" wholly away. If all that is meant by such representations be, that early childhood is the state of innocence and simplicity, that there is no falsehood or imagination of deceit in its transparent eye, no stain or line of actual sin in that ingenuous face, no selfishness in the little one that has not conceived of itself as a distinct creature, its very identity not yet separate from its divine or human parentage ; — if it be meant that there is an unspeakable beauty and charm to the soul in that confiding helplessness, clinging dependence, and freedom from guile ; and that these natural traits are often not transformed, as they should be, into moral and spiritual virtues in advancing years, but wholly left behind as the dew of youth is exhaled ; the statement may be accepted as true, and equivalent to what our Saviour himself intended by exhorting us to become like little children, and declaring that of such is the kingdom of heaven. That is, the great problem is for manhood, in the midst of knowledge, excitement, and temptation, to be from choice as guileless as the infant is from necessity ; and the true subjects of Christ's kingdom are to be gained by training up infancy to this end in the way of his precepts. But if it be meant that little children are positively spiritual, virtuous, and devout, at the outset, before they have come to be free and independent agents at all, and while swayed by varying impulse alone, — the doctrine, which would make our office of moral instruction a superfluous task and senseless misnomer, is but a chimera, having no ground in experience or in reason.

The very idea of teaching is to bring out from the crude capacity, from the unwrought substance of the soul, these very virtues ; to awaken in the child apprehensions of spiritual things, which have not yet visited its mind; to communicate conceptions, which must be faint and narrow at first, of God, heaven, and immortality ; to withdraw the thoughts from exclusive occupation in outward and sensible things, and fix them on those which are unseen ; to strengthen and set up conscience as supreme ruler in the breast, royally armed and enthroned to resist the seduction of the world, and the rebellion of the passions ; to form these creatures of sense and fancy,

and wandering desire, into the intelligent and determined followers of Jesus Christ ; to prepare them to
act well their several parts in the various stations of
social existence here ; to fit them to bid at last a
willing adieu to all lower scenes, and enter on a
loftier and more blessed stage of being after death.
And there is nothing sublimer in after years, in all
the later experience of the advanced Christian, than
in the first dawning of such thoughts and purposes
upon the soul standing on the very shore of being.
It is indeed a great idea, to be realized only by a
long and arduous process, carrying the soul not only
far away from, but infinitely above, its original rudi-
mental state, where the powers of good and evil, as
yet unstirred, slumber together.   To the negative
care of not hurting the child must be added the
positive, of helping him according to his great,
pressing want.   We need not fear to lay a vigorous
hand upon his spirit, in prosecuting this work.   For
that spirit is not the already delicately shaped, perfect excellence some suppose, like beautiful frost-
work, which a breath may mar ; or frail porcelain,
exquisitely fashioned, which is easily shattered ; but
an undeveloped ability to fear and love and serve
God, which we are by all means, and with all our
might, to stimulate and bring forth.

It is a work of difficulty.   As the apostle says,
" First is that which is natural, and afterwards that
which is spiritual."   You who have seriously made
the attempt will all bear witness, that you have found
the making of this road for the child in his own

heart, from the natural to the spiritual, no slight or short enterprise. Were it only to guard against excessive disappointment and discouragement, into which parents and teachers, proceeding on a false theory, are apt to fall, as well as to direct skilfully our efforts, it is desirable, at starting, to consider soberly the whole truth as to the subject we work upon, — the nature of the child. Leaving out extraordinary cases of those, on the one hand, apparently sanctified from birth with singular tenderness of conscience and nobleness of feeling, or, on the other hand, of a strangely stubborn and incorrigible temper,— the being we have to deal with, beheld not as transfigured by our imagination, but in his real condition, is a being of undeveloped spiritual nature. Nor is this all. While the germ of the spirit is in him, the germ of what in Scripture is called the *flesh* is in him too. He is capable, not only of religion, but of selfishness, irreverence, falsehood, unkindness, impurity. Rejecting the theory of original virtue, I do not, of course, propound any theory of original sin, except in the sense, one has suggested, that it is original with the sinner. But neither can I adopt the view apparently entertained by many, that sin is poured even into the youthful mind from without, like water into a vessel. "The traitor is in the heart." Allow me to offer you a conclusion coinciding neither with the extreme liberal view of the dignity of human nature (though I believe in its true dignity), nor with the other extreme of the depravity of human nature ; but regarding the child

13*

as both capable of virtue and capable of vice, as its nature opens, placed in the midst of contradictory inclinations to right and wrong, and so placed on purpose by the Creator because only in this struggle can virtue be born, and God's sublime purpose of a voluntary loyalty and devotion fulfilled. Goodness secured in any other way would be a mechanical, imputed, involuntary goodness, not one's own.

Through this inward struggle, then, must the child pass. Our specific office is to aid him in it ; to see, far as we may, that the lower desires do not triumph ; to side with every thing generous in him ; to invigorate the better principles ; to introduce divine and heavenly influences, which — as, in heathen story, the gods are pictured as coming to the aid of their worshippers on the field of battle, and bearing them safely away — may give him the victory in this sorer contest between the mind and the flesh. You may have seen the German drawing of "the game of chess," in which a youth plays with the devil, the stake being his soul ; while the guardian angel bends, as a good genius, over the contest. That game is in the heart : our task is to encourage and assist the good principle against the bad.

But the difficulty is not only within. From the evil that is in the world too, from the general level of human conduct, flows a mighty stream of influence, tending to carry the child either into sin or a mean mediocrity of character. How lift him out of that stream ? How get him above the unworthy temper that not only arises within, but predominates around and insinuates itself into him, like an unwholesome atmosphere, at every pore? So far as that mighty influence is concerned, can the effect be superior to the cause?—the current rise above the fountain?—the instructed be any better than his instructor?— the new generation excel the old generation that trains it? Of what use, in fact, is ingenious speculation and long discoursing on such a subject? Is not the child, by an inevitable law, fastened to the same plane with the parent, and the pupil with the teacher; mutually entangled in what is base, or alike soaring into what is noble; a continual inheritance of good or evil, transmitted to the rising race from the living manners, customs, words, faces, all around them?

Such, then, is the problem to be solved, as presented in the nature and difficulty of our work. How shall we grapple at once with this subtle foe in the heart, and this boastful Goliath of the world, together assailing the charge in our hands? I have but one comprehensive means or instrument to propose, and that is truth,—religious, divine, Christian truth,—truth, which Christ in his own prayer relies upon to sanctify his disciples. Truth is the magazine and armory, by winning which into our possession and vigorously bringing to bear upon our object, we can, I believe, effect our three-fold object of developing the spiritual nature, subordinating the animal nature to its right place and proportions, and giving a check or antidote to the corruptions of the world. But it must be truth taught and truth exemplified; for

otherwise it is hardly the truth, but only its body
without the soul, — truth flowing audibly from the
lips, and silently from the character, — truth in our
conduct, feelings, affections, and principles, as well
as in our patient speech and persuasion. Let us
remember, no one can give what he has not. We
must first ourselves get the truth, before we shall be
able to communicate it ; and we may bear in mind,
for our comfort and the peculiar attraction of our
work, that we are thus saving our own selves, just so
far as we save others. No mere words of truth,
which we may read from a catechism, a manual, or
the Bible itself, will ever be effectual. " The letter
killeth ; " — " the spirit only giveth life." There is
all the difference between truth set forth in its merely
verbal signs and truth realized, that there is between
the galvanic battery with its material apparatus lying
coldly round, and the same machinery sparkling,
darting electric shocks, and melting the hardest substances as the invisible fluid runs through every jar
and wire ; or between the volcanic crater when it
is ice and when it is flame.

In the religious education of a child, you aim at a
great effect. Do you complain that you see little
fruit from your exertions ? But have you put in
motion a power or cause, great in correspondence
to the effect you would produce ? If not, you are
as unreasonable as the man spoken of in Scripture
who would build a tower without counting the cost,
or as it would have been to expect the fountain of
refreshing waters to gush up in our sight, before the

rock had been bored and the quicksand bridged to conduct the stream. The moral faculty, in an immortal soul, is not a flower like that which opens in the morning to shut at night, but nearer resembling the century-plant; and we must be content to nurse it through grade after grade of growth, slowly approximating the bright consummation, which, even in the saint, is but partially revealed in this earthly life. Only for our good cheer, in this gradual and perhaps tardy process, let us have faith in the law of cause and effect, as operating no less surely in the moral than in the material world. No visible impression or audible echo proves that our aim has been sure, and our mark reached. We strike into the invisible; we embrace the intangible: verily, it is a spirit that we are treating with. We work much in the dark, and we may feel sometimes that we are beating the air. But not so: so far as we really employ the living truth of God, and bring that' into action in our words or deeds; so far as it shines in our countenance or breathes in our tones, it does and must needs produce an effect. No more certainly will the sonorous church-bell answer to its clanging tongue, calling us to worship, or the liquid water spread its successive circles from the falling stone, or our own voice penetrate the listening ear, than, sooner or later, will the sincere and vital truth we utter or practically manifest produce an influence upon all within our sphere, especially upon the susceptible young. Let them smile or be serious, assent or question, agree or profess to reject, they experience an unavoidable effect according to the nature of the cause. This is the law of life, illustrated by all influence, from the humblest act up to the example of Jesus Christ, flooding the world with new light and love through a hundred generations.

Here, then, is the criterion and measure of our legitimate faith in religious instruction. Just so far as by study and meditation, by prayer and toil, by fidelity and adherence to a lofty standard, we ourselves have learned the truth ; just so far as our own hearts, like the disciples' on that famous walk to Emmaus, have burned within us at its revelations in the gospel ; just so far as we have grown upon its nourishment, incorporated it into our motives, or exhibited it in our behavior, — just so far shall we have therefor the best reward and privilege of introducing it into the souls of those committed to our care, and by it awakening in them all good affections and principles. Nor are there any mathematical axioms by which the man of science can anticipate the result of his combinations, or trace the course of material revolutions, more certain than to the eye of Omniscience, in the issues of eternity, are the demonstrations of this law.

Our remedy, then, for the fear and doubt and dejection so apt to come over us in our spiritual labor, is an ever-new personal resort to the fountains of strength in the word and spirit of God. As the engineer in the steam-ship or at the locomotive, if he observe the wheels slacken, increases the speed by increasing the power, acts on the circumference by first acting on the centre, and quickens the pulsations of that great heart of brass and iron which he wields, that he may hasten the motions of his car or vessel; or as the aeronaut, if his balloon will not carry the given weight into the atmosphere, does not sceptically sit down to repine, but only sets to work to generate more of the buoyant force; so are we not to be dispirited and unbelieving, when our moral ends in the minds and lives of the young are not accomplished as rapidly as we desire, and they do not rise to the height of purity above the world we would fain see them maintain: but we are to replenish our own spiritual stores, and clear a new passage for the perhaps obstructed waters of that well within, which springeth up into everlasting life. We are to go to the "closet" to revive in our prostrate hearts the spirit of faith and devotion. As one said that the Bible was his church, and Christ his preacher, we must frequent the ministrations of that divine sanctuary and that great High Priest; and the truth of God, his own immortal truth, will thus again flow into us, and through us into those, the instruments of whose regeneration and salvation we are set to be.

In short, we, as teachers of the young, are aiming at a particular result, which we cannot, of course, expect to reach without a careful and patient observance of the exact conditions on which it depends. If the explosion, the precipitate, or the transparency does not follow upon the mingling of the chemist's ingredients, as he expects, he attributes the failure of his experiment, not to any mysterious fatality or insuperable hinderance, but at once to his neglect of some of the requisite conditions ; for nature does not lie, or ever prove treacherous. If the architect's roof settles or his tower leans, he judges he has made some mistake in his foundation, his materials, or construction. If the artist's canvas presents an untrue portraiture, his eye has been at fault as to the coloring, or his hand in the proportions. If a political movement, business-plan, worldly speculation, or trial in husbandry, turns out badly, there has been some want of discernment, contrivance, or forecast. So the *failure of our moral experiment upon the hearts of the young indicates the absence of some necessary ingredient. The weakness of our spiritual building proves that we have taken the sand for our basis, instead of having been at the pains to penetrate to the rock. And if there be no success, no return, no fruit, from our religious calculation and culture, the first and most likely inference is, that we have not endeavored wisely, anticipated prudently, grappled with the real difficulties, taken advantage of favoring circumstances, or well prepared this living soil for the seed of God's word. We are mixers and combiners of motives, edifiers of a spiritual and immortal temple, painters of a picture whose hues may harden for an eternal duration, adventurers for a gain beyond the gold of California, cultivators of a ground which may bloom with beauty, and be luxuriant with fruit on earth, and bring forth more abundantly in the upper paradise of God.

Do we, then (for this one question covers the whole ground of this subject), — do we observe the strict conditions of our vast and unsurpassably momentous work? I know, and do not forget the peculiarity involved in the fact, that we are not working in gross matter, as wood or stone, or dealing with such things as the wind and the rain in our planting, or wielding the mechanical elements of any earthly economy; but trying to impress a spiritual substance, essaying to guide a self-moving and free being, whose liberty and inclination and individuality of nature, whose situation and exposure to change and temptation beyond our reach, give a singular character to the terms upon which we can stand with or approach him.

But all this does not make void, or even for a moment bring into the slightest question, the principle that has been laid down. Whatever may be done to the child by others, or whatever he may do to himself, our action upon him will nevertheless tell the full tale of its own quality and amount. The ship sailing across Atlantic seas may be retarded by the shell-fish that fastens on her smooth sides, or be swept out of her course by the Gulf-stream: nevertheless, the breezes of heaven, that have blown upon her, have produced their entire effect; and she would have been more retarded or further diverted, had those breezes intermitted their constancy, or abated their stress. Much of the force in all machinery is lost in friction; but the artisan does not therefore doubt the virtue of the central motive-power, how-

14

ever much of it may be neutralized on the way.   So
our exertions, whether cancelled by hindrances or
producing their free results, are fully reckoned in a
positive or negative way.   And we know that God
himself conspires with our enterprise ; that we are
humble, privileged co-workers with him ; setting our
action in the line with his friendly providence ; ful-
filling what will ever more reveal itself, as dearer to
him than the making of worlds, kindling of suns, and
balancing of constellations ; sowing our seed, and
preparing its tender sprout and blade for the dew he
promises of his Spirit, and the rain that will descend
of his grace.   And, as regards this mysterious power
of free-will, it as yet but feebly stirs itself, suffering the bosom of childhood to lie often free and
open to our influence, and giving precious opportunity how earnestly and eagerly to be improved, as
we remember that the time of freedom — and, if we
watch and prevent not, it may be wilful, wayward
freedom — is indeed soon coming when

> " The wintry hour
> Of man's maturer age
> Will shake the soul with sorrow's power,
> And stormy passion's rage ; "

while we may so now operate on the pliable purposes and ductile dispositions of the soul, that the
energy of will and passion may run in the way of
duty, consecrate itself to religion, and promote the
glory of God.

The question, to which our preliminary reflections

have brought us, grows only more fearfully weighty
with every consideration that can be proposed. Do
we fulfil the conditions of our work ; — fulfil them in
regular and faithful preparation for our office, preparation of our lesson and preparation of our soul ; —
fulfil them in giving the flower and strength of our
interest and zeal to a matter of such unspeakable
concern ; — fulfil them in nourishing an earnest and
tender love for every one of our children or pupils,
carrying them in our hearts through the week, bearing them to God in our prayers, coming to them in
the fullness of the blessing of the gospel of Christ ;
adapting our instructions to their individual capacities and sensibilities ; convincing them, by our
whole temper and deportment, that we really seek
their good ; showing to them, by our own constant
attendance on the institutions of religious worship,
that our example is as good as our precept, and
does not shamefully contradict it ; pursuing their
souls the more affectionately, as what has been called
" the dark age " of boyhood comes over them ; and
being continually to them as those fresh from the
presence of God, and encircled with the light of religion ? If we fulfil these conditions, if we stand to
them for what is right and pure and godly, we shall
not labor in vain, however gradually we accomplish
our end ; not in vain, any more than they who per-
severingly, though slowly, cut away the hill for their
iron road, or clear the forest for their farm and
habitation. Said a wise elder in the ministry of the
gospel to a younger laborer in the vineyard, " If you

want to save the souls of your people, you will."
So, if it be the real absorbing object of your desire
and devotion to lead your little flocks into the ways
of pleasantness and peace, you will at least set them
in that blessed direction.

And what reward of your labors greater that even
their partial and commencing success? What should
one so desire to do in the life he lives in this world,
as to give to a soul the tendency of virtue, and in-
flame it with the love of God? What ambition
beneath the sky so great and far-reaching, upon
whose achievements and empire the sun will not set,
nor the heavens themselves close when they are
wrapt together like a scroll! As I sit in the Sunday-
school, and think of it; as I look over the written
lessons, many of which hands but little practised
have prepared, perhaps the first lines they ever
traced; or cast my eye around to mark the fixed
attention that has drawn all the members of a class
here and there into a living cluster about the teacher,
from whom, in the apostle's phrase, they "desire the
sincere milk of the word," that they "may grow
thereby;" and then, as I gaze forward upon their
future career, and see their earthly relations, domestic, social, and civil, blessed and sanctified by this
early nurture; or, glancing still further on beyond
the grave into the world of spirits, behold, what I
doubt not is the very fact while we here meet and
meditate, many an angel of God tracing back to
such a beginning the crown and palm and harp of
his glory, joy, and praise, and pointing his brother-

angel to what he did for him in that beginning, following the lines of influence from a little room to that measureless canopy on high, — the material vocations, the perishable accumulations, the shining reputations of this world, fade and dwindle before the solid, everlasting work.

> " The cloud-capped towers, the gorgeous palaces,
>   The solemn temples, the great globe itself,
>   Yea, all which it inherit, shall dissolve ;
>   And, like an insubstantial pageant faded,
>   Leave not a rack behind."

But the virtue to which you have trained a living soul, the great thought of God you have awakened, the sentiment of worship you have inspired, the devotion to duty you have kindled, the love you have made to glow for a heavenly Father and his rational offspring, — oh! these things will outlast all, and abide for ever.

14*

DISCOURSE X.

FAITH THE SUBSTANCE AND EVIDENCE.

Heb. xi. 1. — NOW, FAITH IS THE SUBSTANCE OF THINGS HOPED FOR, THE EVIDENCE OF THINGS NOT SEEN.

How shall we prove the reality of things which we denominate spiritual and unseen ? We talk much about such spiritual things ; but how show that there is any substance corresponding with our language ; that it is not, after all, mere shadow and illusion, on which we feed our thoughts ? The author of our text answers this question, by declaring that faith is itself the substance or ground of things hoped for, — the evidence of things not seen.

In an age characterized as an age of scepticism, — certainly an age of extensive questioning of long-received dogmas ; with a deep feeling, on the part of many, of great uncertainty in the religious views in which they have been bred, or which are proposed for their acceptance ; and a persuasion, on the part of others, that every thing put forth and canvassed among men about a spiritual and invisible world is mere cant and superstition ; when doubts about the Scriptures, and denial of all that is supernatural, busily pave the way for sweeping infidelity and utter irreligion, — at such a time, it may be well to examine what real foundation there is at all for faith in spiritual things.

As the text declares, so I would maintain, that faith itself, the believing faculty, as a power and native tendency of the human mind, belonging to us originally and fundamentally, but best developed by our religion, is the basis and evidence of what we hope for. In other words, an unseen and heavenly world is required to correspond to our faith, just as much as a material world to correspond to our senses. I stand in the midst of nature on some lovely spring-morning. The sweet and pleasant light salutes my eyes. The fresh and bland breeze mingles with the warmth of the sun, fanning his beams as they fall to give that perfect and temperate luxury which makes the feeling even of physical life a delight. The fragrance of flowers from every bright and waving branch, dressed in pale and crimson, floats to me. The song of matin birds falls on my ear. All this beauty, melody, and richness are the correspondence to my nature of the material world through my senses.

Now, there are inward perceptions and intuitions, just as real as these outward ones, and requiring spiritual realities to correspond with them, just as much as the eye requires the landscape, or as the ear asks for sounds of the winds and woods and streams, for the song of birds, or the dearer accents of the human voice. To meet and answer the very nature of man, a spiritual world, more refined modes of existence, action, happiness, must be, — just as there must be space without for his physical motions, and color for the discriminations of his sight, and modulation of tones for his hearing, — else his nature, satisfied and fed in one direction, and that the lowest, is balked, belied, and starved in another direction, and that the highest.

But, without illustrating further, in this general way, the rooting of faith in the primary ground of our being, let me show the peculiar light in which the great doctrines and practical influences of religion are brought to us, by thus considering "faith" itself as " the substance of things hoped for, the evidence of things not seen."

And first the great doctrine or fact of the being of a God is one of the things that corresponds to our faith, of which faith itself, as a faculty of the soul, is the basis and evidence.   Much is said of proving the existence of a God.   Belief itself, I would say (in the spirit of my text), as a power and disposition of the human soul, is a proof and the great proof. No logical argument, metaphysical or natural, is so strong.   How do I prove the existence of the material world ?   By any syllogisms of reasoning, or steps of philosophic demonstration ?   No : such proof is impossible.   I prove it by my eyes, by my ears, and all the senses that bring me into correspondence with it.   Seeing, hearing, feeling, I cannot doubt, I cannot argue.   The world is a bright and glorious reality with which I am in contact.   I experience the world, and so need not demonstrate it.

Even such is the true proof of the being of God. It is to see and feel and commune with him. The most cunning ladder which speculation ever wove, the firmest bridge that natural theology ever constructed, will not carry us to him so surely as the direct discernment, the holy consciousness, the immediate beholding, of our faith. Moses, we are told, lived as seeing Him that is invisible ; and Christ has assured us that " the pure in heart shall see God." It is the moral and spiritual intuition of a justly exercised and exalted faith. We want no other reason for believing in God. Faith itself is the reason, and the best reason. As the beloved apostle declares, " He that believeth hath the witness in himself." We need nothing put under our faith to support that, any more than under our direct outward perceptions, our positive knowledge, the dictates of our consciences, or the affections of our hearts, going forth to fix upon their appropriate objects. Like them, it is a radical part of our very constitution,— only a part which Christ has come specially to bring out, enrich, and ennoble with the truth he utters, and the actual objects he presents.

To the man in whom this principle or sentiment of faith is thus enlivened by meditation, prayer, and the whole stimulus of the gospel, the Supreme One does not appear simply as a first Cause, an original Creator, far back out of our present reach, but as the perpetual Sustainer and Renewer of all things, to whom he joins with the angelic choir of the poet in singing, "Thy works are beautiful as on the first day." His God is near him, nay, with him; breathes upon him in the freshness of the morning; folds him tenderly in the shades of night; whispers to him in the awed stillness and loving aspirations of his heart; and answers every entreating or confiding desire which he silently ejaculates, with peace, sanctity, assurance that can be felt; "the benediction from these covering heavens falling upon him like dew." As, sailing in northern latitudes, the needle dips to an unseen power, so his heart inclines to the unseen Power of heaven and earth. Observe that I do not here speak of faith separate from the influence and unfolding power of the gospel. I admit the need of the light of a supernatural revelation. But that light operates in the soul as the light of the sun in nature; not being lodged mechanically in the place where it falls, but mixing with, to expand, the primitive germs of thought; opening the native sense of a superior Power, not into polytheism, or the beautiful idolatry of fire-worship, but the adoration of one Father.

With an ever-quickening sense of the Divine Being, comes also, through this vitally unfolded power of faith, the feeling of a share in the permanence of that Being; a persuasion, and, so far as in the flesh such a thing can be, realization of the immortality of the soul. There are arguments, many and strong, for the immortality of the soul; but that immortality never will become vivid and real to us, without the development of the principle itself of faith, or of the capacity for apprehending spiritual and heavenly things. Nay, does not the Scripture itself declare, that they who are thus insensible would not be persuaded "though one rose from the dead"? And they are not persuaded by Christ's raising the dead or by his own resurrection, because they are earthly-minded, intent on worldly and carnal things, having hands only for gross and material works, and none of finer make to lay hold of eternal life. The spiritual nature, which allies them to God and the upper sphere, being dead or asleep, immortality is, of course and necessarily, to them but a vague dream, an absurd vision of the night, a groundless, incredible fancy. All the descriptions of that celestial region to them are like showing colors and beautiful pictures to the blind; or playing on harp or organ sweet tunes, harmonious and sublime anthems, to the deaf. They do not appreciate the matter, more than a rude savage, in whom the principle of taste had never been cultivated, would the masterpieces of the fine arts.

When a man, whose life has been devoted to pleasure, who has had, morning and night, only the one thought of riches, or who has been assiduously all his days climbing up the ladder of earthly ambition, — when such a one tells me he does not believe in the immortality of the soul, I am not surprised. I believe it none the less, nor is it the less credible, for his disbelief. The wonder would be if he did believe it. His scepticism is his inward condition; it is the retribution and punishment of his selfish, fleshly course. Though heaven's gates should fly open before him, he could not properly enter into its joy and glory, till the spiritual faculty of faith should be developed. So the tribes of the field walk about untouched, and in dull stupidity behold with the outward eye those splendors of the creation, whose matchless order thrills the musing and devout human heart with rapture.

These views are confirmed by the manner in which Christ himself regards and presents the soul's immortality. He does not dwell on it as a special theme. He does not undertake to assert it as a separate doctrine. He grandly assumes it in all his teaching. Nothing, he says, would be true and complete without it. It is something he sees and feels continually; an air he breathes; an element that bathes his very being. We feel, as we read his words, that he is immortal; not is to become so. We behold the divine and deathless in him, when truly we behold him at all. We see a being from heaven walking on the earth, not so much reasoning upon and enforcing, as illustrating and exhibiting, the fact of immortality; all his deeds and motions savoring of the celestial courts whence he came down; and his rising from the sepulchre seeming in him no strange thing, but what naturally and inevitably must be.

And, when we walk in the atmosphere of his truth and life, are in his holy familiarity and companionship, our faith puts forth like a blossom in the spring. Our hearts catch from him a sense of spiritual things, as it were a heavenly fire.   The doors of an endless existence, bolted to the worldling, open of their own accord.   We believe in immortality, because the soul within us thus unfolded claims it as its portion, and cannot conceive of any other fate.   Its proof is not the reasoning of Plato or Butler.   Its demonstration is not even " the letter " of any single text of Scripture.   Its faith, its Christian faith, is all the argument it needs.   Its inward, spiritual, vital premises involve the conclusion more surely than any curious and subtle analysis of the understanding can reach it. " Faith " itself, as our text avers, " is the basis of things hoped for, the evidence of things not seen," and needs not that any other foundation though of rock, or pillars though of iron, should be put underneath it.   As we believe in the world below because we have senses, and not because somebody attempts logically to prove it to us, so we believe in the world above by the inner perceptions of faith.

In fine, the same faith, while convincing us of this durableness of our real life, redeems us from the bondage of death, to which many, all their lifetime, are subject.   Thus the apostle declares of Christ, that he " abolished death."   For just in the degree that, through a religious faith, the feeling of immortality grows in the soul, the death of the body loses power to disturb or alarm it.   Principles and affections are developed, on which, we know and are inwardly assured, death cannot lay that icy finger which must chill every flowing drop in the circulation of animal life.   The spirit, alive to its relations

15

to God and to all pure beings, is conscious of nothing in common with the grave, has nothing that can be put into the grave save the temporary garment that it wears; and its mounting desires, its ardent love, its swelling hopes, its holy communings, are not stuff woven into the texture of that garment, but are as separable from it as the lamp from its clay vase, as the light of heaven from the clod it for a passing moment illumines. In fact, in this state of inward life, the ideas of the spirit and death, of dust and the soul, cannot be brought together, any more than can the ideas of virtue and color, thought and material size.

Death is dreadful to the man in whom no such soaring wishes and expectations have been born, whose spirit slumbers, whose faith is dead, the active principles of whose nature are sunk in the flesh and the material world; who, by love of pleasure, has identified himself with the body, nor can clearly, even in thought, disentangle his soul therefrom; or has gazed on no prospects beyond houses and lands and earthly goods. Death must be dreadful to him; for it must seem to be the death of all: it must look like annihilation. As a candle goes out in a deep pit, so he must fear lest his life should be quenched as he is lowered into the tomb; nothing being as yet distinctly unfolded in him which can live, and, as a triumphant survivor, ascend from the wreck of matter and mortal decay; no " faith " now, when all other props fail, to be the " basis of things hoped for, the evidence of things not seen."

But to the believer, who has cherished and cultivated a spiritual, evangelical faith, death, robbed of
these terrors, comes not as a destroyer, but a deliverer ; finds in him, not a victim, but a victor through
his Lord Jesus Christ.   The life that is in his spirit
from God is the pledge of its own endless continuance.   God help us to secure that basis nothing on
earth can shake, that evidence nothing can refute !

DISCOURSE XI.

POSITIVE FAITH.

Acts xvii. 19. — MAY WE KNOW WHAT THIS NEW DOCTRINE, WHEREOF THOU SPEAKEST, IS ?

PAUL was in Athens, and Athens was another name for a place of philosophic and religious speculation; the "air full of noises" of disputing sects and schools, — Stoic, Epicurean, Greek and Jew, with their doctrines of one God and many gods; of cold destiny as the guide, or mere pleasure as the end, of life. The apostle, with his characteristic ardor, plunges into the midst of every little gathering swarm of debaters in the synagogue and the market; and, either by the superiority of his power or the singularity of his views, soon attracts general attention, and becomes the central figure in that motley, many-tongued group of citizens and strangers. They take him, carry him to their high court of Areopagus, and ask of him a fuller exposition of his faith; which, from Mars' Hill as his pulpit, he preaches to the whole assembly and to the world. The calm utterance of his unwavering convictions in that scene of scepticism, contradiction, and intel-

lectual curiosity, suggests to us the importance of a
positive religious faith ; and to this subject I invite
your attention.

Passing in review the various forms of opinion
that have prevailed from age to age, or that now have
dominion in one or another section of the church
or the world, it is easy to see how much they
express which we do not believe ; easy to reject the
loudest and most pretending theories ; to smile at
and scorn modes and judgments, once supremely
potential over the human mind ; to brand much as
obsolete or exploded, and much as exercising sway
only over ignorant, superstitious, and bigoted minds.
But, meantime, amid all this negation and contempt,
the question comes back and thunders upon us, —
What do you believe ? What is your true substitute
for the supposed erroneous ideas of past centuries or
present millions ? May we know what your doctrine
is respecting these high themes, God and man, life,
death, and eternity ?

You disown, as absurd or groundless, this or that
notion or dogma, or mass of notions and dogmas.
Let them pass, as unworthy further notice, into the
receptacle of things forgotten and " lost on earth ; "
but recall your attention to the substantial and positive principles, if any such there be, which you
maintain ; and, if none such there be, consider how
much you gain, or how lofty a height of reason you
reach, by merely sitting in the seat of the sceptic
and scorner, and not burning with the enthusiasm
and love and devotion of the religious believer.

15*

You disallow perhaps the Hindoo's doctrine of manifold successive incarnations, from age to age, of the Supreme Being. Do you accept, with all its consequences, the New Testament teaching of one incarnation, or manifestation in the flesh, of God in Jesus Christ? You deny the blind fate of the Greek and the Turk. Have you trembled in mingled awe and joy at the thought and in the use of your moral freedom? For herein is the importance of a real positive faith on any point; its tendency to pass into disposition and act, moulding the heart and life. And here is the misery of having an unbelieving or indifferent mind about religious truth, that the heart becomes a prey to mere inclination and the present world, and that the powers of the world to come are unloosed from it. Positive faith, even though we have but a little, a few sentences, a creed of a handbreadth, including simple and grand points, only embraced and possessed vitally, — as dying martyrs have clasped the Bible or the Cross to their bosoms, — will exert an astonishing influence. And it is said there is electricity enough latent in a drop of water, could it be developed from all its affinities, to charge a cloud, and make a shining thunderbolt; so there is power in the shortest and most obvious doctrines of our religion, in the very particles of faith, if practically brought out and applied, to dissolve our earthly reliances, and revolutionize our lives.

Do you believe in so plain a thing as this, "Thou God seest me"?—that, in every thought and deed and purpose, you are seen by God? What, then, is the deed you do, the thought you think, the purpose you intend, under that close, blazing inspection? What the sentiment you express, upon the faintest feature of whose expression that unearthly, penetrating light falls? What the covert from observation you retreat into, which that undeceivable search instantly unroofs and exposes? What the defences and fortifications you rear, what the tissue of fraud or veil of self-deception you weave, before motives, which, beneath any entrenchments and all illusions, that Omniscience so easily grasps? What good and righteous purpose shall I not make predominant in all the frame of my mind, and all the work of my hands, if " Thou God seest me " ?

Or take any other simple doctrine, thus positively held. Do you believe in the influence of the Holy Spirit? that, as Christ declares, you, as a parent, are not so ready to give a good thing to your children, as God is to give, to them who ask, his Holy Spirit? And will you not ask? Your faith being positive, you will. An earthly office, a place of patronage, is sued for; opportunity and means begged to seek far-off climes of promise; a situation of any profit or political advancement swells into a vast allurement of magnificence; and all the time, as day passes after day, and week succeeds upon week, and rolling years move on, have you never asked for the Holy Spirit? It may be had for the asking; with no rebuffs or procrastinations, no "law's delay." or "proud man's contumely." But, oh! that asking,— it is, indeed, no formal motion of the lips, no merely intellectual framing of the thoughts, no hasty and transitory breath of superficial desire; but a deep longing, a needy yearning, a continued besieging of the mercy-seat of the divine dispensing Power. To those thus asking, as though they meant what they said, prized what they requested, believed what they professed, and wanted what they prayed for, the communication shall be made; the door in their heart, made mysteriously into the spiritual world when their heart was fashioned, shall open at God's own touch; heavenly peace and purity shall flow in; they shall be inspired; perceive the motion of another mind, and that the Divine Mind, upon their own; that they are not shut up to their own poor supplies and individual nature, but can draw upon the wisdom and riches of an Almighty Father, and feel the light of his countenance play refreshing upon them. Even so mighty and prevailing is a positive faith.

Do you believe, once more, a thing so worthy of all acceptation as that Jesus Christ came to save and reconcile you to God? Take ancient statements of the doctrine, or modern ones, or put aside as faulty all the speculations upon it ever clothed in human speech: disbelieve what you will in theories respecting the cause or the process; but do you believe positively the thing? If you do, your faith will have irresistible power over you. It is proved to be but infidelity's dead profession, if it do not. The man who is assured and positively believes that some European relative has left him an immense fortune, which personal attention is necessary to secure, sits not down to rest upon this as an abstract speculation, amusing with it his thoughts, but rises, departs, crosses the sea, with energetic and nice procedure, to fulfil the conditions of the case. The adventurer, listening to a tale of rivers, which, like the ancient Pactolus, flow over golden sands on the far Pacific coast, is not satisfied with it as a tale that he can pleasantly relate to other greedy ears, but embarks, throwing himself and his all on the single cast. The sick man, learning of sunny climes which have a balsam in the very air to pour healing through the avenues of disease, bids adieu to all, however dear in home and friends and native land, — for the sake of the body, the poor perishing body, that must here, there, or somewhere find and fall into its earthly grave, — to seek the warm isle or southern continental shore. And, oh! the sinner, spiritually poor, empty, sickly, if he believe in a Redeemer who can break the power of sin, and raise him above his own selfish and wayward will into the life of virtue and of God, will not stay long in cool debate respecting the original rank and person of that Redeemer, but will run to him, as, in all his instructions and precepts, life and death, the enricher, benefactor, physician, of his soul.

You dissent perhaps from the doctrine of an absolute eternity of fiery torments to those who die impenitent, and call it incredible that they should be forever forbidden to raise an eye of supplication to the Father, who has said, "All souls are mine." But do you believe in a just retribution, by which present character is inevitably linked to future destiny? And is there not solemnity enough in this as a positive doctrine to make you avoid all wrong-doing, as the bane of peace and the very seed of wretchedness? Would you have any thing more fearful than that in Paul's own answer to his questioners on the famous hill of Areopagus, "Because he hath appointed a day in the which he will judge the world in righteousness"? To a rational soul, what particular threat could be so grave as this general declaration?

But I must occupy no more time with illustrations. Returning to the general subject, we may say in the most level, unimpassioned tone, so marvellous is this principle of faith by means of that element of divine truth it lays hold on, that, as our Saviour declared, an amount of it so small, as to be fitly symbolized by a grain of mustard-seed, can "remove mountains," operating in the moral world as in the material do the most potent substances of nature. Accept any doctrine of God's revelation vitally, whether a doctrine of his attributes and purposes, or any one of his attributes or purposes, or of our own nature, capacity, responsibility, and destiny; and it will leave nothing in us, from the foundation to the summit of character, untouched; but noiselessly penetrating like light and air, and cleansing as a baptism of water and fire, it will alter and improve our whole being. Like the single grain, that has sown a continent; like the particle of odor, whose perfume has lasted for a century; like the well-worn instrument,

that has served in unnumbered scenes of trial, so its
virtue will spread and pierce and last. Under its
ennobling influence, we shall feel we have the best
of God's gifts; envying no man's wit or learning
or genius, but adopting the sentiment of the great
philosopher, who, in the midst of the treasures of
science of all ages and the added results of his own
search and study, declared he regarded a firm religious faith as the greatest of blessings.

But am I mistaken in supposing there is a considerable class of persons who have no such decided
religious belief; whose mind on the whole subject is
in a state of indifference and doubt, rather than of
interest and determination; to whom Christianity
is a sort of general atmosphere, not a direct power;
a vague adumbration, like that you saw the other
night in the moon's eclipse, not a piercing beam of
the sun; who are going, like the famous unbeliever
we read of, to take at death a leap into the dark;
who conform, it may be, to certain modes of proceeding, and assent to certain common-place declarations; but, if asked what their faith is, would not be
ready with its reality or reason, there having been
no inward exercise and struggle of mind and heart
for the truth, but religious appeals and representations falling only on their passive attention, like a
poem or song or rhetorical display upon their ear?

To whoever partakes at all of such a character,
our subject sends from the Most High God its summons. It invokes every such one to come to some
conclusion on this matter, which, if it be more than

a dream, is a matter of infinite consequence. A positive faith, though alloyed with superstition and error, is better than dull apathy or a negative unbelief; for it at least brings the eternal world near to move with luminous, attractive weight on the soul, however it may be misjudged in some of its features. And who of us can judge aright the whole height and depth, length and breadth, of those features? The most unenlightened believer, who beholds religion covered with a load of ceremonial pomp, who comes to its outward altar as alone or above all other things sacred, who listens to the voice of its priests speaking in an unknown tongue, and sees the Saviour's broken body and streaming blood literally in the symbolic wafer and cup ; — nay, the supposition is poor and weak ; I go further and say, the man who, wholly out of the pale of Christendom, cries from a full heart, "There is one God, and Mohammed is his prophet ; " or the pagan sage, who, ignorant of one Infinite Spirit, trusts only the good demon in his breast, is nearer heaven while on earth, and more likely to have an entrance into it ministered to him hereafter, than the nominal Christian, who has no vital, regenerating faith in truths familiar as household words to his understanding, flowing around like the air he has breathed from infancy, and the light that shines upon him from heaven.

Let us lay aside, then, as of inferior import, our doubts, disbeliefs, denials, and questionings, upon which we may have falsely prided ourselves ; and let us gather up our convictions, as wheat sifted from the chaff. Let us positively establish our faith, and enthrone it over our life. If it be only so brief as to say, not as mere phrases, but with a living significance, that Christ is our Saviour, and God our Father, and God's Holy Spirit our accepted Sanctifier, and immortality, running over these graves we must lie down in, our destined career; let it take its seat to preside in us, and rule with a rightful sceptre our thoughts and conduct. Let it make us walk as on the borders of an unseen state, guarded by a lofty companionship that shall give us victory over temptation, deliverance from sin, and pluck out the sting of death! Then shall it fulfil its office, and be transformed into, or succeeded by, nobler and as yet unknown exercises of our immortal nature in the world which is to come.

DISCOURSE XII.

PUTTING ON THE LORD JESUS CHRIST.

Rom. xiii. 14. — BUT PUT YE ON THE LORD JESUS CHRIST.

THERE are two methods of moral improvement: first, acting from ourselves according to an abstract principle; and, secondly, living over again the example of actual excellence. It is the latter method to which the text points. It is certainly a very remarkable power which God has given us, of representing to and realizing in ourselves a character different from our own; of putting on, becoming another person, another soul. We cannot fail to see in such a constitution the divine purpose, not only that we should enter into the feelings of others, but moreover that we should enlarge and enrich our own nature; not be confined strictly to our native tendencies and original biases, but borrow others' wisdom, copy others' virtue, imitate all good examples, assimilate every right quality, and incorporate into our own being a thousand exotic and foreign excellences. He who exercises not his imagination and sentiment to this end, but, in the grave and forbidding, proud or exclusive way we sometimes notice, shuts up his heart to his own independent resources, becomes meagre and impoverished, and is on the way at last even to idiocy, lack of common feeling, lack of common sense. A consideration of some of the modes in which this representing, realizing power operates may help us to understand it as a moral faculty, and consecrate it to the highest uses.

Do we not see a very familiar display of it in the genius of the poet, by which he conceives of characters — creatures of his imagination, yet true to nature and drawn from nature — distinguished from one another and from himself in their modes of thought and actuating passions, and, through all the variety of situations in which they may be placed, severally well sustained? Nothing is more common than this representation in the Bible itself. Sacred historian, psalmist, and prophet are continually figuring certain characters before our minds, as examples or warnings. The whole book of Job is, not improbably, thought by many critics to be a dramatic poem; and certainly, if so, the sublimest ever written; grander than the epic of Homer, with pictures more vivid than ever dropped from the pencil of Milton or Dante, and delineations that strike deeper into the immortal essence that we are than the tragedies of Shakspeare. The parables of our Lord are commonly but portraitures to our spiritual fancy of diverse moral characters; and we can learn the lesson he intends, only by a vigorous use of this representing and reproducing power.

The exercises, too, of the human voice in recita-

tion and oratory, only set before us in tones what
the pen has first traced in simple words.   From the
child that is taught to speak the sentiments of some
hero, saint, or martyr, in his earliest declamations at
school, to the grave debater in legislative halls ; from
the narrator at the fireside, to the lively rehearser of
inspired pages of human composition, or the edify-
ing reader of the sacred word of God, what do we
see throughout but this very endeavor of the soul to
personate and put on, or accurately to report the
meaning and feeling of, some other character ; and,
so far as it is understood and believed to be a noble
character, to adopt, appropriate, and live over again,
its nobleness.   Here, again, is the main office and
talent of the historian and biographer, to enter into
the very heart and secret life-springs of those who
have animated the events of a period, and set them
forth in their true shapes ; as Paul, speaking of a
record of his own thus made, says, " These things
happened for ensamples."

It is to give a lesson through the same personating, pictorial power of the soul, that the artist puts
before us his creations, — the loveliness of the Holy
Family, the purity of the Virgin Mother, the devotion of dying confessors, or the courage of bold
apostles ; the true end being to stir a holy rivalry in
us to put on such virtue and sanctity, and enter with
a glorious jealousy into competition with every form
of excellence.

Or, to illustrate the subject from more homely,
universally known facts, the reality and strong work-

ing of this imitative and assimilating power of the
soul will not be doubted by any who have noticed
how in daily life we continually fashion each other,
and are fashioned by those we are with ; who have
observed the contagion of custom in a community,
the transfer and diffusion of manners, the mutual
likeness often obtaining both of moral traits and visible expression between husband and wife, and more
or less all the dwellers under a single roof, the degree to which one can be known by the company he
keeps, and, in short, the transforming force upon our
own hearts from the scenes we enter, the presence
we stand in, the books we read, the images we contemplate. The votary of any great leader in science
or action, in arts or arms, becomes filled with his
master's spirit. The soldiers of Napoleon were said
to become, in some sense, like their captain : they
put on Napoleon. In truth, we are continually en-
acting, and, by an art and practice deep as life, and
made perfect from infancy, working into ourselves,
the feelings, prepossessions, purposes, characters, of
all those around us. This impersonation of the soul
and spirit, in the use and actual bearing of every
man, exceeds in subtlety and extent all the imaginations that poetry has ever expressed. Therefore
is not the divine wisdom toward us shown, when the
Scripture fixes on this great, fundamental instinct as
a moral power to be dedicated, for its main employ-
ment and final cause, to our spiritual growth ?

It operates, indeed, to a degree involuntarily, and
upon all subjects good or bad. But, by a religious

16*

discipline, we can so hold base and wicked characters as spectacles before the mind, that they shall not be allowed to penetrate beneath the imagination into the affections, and seize upon the active powers, but be alarming figures in our speculation, not chosen ideals to captivate our person and life. As the poet shows his art by making his villains and mean personages hateful and disgusting, though he paint them as perfectly as the noble and pure, and the dressing by any writer of fiction of his unprincipled characters in winning charms, draws down upon him for so corrupting an influence a peculiar moral indignation; as the reciter and orator, by their very accents, hold off at a certain despicable and condemned distance the worthless whom they describe; as the historian and biographer, even in their sober narrations, and when pronouncing no dogmatic judgments, yet contrive to fasten a subtle sentence of disapproval on the actors that have performed an unworthy part in the great theatre of human life; as sensuality and hypocrisy on the artist's canvas gain no attraction over us, though clothed in an equal strength and splendor of coloring with the holy and the just; nay, as our Lord himself, with his brief but matchless strokes, carves in his immortal language the appearance of the ungodly for an admonition, and of the righteous to work a gracious and benignant spell upon our thoughts: so, while imagining the whole variety of human dispositions, we may enact by our will, personate in our love, and work into our feeling for the alteration of our character and soul, only those patterns which fancy or true story, actual observation or holy apologue, has unfolded in features of all that is beautiful, admirable, and exalting.

Like the painter who drew in a single likeness the transcript of what was best in each selected countenance, we shall be continually transferring from the vast galleries of Providence and Holy Writ, from the society of the present and the past, and from the face of those on earth or in heaven, the manifold moral beauty which is "every creature's best;" and thus put that imitative and personating faculty, by which we pass into another's heart, to its highest designed use.   And doing this, we shall do a work incomparable in its importance and solidity. Yea, the poet's time-defying page shall be but a poor, perishable production; the orator's accents of fire and softness, which have kept until now the name of a Cicero as "the very mocking-bird of eloquence," — so had he inwrought the natural language of all human emotion into his marvellous speech, — shall be but a transient sound in the air; the fresco of holy temples shall be a fading picture on their old, venerable walls; the statue of marble, a crumbling stone on its firm pedestal; and all historic facts turn to a fabulous tale, as historic facts have done, — in comparison with those durable and everlasting realizations of whatever is true, pure, lovely, with which, from every earthly source and lofty example, we shall have adorned the chambers and inlaid the very substance of the heart.   For our imitation is not in words or tones, colors or forms, but in living thoughts and affections. The lofty worth we steadily hold up before our emulous soul, like the landscape through the daguerreotyper's lens, leaves a more indelible print. The justice we admire, the charity we love, the holy zeal and endurance we revere, the fervent adoration and self-devotion which make our hearts burn, — all these we possess and become, "growing in grace," and translated out of the poor limitations of our individual or merely private nature, "from glory to glory;" blessing God, as we advance, for this privilege of increase which he has afforded, not only in the native germs and individual qualities of our own being, but more abundantly in communication with all the spiritual riches of his rational universe; especially saying, — "Thanks to God for his unspeakable gift."

For all that has gone before in this exposition has been but the construction of a ladder to the height of our text, — "Put ye on the Lord Jesus Christ." The whole gospel is preached and summed up in that single exhortation. Its difficulties, which have furnished subjects of disputation for centuries, are here explained. "To put on Christ;" "to be found in him, not having our own righteousness;" to be "clothed" with his meekness and humility; to have "his spirit," and "the same mind in us that was also in him;" to open our hearts for his "abode," and have him "formed within us, the hope of glory;" — who but recognizes at once, in this so controverted and abused language, the burden of the

New Testament? And wherein is the sense of this language, if not in the appropriation of his worth to our nature, by the force of sympathy, and of a two-fold spiritual consciousness operating to unite him to ourselves? Is not here, too, the true rational as well as scriptural meaning of "the merits of Christ," as, in the technical language of creeds, "imputed" to us, of his "sacrifice" and "atonement" for us, of his "becoming wisdom and righteousness and sanctification and redemption" unto us? What is it all but the impersonation and inward putting on of the Lord Jesus Christ? not a conceit of speculation, as has been so much supposed; not a figment of the theological brain, the scholastic inheritance of a thousand years; not a forensic, technical transaction with God; not a vicarious offering, independent of our participation; not, in the Romanist's notion, an eating of the Lord's real flesh in the bread, and drinking of his real blood in the wine; — but a practical, vital assimilation of him, of his mind and spirit and undying love, according to the simplest laws of our being. This, verily, is Christ's life and example, Christ's cup and cross, Christ's crown of thorns and bloody sweat, "his stripes by which we are healed," his death in which we live; all dependent for their virtue and efficacy upon the exercise of this sympathetic and reproducing power, through which his majesty and lowliness, his submission and self-sacrifice, his sinless virtue and everlasting love, melt like the expressive traits of some grand and pathetic picture into our souls.

Thus, the divine graces of his character are not impressed in the way of mere commandment alone ; but, as the beauty of the landscape and the fragrance of flowers possess our outward senses, so these finer influences sink into the deeper perceptions of the spirit.   No poet's imagination, no speaker's expression, no artist's fancy, no friendship's experience, and no other character on the historic page, can work on us the elevating transformation which we feel in gazing on our Master as he appears in the artless evangelic accounts, till our whole thought becomes engrossed in and identified with the object of our regard, and he appears to us, not in human articles of theoretic belief, but shines with a living glory into our real knowledge and love.   Neither can any simple self-culture, which has perhaps been too much our method, any laborious efforts of will, any works or merits of ours, suffice for our salvation, and lift us into the highest divine frame, without this admiring absorption of mind into the model and mould of perfection, by which we "put on Jesus Christ."

Here is the point of our whole meditation, to devote to its highest and most precious purpose that impersonating, reproducing energy of the soul, which may be abused or spent for trivial ends. The hypocrite and dissembler employs it for the masking of his real character, or the pretence of an unreal one.   The playful mimic puts it to a superficial use in catching the mere looks and vocal inflections of another.   The poet, with a profounder reach, makes it his instrument to dissect and delineate the very workings of design and passion in the human breast. And the performer, by voice and gesture, wields it as his talent to set forth, by an illusion of likeness and motion in the very air, the poet's marvellous scenes. But the seeker for truth, and for a regenerative, ever-growing enlargement of his own soul, engages it more grandly to import into and re-create in himself every thing right, generous, excellent, holy, and religious, witnessed or learned, far or near, in the whole scope of human knowledge and social action. So beholding, in the person of the Saviour of the world, the noblest and most spotless portrait of whatever is venerable and lovely in character, hung up in the frame of history or human imagination, beyond all other contemplation of fact or fiction, let us dwell in the sight of those matchless features, and " put on the Lord Jesus Christ."

DISCOURSE XIII.

DEATH IS YOURS.

1 Cor. iii. 21, 22. — ALL THINGS ARE YOURS, WHETHER PAUL, OR APOL-
LOS, OR CEPHAS, OR THE WORLD, OR LIFE, OR DEATH, OR THINGS
PRESENT, OR THINGS TO COME; ALL ARE YOURS.

THE apostle is exhorting the Corinthians to take no
narrow, sectarian view of their religious position;
and he goes on to make some general enumeration
of their large privileges and lofty opportunities. All
the living teachers of the Christian faith were theirs;
the world, with its beautiful and glorious revelations
of God, was theirs; life, full of promise and occasion,
was theirs; death, too, was theirs, — things present
and things to come. He reckons death among
their treasures and advantages. He encourages and
inspirits them with the consideration, that it, as well
as life, was their right and blessing.

Certainly this is a very peculiar view of death.
Death ordinarily presents itself to us as a misery,
not as a privilege; as the inevitable termination of
all we have experienced, and pursued, and delighted
in, not as itself another boon; as something that
nature recoils from, not welcomes. And, lo! the
apostle would take it into the catalogue of great

possessions! In a rapture of holy joy, and a strain of exalted eloquence, he appropriates it to the rich and boundless estate of his converts. He marvellously calls in " the king of terrors " among the ministers of comfort; puts the last enemy into the list of friends ; and makes the robber, who has laid waste earth's cities and villages, who steals away all that is bright and beautiful and happy, and puts the riches of a million homes and myriad hearts in his unfilled pit, — makes him to be a generous patron, to whom we are in debt and under obligations.

This New Testament representation of death is in striking contrast with any ever given in the famous and splendid Greek or Roman literatures of the world, and far in advance of any thing even hinted at in the Jewish Scriptures. We ourselves are apt to speak and think of death as a dread necessity. Such is often the tone even of Christian literature. So great a man and so humble a believer as the distinguished Samuel Johnson expresses the sentiment, that the only reason why we do not weakly weep at the prospect of death, is, that we know it is of no use ; for we must die. And the pulpit too much echoes the same sentiment, and, in dolorous or threatening accents, declares to the children of men, " You must die ! "

That " it is appointed unto all men once to die " is no doubt a fact to be gravely brought to the notice of the careless, unrepenting transgressor; because "after death is the judgment." Still the event or institution of death is not the Almighty's curse, but

17

his blessing. Strange, indeed, if it were an evil, happening universally as it does to intelligent creatures
under the government of a benevolent God.   No :
death is yours.   I would fain say it to you, my
friends, not in the spirit of melancholy, uncertain
doubt, but of cheerful assurance and hope.   I come
from the funeral-company, from the coffin and the
grave, to say it ; and many of you have come from
the burial of loved and pure ones to hear.   Death is
yours.

What thought can be of more interest and practical power ! Behold the frail mortality with which the
spirit in us is swathed ! Note the perishable vesture,
the worn covering, the perhaps already decaying
frame, drawing in for every instant's need a breath
of air to fan and keep a little longer unextinguished
the flame of life ; the vital current, propelled by
rapid strokes of so slight enginery through a thousand channels, and making each member tremulous
with the constant pulsation that so small an obstruc-
tion could stop ; or sending a quivering into the grasp
and pressure of friendly hands, as though to remind
each other, not of a mighty affection alone, but of
the slender thread on which all earthly tokens hang.
And is it not indeed a consolation and re-assurance
to know that not only life, transient, fading life, but
death, too, is yours ; not an angry, menacing demon,
to dash every good thing from your hold and at last
prostrate yourself, but a good angel, a munificent
donor, an upward leader ?

Far in advance of the worldly or the pagan sentiment is Paul's Christian doctrine,— not of what death robs us, but how much we owe to the dark angel, set by God as the sentinel and conductor between the verge of this world and another. Long before we reach that station, what a purifying power does death exert upon our whole life! Speechless, but how solemn are its admonitions! untold, but how vast its benefits to the individual and to the race! All the preachers in the world utter a voice how feeble in comparison with its real instruction! All rhetoric and art of language are but " sounding brass and a tinkling cymbal " beside its eternal emphasis. Every call to virtue seems to be embraced in its incessant summons. Every warning against vice blends in its terrible alarm. What a blessing and inestimable treasure does death communicate to us in this very influence! What privilege so great and indispensable as this restraint from sin, and incitement to goodness! For what shall we thank God, if not for this awakener of our good purposes, and extinguisher of our evil desires? How dangerous, indeed, and ruinous our state without it! Into what luxuriance, but for this check, would our lower appetites spring! How would our vanity and ambition blossom ; how our pride tower ; how thrifty the love of gain and pleasure become ; and oh ! how cast down from heaven every aspiration, and rooted in the earth every propensity, but for this solemn-breathing air from the everlasting world, mingling with the atmosphere of this world, to suppress the poorer and stimulate the better growth of our minds !

Nay; if, with this serious and perpetual power to move or bind us, moral evil can shoot up so hardy and vigorous, what would be our condition were it withdrawn, to leave us subject to the unmitigated forces of seduction from the world, the flesh, and the devil, — tempting whispers from without, and evil inclinations within?

We may indeed, then, be grateful, and in the highest energies of our nature sublimely cheerful, that death, no less than life, is ours, — ours as a spiritual helper and sanctifier. The king of terrors becomes thus a rightful prince and minister of good to us from and under the Supreme Ruler. The harsh lines of his countenance are softened into traits of wisdom, and even of love. And through the shadows of the picture in which he stands on the brink of all things earthly, brilliant flashes of blessedness and glory dart forth from the immortal scene.

Young man, whom the solicitations of sense would allure into sin! look at death so standing. See his monitory finger; hear his wordless but stirring counsel; receive his sober but real benediction. For he can speak a benediction to the tempted, yielding heart, such as never fell from mortal lips, and that grim spectre bless you, as never could human being, however ready to bless.

Man in middle life, at the point equi-distant from the cradle and the grave! new-born existence was at first all you could feel, or receive any notions from. But, since, a mighty teacher indeed has stepped upon the stage; and, oh! how many lessons of vigilance and preparation he has given you! If you have not yet learned, and well-nigh grown perfect in, the meanings of his advice, how insensible you are! How often have you seen the door of his chapel of instruction opened! What sermons, with the coffin of a child or the bier of manhood for his desk, has he preached to you! How many times, amid assembled mourners, have you sat under his instructions, or, in the long procession, gone up to his sanctuary; and stood and heard, in the falling clod, his inarticulate but significant voice! Has he not, even yet effectually, done for you his office of persuasion? Let him do that office on your heart, ere he come to do his other office upon your outward frame. For, accomplishing this inward service, verily, as the apostle says, he is yours; your deliverer and benefactor; for whose redemption and bounty you are to bless God, even as you do for life or the world, for wise and good human counsellors, or for any thing else in the list of favors which the apostle in the text enumerates or intends. What favors of fortune, wealth, earthly honor and pleasure, can equal those gifts of purity and spirituality which will come to him that seriously and habitually holds converse with death?

But I check this sober, monitory strain; for not these "gifts of purifying" alone do we receive. Death is also a consoler, rewarder, and uplifter to a better state. We speak of death as a sad, unavoidable fate, which has overtaken our friends, and is to overtake ourselves. But suppose it were offered

17*

any of us, with our friends, to be exempt from the dread necessity, and to live for ever in this world. Should we eagerly and unhesitatingly accept this alternative, sit down content with the elements of happiness and means of progress this earth can afford, forego the vast mysterious hope that rises within and runs beyond into a spiritual world, and call back the " thoughts that wander through eternity " ? Sordid, earth-born mediocrity of aspiration, if we did! No: the sentiment of the hymn is just, " We would not live alway " here. The very enterprise, and much more the holy yearning, of our nature would carry us up and on. This life, though by God's goodness it has a large overmeasure of happiness, is yet but a bare beginning, an often painful probation, a sometimes hard and sore battle with evil and sin. It is at most but a preliminary and a promise ; and, were it not for the expectation of something better, its best satisfactions would soon end in weariness and satiety. Therefore, standing on Paul's height and sharing his inspiration, let us say, Thanks to God, that he sends at last death to take off from us this " flesh and blood," which " cannot inherit his kingdom," and to translate us to a more glorious sphere. " For me to die," said the chief apostle, " is gain."

I have looked with a solemn joy on the soul-deserted body and mortal face of the dead. I have heard with gratitude of the release of the Christian, yes, of my own friend, from the infirm and distressed earthly tabernacle. I have, with the eye of faith, followed the spirit to its new home ; and I can conceive of its first thanksgiving to God there as being for the death that broke the bonds of flesh, and raised it for ever above the pains of sense which its patience so faithfully bore. My own soul, in its better moments, refuses not, but would gladly go after. When I think of death as introducing the humble believer, and as our religion teaches, — at once introducing him to those joys and glories, under whose weight God's own word sinks in confessed inadequacy so to describe them that the eye or ear or heart of man could take them in, I cannot view the advent of death to any prepared disciple as to be deplored. I wonder not at the story of the Moravians, with their real faith, as singing their song of praise to God, without one faltering note, as their vessel rocked from side to side amid blinding spray and all the darkening horrors of impending wreck.

I ask nothing more definite about the future state than Infinite Wisdom has seen fit to reveal. The simple Indian, we read of, in his harsh northern climate, may conceive of it as a place " where there is no more snow." The savage, in a temperate zone, may anticipate a nobler field for his hunting. These are dim struggles of the great hope God has planted in his children's breasts. But we, Christians, not curious to know what shall be the sky or what the ground of those heavenly regions, will be content and ardently thankful to look forward, as the gospel encourages, to an everlasting progress in virtue and happiness. And, so looking, we will behold unequal-

led lustre and attraction even in that gloomy portal
of the grave, through which we are to enter on such
glorious progress.

Meantime, let not the duties of this life, however
lowly and homely, be neglected; for they alone can
make us ready for the life to come. Not that death
is an evil even for the man who has lived unfaithful.
When a man has perverted and abused his body and
soul by habits of sin, it may be oftentimes, in God's
mercy, the best thing for him to die, and to have his
present inveterately vicious course interrupted and
broken up, into whatever purgatory of future discipline he may enter.

But the good man's approach to that dark valley,
which alone separates him from the heavenly hills,
should figure itself to us in the likeness of a triumph.
His expiring sighs should sound in our ears but as
the soft prelude of divine exultations; and the groan
with which he dies swell into the shout of victory
over all pain, sickness, temptation and sorrow. "I
have fought the good fight, I have finished my
course, I have kept the faith; henceforth there is
laid up for me a crown of righteousness, which the
Lord, the righteous Judge, shall give me at that
day." Kingdoms may be shaken, old dynasties may
fall, and nations rise in their might to reconstruct the
fabrics of earthly rule; but there is mightier and
more blessed change than this, in the departure of
the good from all transpiring beneath the sun. For,
placed in whatever earthly sphere, — exercising a
holy virtue in the tasks of the busy world, or making

the beautiful sacrifices of love and devotion in the domestic scene; though encountering trouble, and prostrated with anguish, — the good man has ever, as one has said,

" Three firm friends, more sure than day and night,
Himself, his Maker, and the angel Death."

DISCOURSE XIV.

THE DEAD SPEAKING.

Heb. xi. 4. — AND BY IT HE, BEING DEAD, YET SPEAKETH.

THE powers of language have been exhausted in describing the shortness and feebleness of human life. It is a shadow that fleeth. It is a vapor that vanisheth. It is a flower that fadeth. It is grass that withereth. Generation after generation passes away, like the clouds that chase one another over the landscape. Such is the representation, and it expresses truly one aspect of mortal existence. But it does not express the whole. There is a very large and important exception to be made to it, and that exception it is my purpose now to state.

Human creatures die, but the dead speak: they exert an influence on the living world. Six thousand years ago, and four thousand years before the words of our text were written, Abel, a keeper of sheep, brought of the firstlings of his flock an offering unto the Lord, an outward expression of the reverence of heart with which his spirit bowed before the majesty of heaven and earth. He laid his sacrifice on the altar, and died in the morning of existence, in the dew of his youth; his fair and glorious promise blasted before his parents' eyes, his innocent blood shed by an envious brother's hands. Even like the tender stalk he was cut off, and no man knoweth the place of his burial. But, though dead, he spoke; spoke through the sincere fervor of his worship to God; spoke through the unresisting meekness with which he sank under the smiting murderer; spoke in the voice of his blood that cried from the ground. And that first altar of the race which he reared seems still to smoke up to heaven; it excites feelings of adoration, even to this day, in unnumbered bosoms; it makes our hearts throb with the self-same worship.

Every religious act will not operate so strongly; but it may operate as long. This is the nature of all influence, physical or moral. A motion, once begun, continues in some shape or combination for ever; and so moral character is self-productive without end, and our temporary existence will leave behind an element of power for the permanent weal or woe of our fellow-men. What consideration should so affect us? What is the posthumous fame which some hope to secure in the mouths and mention of men, compared with the privilege of working a purifying principle into the mind and heart of those who shall come after us? But there is another side to the picture. The evil that we do shall also live after us. Cain spoke as well as Abel; spoke in the voice, not of piety, but of unholy passion; not of meeknese, but of revenge; not of solemn appeal to God's mercy, but of impious defiance to his justice.

There is thus a double solemnity in the life that we lead. We believe we are to be judged at God's bar for the deeds done in the body; but by those same deeds we are doomed to help or hurt all with whom we are or shall be connected here below, till the last circulation and throbbing of a heart that shall claim kindred with or be cognizant of our own. This is not an arbitrary decree : it is the necessary condition of human life. We influence others according to our characters continually while we live. But death has a peculiar power of bringing out distinctly the characters of the departed. With what lively and deep impression it paints their portraits! Resisting the effacing fingers of time and mortality, how it clears up the features and deepens the lines, perhaps before dim to us, in the chambers of the heart! No pencil has truth and force like that of death. Nothing will reveal us like death to those we are to leave behind.

The subject requires you to take a position which perhaps you have not attempted ; to transport yourselves in imagination to the other side of the grave, and from that point contemplate the continued effects of your life. It is a sober and monitory, and at the same time a cheering and inspiring doctrine. By the force of mingled alarm and exultation, it calls on us to take heed to our ways. One might think the joyful side of the alternative would alone suffice to make every man good and faithful. Think of it. Your example of fidelity in the earthly post of duty where Providence has placed you, shall not only adorn the station itself, but send light along the track of your successive co-workers in it. It shall be a voice of good cheer, a reviving word to them, like that flung out from the watchman's trumpet to the tempest-tossed and benighted sailor, a word of guidance and safety.

It is not true, then, that while

> " The evil that men do lives after them,
>   The good is oft interred with their bones."

The good work you build shall stand when the earthly workman is dead. As the tree dies, but in its very decay nourishes the roots of a new forest; as the little silkworm dies, but his fine fabric does not perish; as the coral-insect dies, but his edifice breaks the angry wave that has traversed the ocean, and becomes the foundation of greenness and future harvests: so, when you die, be your place lofty or lowly, your self-sacrificing endeavors shall leave enduring riches and a moral bulwark. Being dead, we shall yet speak in some way. If faithful, while our cheerful tones mingle in the praises around God's throne, some authentic word shall also sound harmonious and peace-making among the lower circles of earth.

With what new interest does this thought clothe all the relations of human life! It speaks to you, parents. You are now instilling into the tender heart, principles that shall survive this mortal existence; and you shall speak to your posterity with the whole power, and according to the precise char-

18

acter, of the influence you are now exerting. What is taken in "with the milk and first circulations of the blood" is a living principle, to grow with the growth, and strengthen with the strength. Your very look, your tone, your manner, your expression, are embalmed and alive in your child's mind. Your own spirit shall expand in it with its expanding frame ; and all your influence shall come back to act with new power after you are gone. Your child, when it comes to stand over your grave, shall be governed by feelings which you infused. It shall know that it is, in great measure, what you have made it. Out of the silent chambers of death, mingling with their hollow-sounding echo to the tread, your voice shall return to it in familiar tones. If you have neglected or misguided its early affections and budding desires, the chilling remembrance coming back, when it stops there to muse, may check the thanks to God which, for a good parent, burst from every filial heart, as for the great blessing of life. If you have unfolded the better nature in your child, you will live and speak to it, as with angel-accents, after you are dead. It has been said of those engaged in some great literary or civil undertaking, that they were working for immortality. The good parent is working well for immortality ; ay, for that earthly immortality, which the expression, in its vulgar use, intends, no less than for the more glorious and truly endless immortality in heaven.

The dead speak, however brief the term of the mortal career, and even though that career be closed while the moral nature still sleeps in God's own charge. The little child, fading like a tender plant, has not wholly perished even from the earth. Though it came but to smile and die, yet has it left its influence; an influence not fleeting, like the shadow of its earthly existence, but long abiding. That gentle image of innocence, that strange power of patience, shall soften your heart, and make it move with tender sympathy to the distresses of your kind, even to the end of your own days. But a peculiar power belongs to those who have been wayfarers upon earth, who have fought the battle of life, and gained the victory over temptation. Let me bear witness that it is not the living alone who move me; but the faces of the dead, especially the excellent departed, mingle in the company. I feel ever environed and attended by the ghostly, witnessing band. Faith and imagination have removed from those faces every vestige of weariness and pain, and have touched their cold marble hues with the animation of undecaying health. They come not in funereal garments and with the chill damps of the grave clinging to their forms, but "clothed upon" with robes of light, and that "house which is from heaven." I feel,— and do not they feel? — the unbroken cords by which we are still knit together. I seem to be with them; our intercourse renewed or continued; and I gather instruction and take in affection from their presence. They encourage me in my toils; they say to me, "Here is the end of thy griefs;" they warn me against the indulgence of my errors and sins;

" Soft rebukes in blessings ended,
Breathing from their lips of air."

But, in a matter so momentous, I cannot give
place to merely pleasant or moving description. It
is a practical purpose for which we meet, and there
is a seriousness in the truth we are considering, that
ought to come home with pungent and awakening
force to every conscience. When these tongues are
still, and these arms are wasting ashes, shall our
spirits walk the earth, not, according to the old
dream of crazy superstition, as apparitions to the
eye, but in the survival of our characters to work in
the inward hearts of men? What, then, are we
doing, what principles cherishing, what dispositions
manifesting? How shall we re-appear to the contemplative eye of those who shall here outlive us?
Were it only ourselves that we had charge of, only
our own destiny that we could affect, we might, with
less aggravated and peculiar guilt, take the fearful
hazards of moral negligence. But we cannot stand
alone. It is the law of our life and nature that we
shall not stand alone. Our hearts are knit to the
hearts of our kind ; as our hearts throb with good
affections or evil passions, their hearts will partake
of the impulse. And "when our tale is told," and
we have no more to do beneath the sun, our characters will be summed up, a living reckoning in the
natural and necessary effect of their confirmed tendencies and accumulated manifestations ; no drop
that ever fell, left out of the stream, no grain of our
slightest act missing from the vital deposit.

It becomes me to ask that you should ponder it, and make a scrutiny into your own breasts in view of it. Let me give voice to your self-examination. How would you return in the survivor's memory, were you now to receive from God your summons? As a faithful father, who let slip no opportunity to train up his offspring in the way of virtue and honor, who never sacrificed the welfare of his family to his own pursuit of profit and pelf, but sought for them the treasure that is better than gold? — How would you appear? As a good mother, who never in time of need forsook her child for the gay scene of selfish mirth and pleasure, in that silent return, as when a spirit passed before the face of Job, coming and standing before it as one guiltless of any injury to its body or mind? nay, more, as an object of worthy veneration for those early benefits of parental care and counsel for which there can be in after years no substitute? And how would it be with you, children, were you, like some who have been your companions, called out of the world? You would not utterly vanish from view. Oh! no: your parents, at least, would still behold you; — and how behold you? Would it be with emotions of unmingled satisfaction that your re-appearing images would inspire them? Would they have that greatest of consolations in your departure, that you had exhibited a uniform affection and obedience while you lived? Would this recollection dry their tears, or mingle sweetness and gladness in the tears they might shed?

18*

But the appeal is to every mortal. "No man liveth to himself, and no man dieth to himself." In whatever relation of life thou mayest stand, let thy soul now speak to thee, and say, if, when thy bodily presence ceases, thou wilt leave a holy and hallowing influence in its room; if, whether or not thou bequeath wealth to thy heirs, they shall receive from thee what is more precious than rubies?

I have now discharged my commission. I have set the truth of the text before thee. The responsibility becomes thine, how thou wilt consider it. Go, I pray thee, and take heed to it. Reflect on that in the temper of thy soul which will survive thee. Place thyself in thought on the other side of the grave, and, with reverted eye, mark how it will be. From that position, now imaginary, — but how soon for each one of us to be real! — dost thou look back, and see selfishness, meanness, pride, envy, lust, passion, absorbing love of the world, all from thy life working ruin, according to their nature, on thy associates and fellow-men? God forbid!

DISCOURSE XV.

THE THREE TABERNACLES.

Matt. xvii. 4. — LORD, IT IS GOOD FOR US TO BE HERE: IF THOU WILT, LET US MAKE HERE THREE TABERNACLES.

THE disciples who had followed Jesus from their homes far and long through town and desert, when he took three of them, as it is supposed, to the top of Mount Tabor, to behold his transfiguration, might be pardoned for wishing to shake the dust from their way-worn sandals, and to rest in such a scene. They perhaps fancied that all their glowing though indefinite anticipations were now on the eve of accomplishment. No more exposure and hardship! The world is to be a wilderness no more! The Master's triumphant manifestation, his longed-for kingdom, is at hand; and this sacred effulgence, these celestial visitants, announce his grand coronation.

Empty dream of temporal display! Foolish confidence of ended toil and blissful security! At that moment, Moses and Elias were speaking to Jesus of that departure in agony from the world he himself had predicted. In an hour, they were to descend from that mount, gleaming with a lustre more beau-

tiful than the ancient crown of Sinai. These golden
clouds but hid the bare earth, along which still
further they must wend their toilsome way, and
were but as a yellow haze over the midnight cold-
ness of Gethsemane and the wild desolateness of
Golgotha. That lightning-clad summit must be
exchanged for the low vale of yet sorer privation
and anguish than they had ever known. But were
they to sink thus into final prostration? No : the
near vale but intervened between Tabor and a height
more glorious for their future ascension. The bright
mountain-cloud that veiled the lonely garden, and
hung between them and Calvary, shadowed forth,
beyond all the towerings of earthly sublimity, and
infinitely above the disciples' present idea of the
kingdom of God, that heavenly Jerusalem, whence
Moses and Elias came, whither Christ was going,
and where Peter, James, John, and others innumerable, would at last rejoice with them together.

Is not this scene from our Saviour's history a
picture of human life and of human love? When
the bright, heavenly cloud of unbroken domestic joy
has overshadowed us, we, in our sweet converse,
have said with Peter, " It is good for us to be here."
Like the disciples, we have reached the spot of our
desire, after much fatigue and anxiety. To this
day the traveller approaches Mount Tabor over a
range of stony hills. So come we to the mountain
of our social peace and prosperity. " Why should
we not remain ? " we ask with almost a bold exultation, as we cast our eye backward over the long,

rough passages through which, on our progress, we have wound. We have paid the costly price which only endears to us our invaluable boon. "Sweet is pleasure after pain." Labor gladdens ease, difficulty burnishes acquisition, suffering blesses affection. And, after we have taken every hard step, — after care has chiselled its lines in the face, and the sinews remain stretched from habitual toil, why should we not build tabernacles for a permanent abode?

It is, indeed, like the old paradise, a scene at which even an enemy might pause, and gaze with delight. Beautiful it is to contemplate the work love does for this world only. What tabernacles like those it builds! How it moves to effort, spurs to success, kindles the desire of gain, else sordid, and cherishes a tenderness for reputation! It dignifies even the gaudy show of earthly luxury and splendor, to remember how far this is the gift of a prompting affection; how many of the beautiful adornments are tokens of love; how much that would be folly, if spent on selfish and sensual desires, is sanctified and immortalized by disinterested kindness; for how much lavish profusion a true sentiment gravely pleads; how it alone keeps the splendor undimmed on the diamond's point, and the fine gold unchanged in the bracelet's polish; how the weaving in of its filaments preserves beauty in the band, which cunningly, of half invisible threads, the loom has fashioned; and allows us to keep, wear, or enjoy what we should be ashamed to procure! Love prompts us to toil, to endure, to forego, and to sac-

rifice. Its children are patience, devotion, and heroism.   Second only to religion is its motive and inspiration.   How it surrounds the dear object with
every comfort, privilege, and social advantage ; with
all the means of solid education and various accomplishment !   How it builds up the precious heart
with the granite strength of principle, and on the
front of sincerity shapes the ornaments of grace !
Alas ! does it make but a momentary transfiguration ?
Is it building for the grave, at service under death,
decorating a victim and an offering ?   Did our discernment and solicitude overlook this ?   Saw we
not the stamp of mortality in the face so dear, and
death's mark of property on the palms we clasped
as our own ?   Supposed we the beloved head in-
sured, at least for a term beyond our own decline ?
Or, in our solitary, self-examining hours, have we
seemed to make a covenant with God to spare our
jewel ?   In the petitions which cannot be uttered
aloud, have we secretly cried, " O God ! thy will
be done !   Yet, quench not the light of my eyes !
Remove not the joy of my heart !   Take all but
that, without which goods and possessions turn to
ashes ! "   Our prayer anticipates David's wish of
helpless supplication, that he had died for his son
Absalom ; and, from such secret wrestlings with the
Almighty Providence, fond creatures, we turn to look
at the precious countenance.   " Oh ! it is mine, my
fine gold, my pure treasure ; a heart warmer than
mine ; a life better than mine ; that which makes
achievement bright, and honor dear, and virtue itself

strenuous! I am not to give it to the dust; it is part of my own soul; vitally—I know not where—it joins with the inmost fibres and circulations of my being."

But we cannot decide such a question, of the outward form and tabernacle of our life. We may say, "Send other trials of weakness and disease upon us, — steep us in poverty to the very lips;" but we cannot thus deal with God in compensations and substitutions. He must appoint both the measure and the kind of our discipline; while we can gain the benefit he intends, only by willingly submitting to the allotment, and rob the thunderbolt of something of its sharpness, by a wisely previous and habitual principle of resignation.

Let us not, then, build our tabernacle with a vain feeling of its sure continuance; nor foolishly say, as our solid fabric of domestic comfort rises, "This is for us and our friends, and we build it strongly, as of enduring stone, because we would have it last us our lives." Alas! how the building survives the builder! The traveller in foreign lands tells us the most striking impression of the great works of art is the shadowy, transitory life of their framers. We rear monuments in our church-yards and in our beautiful city of the dead; yet what are our houses but mausoleums, and our streets but lines of memorial structures, in which have lain corpses unnumbered? Our dwellings cry to us with the Scripture, "Arise and depart, for this is not your rest!" Let the sense of life's uncertainty breathe through us, not only when we tread the silent aisles of man's final resting-place, but as we walk amid the bustling crowd, so soon to be hushed into what stillness! Within the door, upon which, as we go by, our eye carelessly falls, the last sands of life may be running. So have I passed the gate of my friend, and knew not it could never open again at his touch. Wait not till church-yards and graves come into your mind, but look upon the chamber where you lie at rest as to be soon the witness of your mortality, the container of your clay. Think of the threshold at which you daily enter as that from which soon, in your coffin, you must be borne. Oh! could "the stone cry out from the wall, and the beam out of the timber answer," as in the vision of Habakkuk, would not a low murmur from every human abode, reared long enough for the weather-stain, through all your daily walks, be continually saluting your ears, "Set thine house in order;"—"Prepare to meet thy God"?

To the thoughtless, this whispered summons is a piercing alarm. Heavily tolls the bell in their ears. But to those who have truly loved, the thought of death is made happy by the rending of their own heart-strings; mortality is embalmed by the dear members that have passed under it; the mansion of wood and stone is hallowed by the expiring sigh on which the faithful spirit fled; and the grave, which joins to that of partner or child, looks winning and pleasant. In another sense than that of the sacred poet, —

> "Sweet is the savor of their names,
> And soft their dying bed."

Such is the peculiar privilege of affliction. Its earthly tabernacle is not only darkened, but glorified. Precious, indeed, are the forms, the faces, and voices of our friends. As these, so long familiar, vanish and die away, we can hardly realize to ourselves the loss. When the door opens, we expect to see the well-known countenance, and to hear the wonted greeting. The near and seen love of kindred and companions has warmed and enlightened the common ground on which we tread. It has made of the whole cold earth a mountain of transfiguration. It is a sad and painful descent to go down from this beautiful height. But, if our souls be true, we do not go down merely, any more than did our Saviour from that old summit of celestial converse. We do not go to the chamber of agony and the deposit of dust alone, any more than he did to his rough cross and to Joseph's new sepulchre. He went down to rise again, and how far more gloriously! Tabor was the dim illumination of a night, and the splendor of a narrow tent, compared to that transfiguration coming from no sudden blaze of light, no transient emotion of joy, but essential and everlasting, in a tabernacle that cannot be moved, and a city which hath foundations. And so all the joys of present affection, satisfying as they may sometimes be, are but as a low height and feeble brilliance compared with those which God hath prepared for them that love him, where none of this earth's misunderstandings, distrusts, or sins can come.

Can ye not believe this, ye that bow and agonize

19

with sorrow ?   If you have been loyal in your human love, I know that you can.   The man that pines
and despairs merely cannot have known the depth,
purity, and spirituality of real affection even here ;
for such affection is no sceptic.   It is essentially
believing.   Faith and hope are its own offspring,
that come into its desolate room as the best con-
solers, and cheer it with promises and longings,
against which the grave is no bar, but a door " to
that within the veil."   True affection lifts up its
objects from the sod.   It rescues them from the
corruption of the charnel-house.   It enshrines them
in happier spheres, suited to the unfolding of all
their holy faculties.   How such affection welcomes
the revelations of Jesus, and can accept his largest
prophecies, and can go on by anticipation to occupy
the glorious mansions he prepares in his Father's
house !   Did I say that all your training and adorning of those dear to you were but the decoration of
victims for the tomb ?   Let me recall those words,
or rather let me add a more glorious, predominant
truth, which finds not its period in the grave, but
runs immeasurably beyond it.   No : all the true
instruction, all the beautiful accomplishment, all the
enriching of the mind, and unfolding of the soul,
are not the garlands of a corpse !   They cannot be
sculptured on a tomb !   They cannot wither when
the world's beauty has forever faded, or when the
places that have known you are themselves no longer
known, and the tombs you have builded can no more
be distinguished from the dust they were meant to

cover. They will bloom in immortal beauty in a region where nothing decays. They shall shine where both the light and the shade of the earthly picture are lost in an unmingled lustre ; for no clouds can come, and no ·shadows fall, where "God and the Lamb," in the beaming of their universal presence and goodness, "are the light." Peter himself, who would so readily have made tabernacles of ease and comfort in which to abide upon the mountain, could afterwards rejoice in his sufferings for his converts. The voice he heard through the splendor of the transfiguration, — "This is my beloved Son, in whom I am well pleased : hear ye him," — could cheer him on in a path where was no comfort or ease, but which, lined with the thorns of hardship and persecution, was to end in a bloody death. Let that voice though uttered eighteen centuries ago, still animate and move us ; for we shall know no trouble that can be final, no grief that can be desperate, if we heed it whilst we hear !

DISCOURSE XVI.

THE SONG OF THE REDEEMED.

Rev. xiv. 3. — AND THEY SUNG AS IT WERE A NEW SONG BEFORE THE
THRONE, AND BEFORE THE FOUR BEASTS, AND THE ELDERS; AND
NO MAN COULD LEARN THAT SONG BUT THE HUNDRED AND FORTY
AND FOUR THOUSAND, WHICH WERE REDEEMED FROM THE EARTH.

THE Book of Revelation is filled with accounts of
the writer's visions of things above the ordinary perceptions of mortals. He has a second and higher
sight. As he gazes, the veil is drawn aside from
futurity, the gates of heaven and hell are unfolded,
the joys of the blessed and the woes of the lost reach
him. The dispositions of human souls, as they are
exercised in the passing hour, or lurk in the secret
chambers of the mind, are projected, in their final
consequences, upon this broad canvas in the air of
eternity, while the rapt prophet reads and notes them
for the instruction of the living.

According to the tradition of the church, it is the
beloved disciple John who is honored with this
privilege of unearthly insight; and from the lonely
isle of Patmos he looks up, not, like the astronomer
from his observatory, to measure the size and cal-

culate the motions of the stars, but to survey the magnitude and the working of moral beings and causes through the unbounded universe. These things are set forth in the most gorgeous style of poetry, now in pictures presenting definite outlines, and now in obscure cloudy shapes floating in the distance, and looming hugely up from the background. No commentator has ever succeeded in clearly expounding the purpose and meaning of this whole book. But here and there, through dark folds of gloom and vapor, that hide so much of what no human language could convey, gleam out vivid and glorious significations. One of the brightest of these flashes is in the text.

After the messages to the churches, the opening of the seven seals, the sounding of the seven trumpets, the battle of the good angels with the dragon, and the rising of the beasts from the earth and the sea, a scene is disclosed of majesty and beauty unparalleled by any thing that had gone before. This magic lens of a spiritualized imagination reveals to the seer a Lamb standing on Mount Sion, and with him a hundred and forty-four thousand having his Father's name written in their foreheads; and, by this instrument of a prophetic faith, his hearing too is extended, till it catches a voice from heaven, "as the voice of many waters, the voice of a great thunder, and the voice of harpers harping with their harps: and they sung as it were a new song before the throne, and before the four beasts, and the elders; and no one could learn that song but the hundred

19*

and forty and four thousand which were redeemed from the earth."

What can be the meaning of this singular announcement of a song not to be taught even to the other inhabitants of heaven? We require no celestial communications, and no supernatural quickening of our senses of body or mind, in some measure at least, to apprehend it. We need but refer to a familiar principle of the mind's operations, whose religious significance is often not perceived; by which toil, pain, and trial, however hard and sharp and grievous in the experience, turn to comfort and delight in the retrospect. As, by the influence of chemical attraction, the most glossy white is brought out on textures originally of the blackest dye, or as the mere constant falling of the bleaching sunlight makes a dull surface glisten like snow, so do the soul's melancholy passages change as they are acted on by reflection, and the darkest threads of its experience brighten in the steady light of memory. It will suffice, for the illustration of our text, to notice some simple instances.

There are few enjoyments more exquisite than the father feels in telling his son of the hardships of his early life. How he dilates on the efforts and sacrifices with which he began his career! and never tires in repeating the story of the want and destitution in which, with no privileges of learning, he laid the foundations of his prosperity; building in the low places of poverty the fabric of his fortunes, while fixed to his little plot of ground, or tossed to strange shores to gather his materials. But would he spare a single one of those pangs now? one hard day's labor, though it wore and bent his frame? one hour's thirst, with which his lips were parched? or, perchance, of choking hunger, when food was beyond his reach? Not one: not one thrill of pain, not one act of self-denial, not one patient stretch of endurance; for all these, by this transforming principle, have become most pleasant to his mind.

On the same principle, we can understand, without referring to unworthy motives, the soldier's interest in his oft-repeated narratives. Oh! the dark and deadly scene! man lifting his hand against man; brethren turning the engines of destruction against brethren; the ground wet with blood; and the smoke of carnage mounting heavy and slow over the dead and the dying! And how can the old man, in whom the passions are now quenched, if they were ever wrongly kindled, — how can he, with mildness in his eye and benignity in his heart, take any satisfaction in recurring to the frightful encounter? How be pleased to think of the alarms of invasion, the plough left in the furrow, the checked breathing of terror in the domestic circle, the standing still of those loved hearts, in the moment of fearful uncertainty? It is not necessarily that his soul breathes the spirit of war, or that he would encourage the spread of this "flame from hell;" but it is that these, like other trials, turn to joys, as viewed from the height of his present thought, stretching picturesquely through the long valley of the past.

The same principle operates in the hardships of

peaceful life. The sailor has a like gladness from the dangers with which he has been environed on the stormy deep. His rough and flinty experience, too, melts in this crucible of inward recollection, by some wondrous alchemy changed to gold. He would not lose now from mind the rough winter, the perilous voyage, the tempestuous Cape, in doubling which, the biting frost and the bitter wind did their worst upon him, and his bark well nigh foundered in the trough of the sea. Not a hurricane, or season of scant allowance, or exposure to deadly disease, would he part from. Sweeter than the music of harps and organs, the breezes whistle and the billows rage from afar; and more beautiful than the calm inland lake, reflecting the wood and the verdant hill-top near which he was born, that foam still sparkles, and those breakers swell and gleam, into which, as he clomb the giddy mast and grasped the frozen rigging, he had well nigh been plunged. The gloomy patches of the scene charm him more than any spots of sunshine. He interprets the almost intolerable accidents that overtook him into a good and gracious Providence, and sings of his calamity, privation, and fear.

So all the sweetest songs, and all the grandest and most touching poetry, that have ever been on earth breathed into sound or written in characters, have sprung out of such work and strife, sorrow and peril. And why should not a new song, unknown even to the elder seraphs, be so composed and framed in heaven, out of all life's trouble and disaster; while the mercy of God, the atoning influence of Christ, all heavenly help and guidance that they have received in their struggles, shall add depth and melody to those voices of the redeemed? The seraph cannot learn to sing that song; for he has not had, either in its hardship or salvation, this experience. Other hymns, of his own history and early course, he may sing for the redeemed from the earth to hear; but he must listen to songs from them no less sweet and ravishing, though something of the plaintive strain of the minor key, as well as cheerful airs, mingle therein.

Such is the mystery and bounty of the divine Providence laying its hand most heavily upon us. Through our superficial feelings, beneath the hard rock of custom, repeated blows of trouble pierce at last into that vein and fountain of living water which is found nowhere but deeply embedded. Paradoxical as it may seem, God means not only to make us good, but to make us also happy, by sickness, disaster, and disappointment. For the truly happy man is not made such by a pleasant and sunny course only of indulged inclinations and gratified hopes; by a worldly lot, containing every desirable circumstance which a worldly mind could fix on, with a cup full to running over of all that fond mortals choose and strive for. Hard tasks, deferred hopes, though they "make the heart sick," the beating of adverse or the delay of baffling winds, must enter into his composition here below, as they will finally enter into his song on high. There is more than pleasant fancy or cheering prediction in that language about beauty being given for ashes, the oil of joy for mourning, and the garment of praise for the spirit of heaviness; for out of dust and ashes alone beauty can grow; supreme gladness glistens nowhere but upon the face where grief hath been sitting; and the highest praise to God is sung when he hath delivered us from the pit of woe and despair. The opening of one of the most strangely beautiful flowers, from the roughest of prickly and unsightly stems, is an emblem of the richest blooming of moral beauty and pleasure from thorns and shapes of ugliness in the growth of the immortal mind.

Our question, then, is answered. The new original song of the redeemed, which cherubim could not learn to chant, which should be an addition even to the rich and infinitely varied melodies of heaven, must arise from the peculiar experience of toil, temptation, and trial, through which the redeemed, under God their Father and Christ their Saviour, pass in their first abode upon earth. But there is a strict condition. They who would blend their voices in that happy choir, to which the hosts of heaven pause to listen, must be faithful in performing this toil, in overcoming this temptation, in enduring this trial. If, recurring to our illustrations, the father cannot with truth refer to any hardships he nobly bore, and sacrifices he freely made, in his early life in building up his fortunes; if his prosperity has been an accident or a gift, or a cunning booty, though it might have been far easier and more pleasant so at the time, he has no such delight of prolonged recollection and no such inclination to repeat the history, which redounds not to his honor. If the soldier can remember only that he was craven when courage breathed high around him, it will be but a gloomy picture that is hung up in his imagination. He will not dwell exultingly on the self-denials which he did not share, or the triumphs he did nothing to secure. And if, when the billows tossed their angry crests, and the whirlwind made dread music among the rattling cords, the sailor slunk to the side or the bottom of the ship, the description of old ocean's fury, and of the motion still felt in every nerve of the rocking and engulfing waters, will lose all its magnificent charm to his fancy. The boast of his adventures will falter on his tongue. For the sweet feeling of safety, as he cowered in the hold and found the means of escape from his post, he has sold the perpetual delight of the mind.

In the "earthly things" behold perfect emblems of the "heavenly." Be faithful through the long work-day of duty, firmly resist in the fierce battle with temptation, and patiently bear under the beating and weltering storm of grief, and the over-payment of bliss shall at last come. Yea, no emigrant from Welsh hills or from Swiss mountains shall sing from his peculiar experience a song like yours! No captive of Arab tribes shall tell a thousand times of his enslaved and thirsty pilgrimage through the endless Sahara marches, with the keen zest of your memory; nor shall Napoleon, from leading his army along the snowy ridges of the Alps, have so great power and command in his own will gladly to remember, as you from your bloodless victories. The temporary roughness of your lot shall soften the progress of your unbounded career. Does not the harbor's sight at break of day, opening its safe seclusion, rejoice the seaman's heart in proportion to the rough and boisterous weather of his course? Can a stout and unbroken constitution give the enjoyment arising from those interruptions of sickness which measure for us the blessing of health, develop new emotions in the spiritual nature, and yield the delight of convalescence greater than that even of bodily soundness and vigor? Such to the redeemed, who have been faithful to their God and Saviour, will be their final health and everlasting refuge. The edge of earthly trial will plane smooth to their feet the floor of heaven. John's Apocalypse, now dim to this sensual, earthly vision of ours, shall gather brightness and power to their translated souls.

An ancient poet says, it is a delight to stand or walk upon the shore, and to see a ship tossed with tempest upon the sea; or to be in a fortified tower, and see hosts mingle upon a plain. But what is such pleasure compared with that felt by those who look down from the firm ground of heaven upon their own tossings in the voyage they have with a sacred and religious faithfulness accomplished, and fix their retrospective eye on the fight they, with a holy obstinacy, waged with their own passions and besetting sins? Overpassing the deluge of time, and discharged from the warfare, they at once join in the new song which they and their companions alone of all God's universe can sing in the common household of the saved. Shall not ours be the toil, the battle, the endurance now, that ours may be the song and the harping then ?

20

DISCOURSE XVII.

I AM A STRANGER ON THE EARTH.

Psalm cxix. 19. — I AM A STRANGER ON THE EARTH.

THERE is something very affecting in this expression.
You can hardly hear it without some moving of
your sensibilities.   In your more serious moods, you
must have paused over it, and had it return to you
with a stirring power.   For, in truth, it comes from
no superficial or accidental chord of feeling, but
swells from the depths of the soul like a solemn dirge.
It is emphatically repeated, at long intervals, in the
Scriptures.   The psalmist says again, " I am a stranger with Thee and a sojourner, as all my fathers
were."   Once more, he speaks in the name of all
the people, " We are strangers before Thee and
sojourners."   Abraham, ages earlier, uses the same
language.   The writer to the Hebrews takes up their
strain of sacred antiquity, and says, " They confessed that they were strangers and pilgrims on the
earth."

The emotion which the very phrase excites, running down from the earliest times to the present
generation, shows that it refers to something perma-

nent in human nature. Plato felt it when he tried to prove, from the nature of the soul's operations, that it was but a mysterious visitor from some pre-existent state. A modern author felt it when he described men as ships passing each other on the ocean, and hailing each other in vain for directions on the way. My friend felt it when he confessed his ignorance before this great question of our being and destiny. Very shallow must have been our experience, very lightly must we have pondered our condition, if we too have never felt it, and responded to the declaration, "I am a stranger on the earth." Very sound must have been that man's spiritual slumber who has not opened his eyes to perceive that his relations to visible objects around him, and to human creatures like himself, do not explain his whole position and being in the world; nay, that his close and endearing connections with kindred and friends do not supply all his wants, and cannot furnish for him a complete home. But to his thoughtful mind, the truth vindicates itself. He is "a stranger." No human love or sympathy, no offices of kindness or earthly respect, can fend off from him the sense of loneliness and need, or give him the feeling here of perfect familiarity and satisfaction.

Even while the fondest ties rest unbroken, the soul in every bosom, as it fully awakes, says to parent, says to husband, says to wife, and says to child, "Ye are very dear to me. God be blessed for the happy and holy bonds that unite us! But, in the so mysterious existence I pass in time, eternity behind and before and immensity around me, I feel like a 'stranger.' Wafted hither, I know not by what wind, in some vessel of incomprehensible power, I am landed on an unknown shore. A few things I have become accustomed to, a few persons I have formed acquaintance with ; but the vast universe around, obscure and shining, stretches beyond this point of my attainment into unfathomed abysses. Pleasant is life, delicious is hope, precious is affection; but my footing is insecure : 'I am a stranger on the earth.' "

So is it while all our fixtures of habitual dependence stand. But, when they are smitten down, and those we leaned on, like props sinking in the flood, vanish away, then the feeling of the " stranger on earth " rises with redoubled power. Under any great disappointment or alteration of our circumstances, this alien feeling will arise, the scene around us put on a look of strangeness, and a voice be heard inwardly exhorting us, " Arise and depart, for this is not your rest." The world is beautiful and glorious: it lies around us, as one has said, " like a bright sea, with boundless fluctuations." But we are not at home in it. We are lost and bewildered amid its splendors. We are unsafe amid its wasting forces. We are but little versed in its capacious stores. Our hold upon it is faint and transient. So, across the gulf of past ages, we enter into eager sympathy with those old believers who confessed that they too were strangers ; and we would seek with them " a city which hath foundations."

But my object is not only to verify the feeling indicated in the text, but to show the deliverance offered us in our religion, from every thing in the feeling that is painful or sad. For it is just this state of ignorance, this sense of exposure, this unquieted search, and this strange and alien feeling of the soul, that the gospel of Christ came to meet. The Christian faith delivers us from such conscious blindness and puzzling insecurity, and defines our position. This authoritative establishment of our actual relations in the universe is the great blessing of the gospel. "In time past," says the apostle, addressing a society of Gentile converts, "ye were aliens from the commonwealth of Israel, and strangers from the covenants of promise. . . . But, in Christ Jesus, ye who sometime were far off are made nigh. . . Now, therefore, ye are no more strangers and foreigners, but fellow-citizens with the saints and of the household of God." Truly not alone to the ancient Gentile or believing Jewish soul did Christ offer this union and rest, but to every solitary, weary wanderer, child of Adam, whom his voice can reach. What an unspeakable gift! Strangers and foreigners have often purchased to themselves, for a great price, the freedom of earthly cities in which they sojourned, or been rewarded with it, in the decoration of golden emblems, for high achievements of heroism and goodness. But the freedom of the city of God, granted through symbols more costly than emblems of jewels and gold, the freedom of the universe, the freedom certified to us of an everlasting progress in

20*

virtue and social blessedness, which no change can interrupt, is bestowed by Jesus Christ. Here is the great point and peculiarity of our religion. This lies not simply in its revelation of the fatherhood of God, and the brotherhood of men, glorious, in- spiring, and fruitful doctrines as these are. Still less does it lie in any theory about human nature, or sin, or salvation. It is to be found rather in the assured direction our religion gives to the long-questioning, searching, doubting faculties of the human mind; and in the clear, broad aim with which it raises the affections of the human heart, so long feeling after, if haply they might find their fate, and too often sadly, in their darkness, groping around the grave- stone and the narrow house as the last distinct objects in their doom. In short, it is in the home among eternal realities provided for the spirit that is in man, and "a stranger on the earth!"

I trust I do not open a vein of sentiment remote from any of you, or point to a source of relief for merely fictitious necessities. Have you never, in your meditation, in your adversity, in your grief, in your satiety, in your uneasy longing, had the ex- perience? As you have finished the ever-recurring routine of the day's labor, while you listened to the monotonous cries of business, or as you heard the sounds of evening gaiety, have you never become aware, that your soul was very much a stranger among these things; that it had "faculties" which could not be "used" upon them, and needed to abide in some higher objects, before it could be truly

at home ? When your capacities of thought and
emotion have been aroused by some special providence of God, have you not realized that the earth
itself, the old familiar earth, was to you as a far
place and foreign country, and you had still to seek
for your native land ? Then have you felt as did
those old Hebrew pilgrims, when " they confessed
that they were strangers on the earth." " For they
that say such things declare plainly that they seek a
country. And " (with what pathos continues the
Scripture !) " truly if they had been mindful of,"
thinking of, " that country whence they came out,
they might have had opportunity to have returned.
But now they desire a better country, that is, an
heavenly."

This is the only solution and satisfaction of the
soul's yearning desire, coeval with its intelligent history, through all Pagan and Christian times. We,
different from the lower creatures, have aspirations
this world cannot limit, spiritual abilities which it
cannot employ, but only that " better " and
" heavenly country " can satisfy ; and never, to the
sojourner in foreign parts, did the songs of his native
land sound so sweetly, as to the soul, really knowing
its own wants, do the teachings of Jesus respecting
the many mansions of the Father's house, and the
place he goes to prepare.

But if you have not had this scripture feeling of
the " stranger on earth," seeking and in Christ finding your true home and country above the skies,
then I would fain stir your hearts from the pressure

of worldly custom up to it. For nothing do you so much need, and nothing will be so rich in holy, practical results, even in your moral conduct among men, as this adjusting, under Christ, of your relations of citizenship in that celestial abode, which the prophecies of Judaism looked forward to, and which gospel and epistle, the mouth of Christ and pen of his messengers, declare. The little child morally sleeps for awhile in the natural, kindred relations of earth; but the unfolding mind that advances to manhood and womanhood will at length transcend them. Unless bound in the stupefactions of sense, or crusted over with habits of worldliness, it will perceive that the conditions and contingencies of this life cannot meet its whole nature, or fill its final need. I would call you to contemplate this simple issue. By the terrors of doubt that cloud the prospect of the unspiritual, I would warn, — by the satisfactions of Christian hope, I would win you, vitally to embrace the peculiarity of the gospel, in the ties of fellowship it offers you, not only with the living and present, but with the unseen beings of another world, — no longer the dim, shadowy, flitting, uncertain phantoms they were to the pagan faith, — with the saints, truly worthy that name, elder and younger, in " the household of God." As the New Testament is true, this association is offered us. Death, terrifier of the world, stands back to let the light stream through his gloomy house, and reveal the holy and happy assembly. Sorrow bends aside her head, so as not to obstruct the inspiring vision. Sickness lifts from

the couch her heavy eyes, to catch a glimpse of it.
What refinement! What elevation! What generosity and joy! What motive and impulse! There,
alive, appear to us the good departed, whom we
have known here below, and those we have not
known; the celebrated in the calendar, and the un-
canonized, as worthy as they; those whose names
stand as monumental exemplars on the page of the
Bible, with names no less pure, written only in the
Lamb's book of life; — and we "strangers on
the earth," in these crumbling garments of clay,
are invited to be fellow-citizens with them all.

But there are conditions. We must give up our
selfishness, we must give up every shape of sin. We
must leave behind our spiritual sloth and our sensual
excess. We cannot accept the invitation so long as
we regard this as our true home; so long as our
most valued interests are concentred in the world;
so long as the visible earthly scene, with its comfort
and pleasure, with its gain and honor, yea, or its
friendship and love, seems to us the only solid
reality. We must have faith in that higher state
before we embark for it our heart's treasure, as
Columbus had faith in this western world before he
risked all to reach it.

But, in fine, whether we have or not the peculiar
and lofty feeling expressed in our text, it is obvious
to you, that not only a feeling is expressed in it, but
a fact. As a matter of fact, our position is that of
"strangers on the earth." Have we not just arrived
here? Are we more than very partially acquainted

with the place we are visiting? Even to a child's question, respecting many things, must we not frankly answer, that " we are strangers," and cannot tell? Is not the conveyance preparing, which is to take us away from the spot where we have transiently alighted? Have we not seen our companions carried out? Will it not soon be our turn to follow? Let us not, then, be blind to the fact, if we are dead to the feeling. Let us be neither blind nor dead. But, if we suffer ourselves so to be, — ah! the immutable reality! — the fact will not thus be negatived, or the feeling finally kept off.

> " Yet a few days, and thee
> The all-beholding sun shall see no more
> In all his course.
>   Thou shalt lie down
> With patriarchs of the infant-world ; with kings,
> The powerful of the earth ; the wise, the good ;
> Fair forms, and hoary seers of ages past, —
> All in one mighty sepulchre.
>   The sons of men,
> The youth in life's green spring, and he who goes
> In the full strength of years, ...
> Shall, one by one, be gathered to thy side
> By those who in their turn shall follow them."

" So live," says our subject to us, cultivate such sympathies with the departed " wise " and " good," that, when the body goes to mingle with theirs in the dust, the soul may meet theirs in the heavens, not as an alien and a stranger, but as a fellow-citizen and a friend.

DISCOURSE XVIII.

NATURE, CONSCIENCE, AND REVELATION, DECLARING GOD, DUTY, AND DESTINY.

Rom. i. 20. — FOR THE INVISIBLE THINGS OF HIM FROM THE CREATION OF THE WORLD ARE CLEARLY SEEN.

Rom. ii. 15. — WHICH SHOW THE WORK OF THE LAW WRITTEN IN THEIR HEARTS, THEIR CONSCIENCE ALSO BEARING WITNESS.

Rom. ii. 16. — IN THE DAY WHEN GOD SHALL JUDGE THE SECRETS OF MEN BY JESUS CHRIST.

In the text, chosen out of several closely related verses, are indicated the three great sources of religious knowledge, — Nature, Conscience, and Revelation. The apostle, writing to the Romans, who were members of the great Gentile nation, citizens of the world more than any others whom he addressed, undertakes a larger account than elsewhere of the whole subject of religion. He is led thus to consider the particular light dispensed respectively in the three directions already named, — Nature, proclaiming God in his "eternal power;" Conscience, while echoing that proclamation, enjoining also duty; and Revelation, while re-echoing God and duty to the soul, disclosing still further human destiny.

God, Duty, and Destiny — these are the great

words severally spoken to man by Nature, Conscience, and Revelation. It becomes us to receive
each and all these messages, through the three
divine voices that convey them, into grateful and
obedient hearts. There is still among religious believers considerable difference of opinion as to the
relative offices and effects upon human life of these
three, — nature, conscience, and revelation. But, if
we effectually learn from the first of God, from
the second of duty, and from the third of our
destiny, we cannot be misusing any one of them,
though the provinces they relatively occupy should
never be exactly defined.

Nature speaks to us indeed, above all things, of
God. Unless our hearts are hard and insensible, we
cannot stop with the outward scene, with the bloom
and plenty, with the order and splendor, of the earth
and the heavens : we must seek for the invisible
Cause. Nor have we to seek long or far. We are
so made as to recognize the necessary existence of
a Superior Power and Wisdom to account for what
we behold. We may look at the sun and moon,
and shining host of the firmament, that beautifully
divide the hours between them in the lofty sky, or
we may survey the smallest flower that opens its
leaves and diffuses its fragrance at our feet, and
equally they declare to us God. His name is written on the immense arch of the universe, but just
as distinctly on a spear of grass or an insect's wing.
His intelligence is proved by the revolution of
the planets, but just as clearly by the sap that

ascends in a plant, or the blood that circulates in
our own veins.   The thunder, the cataract, the roar
of the winds and waves, is his voice, but none the
less the hum that rises from the myriad happy tribes
of animated life.   Verily, nature speaks of God,
shows his abode in the immensity of space, and alike
in the little sparkling crevice of the rock, which only
the microscope can detect.   *God* is the sound that
seems to reach our ear, as we regard any single part
of the creation, but at once returns from the opposite part, and, like a word shouted in the echoing
gorges of the mountains, reverberates in a million
endless repetitions above and below, before and
behind us.   So that, were we left to the religious
influence of nature alone, did not the voice of conscience prescribe duty and prompt us to action, our
own existence would be well nigh overpowered,
swallowed up and lost in the Divine.   Yet, though
thus re-assured by the dictates of responsibility in
our own hearts, by the admonitions of the spirit that
is in man, our existence would still seem precarious
and ready to disappear, but for the light cast by
revelation on human destiny.

The instructions of nature, grand as they are, and
reinforced though they may be by the reflections of
our own moral faculty, do not satisfy.   They proclaim God, and the soul responds duty, obligation,
to this Mighty and Eternal One; but the thought of
God himself and of duty is not enough to give peace,
without some idea also of a future destiny.   That
idea a few minds of peculiar cast and temper may

21

seem to themselves to gather from outward emblems and inward musings; but it cannot so rise to any height of fixed assurance in the common heart of mankind.

Nay, in the most intensely thoughtful and meditative frame of mind, amid the workings of nature, our exposure to decay and death may seem only the more signal and menacing. I have stopped amid the gloom of pathless woods; I have stood on the shore of the sea, and strained my eye to its dim vanishing-point in the far horizon; I have gazed at twilight through the interlacing, indistinguishable branches of the trees, and looked up into the boundless region through which the stars in shining troops hold on their immeasurable careers; and the reality, the vastness, the glory, of all this mighty sum of things have descended with oppressive and insupportable weight upon me. I have trembled, with a shudder of the heart, in the awe of profound worship before the Infinite Being who had laid these foundations, and reared these pillars, and spread out this roof of sparkling worlds. But what am I, and what my life, in this solid and incomprehensible scene? Behold! I am as nothing. My habitation is in the dust. I am crushed before the moth. My life is a vapor, a particle of matter, a flower, vanishing, fading, blown away, and annihilated before the permanent order which an uncreated and everlasting Strength rolls on independently of me; while I, the creature that yesterday brought forth, and to-morrow shall dissolve, even as I look and think, decline and perish.

Nature! with but a handful of her dust, she, by the almighty fiat, made me; and what does she owe me but a place where that animated dust may crumble? My friend hath gone before me, and I know the place of his grave; but whither shall I go, to what point in the boundless scene, to find his spirit? My thought flies forth, but, like the dove over the deluge, finds no rest. There is the sepulchre where the body decays, and, hard by, those pathless woods where the green generations of the forest successively rise and sink; and, on the other side, the ocean dashes with restless and impatient moan against its rocky bounds, and still, at their stations of inconceivable distance above, move on the glittering orbs, amongst whose mazes my imagination strays: but where throughout the vast extent, is the abode of those dear to me? In what chosen spot have their spirits pitched their tents? Or have they yet, — for the doubting question will rise, and has in the greatest minds that ever lived on earth, when looking at nature alone, — have they yet any tabernacles of life and rest, " a local habitation and a name," in any rank of other being?

In the dwelling from whose window, or near whose ancient walls, I thus gaze and meditate, is a fellow-creature slowly wasting away with an incurable disease. Every day she parts with something of her life and frame to the elements, that, continually robbing her of her strength, will soon seize the poor, withered corpse as their lawful prey. Shall the thinking, feeling principle be embodied again? or, as a disbeliever there in Christianity argued with me, is all over and extinct at death? Nature does not answer, save with oracles dubious and above our clear comprehension. The only word she speaks, with distinct and unquestionable utterance, is God. Conscience does not answer, save with fond hopes and irrepressible yearnings. The only additional word she speaks, with deep emphasis and everlasting repetition, is Duty. Revelation *does* answer, adding, that other and final word of Immortal Destiny.

Christianity thus reinstates us in that hold on existence, which, in our connection with outward nature, had seemed so frail and loose. In Christ, our life can no longer be compared with the most fugitive things, as the vapor, the withered flower, the unregarded particle of dust, but outlasts the most abiding features of the creation. Instead of passing away beneath the sun, it shall endure till his flame is extinguished, and the whole material order changed. The ocean shall shift its bed, the primeval forest shall mingle with the clod, the very stars shall grow old or be borne into new cycles of revolution, while the soul of man is yet fresh and youthful, in the morning of its endless career; the grave that seemed to swallow it up being but the entrance, the porch of its loftier and everlasting abode.

How joyful, how inspiring, how almost too great for our hopes, the prospect of that destiny which the Christian revelation opens! How joyful, did I say? How fearful, too, solemnizing, and subduing to the thoughts! Remember the terms in which the text describes that destiny : "In the day when God shall judge the secrets of men." The color of that coming destiny is to be determined by the color of our present life and conduct. What is to pass through that low porch of the grave, appear in that immortal dwelling, and outlive the sea, the sun, the stars, and be the fountain of good or evil to us in the eternal career, is our character. How far it can be changed or improved in that mysterious future, we know not. But Christ and his apostles teach that our condition, on entering the world of spirits, shall be the consequence of what it has been in the past. I call upon you, then, to stand, not with rejoicing only, but with solemn awe, before your destiny, as revelation lays it bare. I call on you to stand with humility, with self-examination, with repentance before it. I exhort you to lead a good and holy life in view of it. I charge you so to listen to the proclamation of duty which conscience makes, as not to rush upon that eternity which the gospel discloses, with a worldly, sinful, and polluted soul.

The Being who is to sit at that judgment of our destiny is the same almighty, wise, true Being whom nature declares, and who is declared by Christ also, as he is intimated by our own conscience, to be a Judge just and holy, no less than gracious and kind. I pray you, my friends, to consider it ; for to this point all religious instructions from all sources respecting God and duty and destiny, with accumulated weight and piercing closeness, converge. Are you living a righteous, prayerful, temperate, faithful

21*

life? Do you cultivate good and spiritual affections in your homes, and with all your fellow-creatures? Are you promoting or injuring the virtue of your fellow-men; helping them on the way of purity and sobriety, or setting before them temptation and a snare? These inquiries are pertinent; they are imperative; they demand a reply from the sincere conviction and most watchful self-knowledge of your hearts.

Man in advancing years! have you so thought of your destiny? Has your course been tending to make that destiny happy, by tending to exalt your own and others' conduct? If not thus, but otherwise, has been the bearing of your actions, trust not to God's mercy to excuse you from the suffering to ensue. God's mercy, like all his other attributes, is pledged to the infliction of that suffering, to purge away, if it yet may be, the baseness of your motives and the rottenness of your life. The word revealed is, Your secrets shall be judged, the inmost parts of your deportment and your spirit probed, in that day.

Man, who standest in that centre-period, on that summit-level, of existence, which seems to command as a high ground of security both what is past and what is to come! do now, before God and your conscience, what will prepare for you a good destiny. Trust not to a future opportunity. You, too, in the prime of life — like one whom I have been used to meet in the ways of business and amid all the bustle of this world's interests, — may be close to that "eternal blazon," which nothing but the veil, the thin and fragile veil we wear, of flesh and blood, hides from any of us. Young man! lend not so dull an ear to the warnings that are wont to be uttered from this place: they concern your destiny.

Children! listen to the voice of God speaking to you from his word and works; listen to the dictates of conscience in your own breast, that, by the grace of God, and the deeds of duty, your destiny, lying as yet all before you, may be blessed. So may God and duty bless to us all for evermore our destiny!

DISCOURSE XIX.

BELSHAZZAR'S FEAST.

Dan. v. 6. — THEN THE KING'S COUNTENANCE WAS CHANGED, AND HIS THOUGHTS TROUBLED HIM, SO THAT THE JOINTS OF HIS LOINS WERE LOOSED, AND HIS KNEES SMOTE ONE AGAINST ANOTHER.

EVERY scripture-narrative is set in a religious light, teaches some moral lesson, and thus deserves the title, sacred history. That we may catch the meaning in our text, let us imagine ourselves present in the scene it describes. Belshazzar was the king of Babylon, one of the most splendid cities in the world. It was built in an immense plain ; and its walls measured a circumference of sixty miles. A hundred gates of brass adorned it ; and hanging gardens, terrace above terrace, clothed its regal palace with living verdure. Through the midst flowed the great river Euphrates, painting in its depths the surrounding magnificence, and shedding beauty on temple and tower, that looked boldly from its banks. Yet the crowned lord himself of this wondrous city was a worthless wretch. He spent his time in luxurious repose, pampering the baser appetites, and permitting all the glory of his great abode to be stained by the debauchery of his people. Many years he went on, and did his pleasure. God permitted him to choose his own course, and work out his own destiny, in the station assigned.

The scene of our text is laid at the return of a certain idolatrous festival. The king had prepared a rich feast to grace it. He called in a thousand of his lords to the sparkling tables. His wives with his concubines came to join the company. And they reclined at the costly viands, spread all around in grateful abundance. Odorous lamps hung above from golden chains, and shed a sweet brilliance through the vast hall, so that the night shone even as the day. Idols, richly carved, bent upon them gracefully from the walls; and gaily those feasters greeted them in their songs. So they went on, hour by hour, intoxicating their senses, and burying their souls in unbounded revelry.

At length, heated with wine, Belshazzar ordered the sacred vessels, taken by Nebuchadnezzar from the temple of God at Jerusalem, to be brought for service in this scene of rioting and drunkenness. And they all, king, princes, wives, and concubines, used these instruments of holiness as their own goblets. They polluted them with their voluptuous lips, and poured out libations to the idols, and sang impious songs in honor of false gods. Then, suddenly, they saw the fingers, as of a man's hand, writing over against the candlestick, upon the plastered wall. Dim grew the lamps before those letters of fire. With the supernatural splendor, a ghastly paleness spread over the features that had been dissolved in mirth; and such was the king's panic, that the joints of his loins were loosed, and his knees smote one against the other. Wherefore those letters written on the wall? Simply to announce a punishment for the crime committed that very night! Thus are they generally understood. But the reference was, doubtless, larger and more solemn. It embraced the king's whole being, and was a final judgment on the long course of his guilty life. There is not a word of reproach for any single offence, but a general decree comprehending every sin of his soul : — " Thou art weighed in the balances, and found wanting."

Was the king utterly at a loss, even at the first, to know the meaning inscribed by that miraculous hand? So it is commonly supposed. And the idea seems to be justified by his offering a reward to any one who should be able to read it. But, affrighted as he was at the terrible appearance, there is reason to believe that he was not altogether surprised. Though he could not read each particular letter and syllable, yet it seemed as if from the whole fearful inscription flashed a meaning that almost maddened him. For, you will observe, it was not the wondrous miracle nor the blinding splendor that most moved the king. No : the text informs us it was his thoughts that troubled him. It was not stupid amazement and blind fear. No : his thoughts, rising clear and strong, and breaking at once through the fumes of intoxication, troubled him. And how was it that the king's thoughts troubled him? Oh! was it not by the interpretation they gave of the miraculous writing?

Did they not translate that burning symbol, whose separate words he could not read, into one large commentary on his whole sinful life ? Yes : guilty conscience woke from her slumber in his bosom, and compelled even the monarch to travel with her far away from the brilliant hall of feasting to scenes of cruel bloodshed and dungeons of unjust imprisonment. Far into years long gone and forgotten, she hurried him as ghosts are said to hurry their victims ; and, once more to the king's awakened mind, they were filled with their own fresh scenes and real characters. The souls of base men he had rewarded, of innocent men he had destroyed, passed again before him in long review. Those letters on the wall his understanding could not indeed distinguish, yet thus he felt their real force within. Though he could not read them, he read himself by them, as by a lamp held in the hand of conscience. In the heat of their flame, the whole page of life which that profligate man had written, as he hoped, in fading traces, was brought out to his eyes in perfect preservation.

Well, then, might the king's thoughts trouble him, so as even to loosen the joints of his loins, and make his knees smite together. For, though there had been no Daniel, wise above all the magicians and soothsayers and astrologers, yet would Belshazzar himself have made out what was essential in this letter written him from the bar of judgment. A solemn account to be rendered, a fearful retribution to be endured, — these ideas, at least, would have been impressed on his mind.

Yet he called in the wise man of God to read the writing, and, as he had promised, rewarded him with a chain of gold about his neck, and by proclaiming him the third ruler in the kingdom. But not for a moment could he stay the righteous goings of the divine law. Hard on the sentence pronounced pressed its dreadful execution. Terrible interruption came to that scene of joy, where "a thousand hearts beat happily, and music arose with its voluptuous swell." That very night the Persian general, having turned the river Euphrates from its course, marched his troops along the empty channel. The drunken Chaldeans had left open their brazen gates. In rushed the besieging army, and the city was filled with confusion and bloodshed. The royal guards were slain; the nobles perished; and the monarch himself, his conscience stinging him for present guilt, his memory arraying before him past iniquities, even like the usurping king of Denmark, "with all his crimes broad-blown and flush as May," was hurried from this final steeping of his soul in lust, and, at an instant's warning, stood before the tribunal of his Maker.

And to what, my friends, have I really been calling your attention? Simply to some events that happened at a far-off place, and in a distant period of history? No; but to a scene perpetually acted over again at all times on the theatre of human life. I have but pictured the operation in a single instance of a law which is universal and eternal,—the law of retribution. It is not Belshazzar alone, and Babylon, and two thousand years ago, of which I have spoken, but of every wilful offender against God's law who walks our own streets. It is the portrait of sin universally, true in every feature : the present mirth, the recklessness of consequences to come, and the sudden destruction with which it is overwhelmed. Into this historic mirror, then, let us look : we may recognize our own faces.

It is to be feared, most of us do not live with a practical regard to this law of retribution. And wherefore ? Is it because we have not found conclusive evidence of its reality ? It cannot be : for not only is it a law expounded in Scripture. It is suggested by all the analogies of nature which Scripture has used for its illustration. It is written everywhere in history. It is taught in all civil regulations. Let some base man outrage society with violence to person, property, or life ; let robbery track and spoil the traveller, or deeds of horror be committed in the pirate-ship ; and how resounds the cry, — not alone among the brave and ardent, but the timid and tender-hearted, — Let the guilty be brought to justice ! Let not night be made horrid, and the sea perilous, by suffering bad men to range unmolested. When the murderous Thugs of India were dislodged from their burrows, when proof of their guilt was brought from secret graves in many a solitary plain and deep jungle, and they were subjected to the rigors of the law, *whose* pang at their execution equalled his joy that a continent was made more safe to the traveller ; and that, for every victim of the law's affronted

22

majesty, the necks of a score of the innocent, the fair, and the manly were saved from the cord of the strangler?

The same thing is seen in the delight taken in fiction or the drama. Why have the tragedies of Shakspeare such enchaining interest, though they abound in scenes of bloodshed and groans of despair? Because of their fulfilments of moral law, that give a solemn exultation to the conscience, and sink all physical pangs into insignificance beside its infinite joy. It loves to see the poisoned chalice commended back to those that mixed it, and the gory locks of the ghost shaken at the murderer, and the stains of guilt refusing to quit the heart of the usurper. The soul demands, in tones sounding of eternity, that virtue have its joy, and vice its woe.

We see the same law governing domestic life. How many families, rising to riches and honor by the path of the virtues, have as surely fallen by that of the vices! Two or three generations measured their ascent, and two or three more have sunk them in poverty and shame; and then men talk of the wheel of fortune. Nay: it is the revolution of Providence; it is the justice of God!

This moral law, too, while exactly adjusting individual fortunes, as easily weighs kingdoms. The Roman empire was built from the feeblest beginnings, by the force of temperance, industry, and valor. She spread her arms over the nations, gave law to savage tribes, made the mention of her citizens a universal joy and terror, and became another name for the world. But luxury flowed in, stagnant sloth extended, corruption prevailed, ambition battled; and she that had ruled mankind by virtue, dissolved in vice, fell a prey to barbarians.

All known religions, too, of merely human invention, have confessed the same principle. How deeply have they sunk caverns of torment in the world of spirits! The Oriental imagination has poured gloom on the future abodes of the wicked, and the pagan mythology has prophesied of infernal regions in which reprobate spirits must wander.

In fine, the vilest sinner himself has fearful anticipations of his doom, as if, in the very highly figurative language of another, "the funeral pyre of the last judgment were already kindled in an unknown distance, and some few flashes of it, darting out beyond the rest, were flying and lighting on the face of his soul."

Retribution, then, is not only a solemn doctrine of holy writ, but a great fact in human nature. And the picture of it which I have presented is but one of a countless number, of which the world, as a vast gallery, is full. Our disregard of it comes not from any want of proof. How, then, is it to be accounted for? Doubtless, we may say generally, by our own guilty negligence. Yet there are more special reasons.

First, the very strength with which it has been believed by some, and the terrific manner in which it has been set forth, have produced unbelief in others. Morbidly excited religionists have averred that the slightest offence is worthy of eternal punishment. Gloomy theologians, impelled by the warmth of narrow and ill-balanced judgment to be more explicit than the Bible, have dogmatically declared, that the sin and suffering of all who now mistake the way of salvation shall go on increasing forever and ever. Men chained to unbending systems have sometimes contended, that even the little child, dying unconscious of its own free-agency, shall taste without relief of the miseries of hell. No wonder that our ideas of God, of justice, of mercy, yea, and our human hearts, should rebel against such representations. But, recoiling in horror from this over-statement and extravagance, many have gone into a perilous extreme of indifference and doubt. Men have lived as if there were to be no day of reckoning at all, and put their souls to imminent hazard. Some philosophize to excess on the subject, and, on speculative grounds merely, extend the season of probation indiscriminately beyond the grave. Others, unscripturally and irrationally, deny any working of the law of retribution after death. How many, too, view retribution simply as a doctrine of the understanding, to be uncertainly reasoned about, refuted, or proved, and a fit subject for sectarians to try their armor upon in theological warfare! We have received it too much as an opinion to be discussed, rather than a reality to be felt in a perpetual pressure on the heart. There is as much difference between these two modes of regarding truth, as between partaking of bread for nourishment and analyzing it to gratify

curiosity. A man may be the finest of biblical
critics, and yet, disobeying what he so well under-
stands, join them who eat the fruits of sin in unseen
abodes of misery.

Thus may we, perhaps, in part account for the
general indifference to this fearful law that binds us.
Exposed to such dangers, it is well for us to be occa-
sionally reminded, that retribution, however we may
make it a knotty point for amusing discussion, is a
clear fact and solemn reality. It is well we should
consider, that the sober law of righteous compensa-
tion, however it may have been caricatured in human
systems, however expounded in dogmas of cruelty,
however clothed in false shapes and addressed in
unreal terrors to the imagination,— yet still remains.
What is plainly important for us to know is evidently the simple fact, just as it is. And I believe
we see this, in its true proportions, in the account
already given of Belshazzar.

This account shows us, in the first place, that men
are generally allowed to go on for a while as they
please, really to enjoy the pleasures of sin for a season. It is sometimes said, guilt always receives its
full punishment immediately, in this life. But this is
plainly not true, as matter of fact ; and, if it were, we
can hardly conceive how sin or virtue should exist
at all. Were the stripes inflicted at once, and for
every even the smallest offence, transgression would
be a thing to be avoided just as we avoid tasting poison, plunging into deep water, or handling coals of
fire. Probation, a trial of men to see whether they

22*

will do right, would be entirely out of the question.
There could be no free moral will but would at
once break down. We should be machines, moving
with regularity as the sun and moon do.

But how was it with Belshazzar? Time was
given him to degrade himself fully, and offer abundant sacrifices to the gods of flesh and sense. Nearly
seventeen years had he reigned. He had gathered
every thing rich and beautiful around him. He had
built towers in the city's splendid squares, and set
up shining idols in the plain. A thousand times had
he feasted with his lords and wives as gaily as when
the feast was interrupted by the blazing letters on the
wall, and the flashing armor of the Persian invaders.
And yet the angel of judgment had not sensibly
touched him. Oh! how terrible, yet true as terrible,
this spectacle, — his being permitted to go on, filling
up the measure of his iniquity, laying up wrath
against the day of wrath! Yet thousands of the
wicked now present the same spectacle, as strongly
as did Belshazzar.

But, secondly, the account from Scripture, while
it shows we have a season of clear and proper probation, makes retribution something equally positive
and distinct. Though not now mingled in equal
proportions with sin, it will at length break in upon
it suddenly and sharply. Probation at an end, exe-
cutions of justice are not indiscriminately mingled
with offers of mercy. If the latter come, it is only
after the former have exhausted their power.

Our own experience will furnish us with cases of

commencing retribution similar to that of the Asiatic
king. We have seen the young man despising wholesome restraints, neglecting regular duties, moving
joyously through all the rounds of sinful pleasure.
Was the sword of vengeance stretched at once over
his head, and his soul summoned to its trial? No:
year after year he went on, and spent his substance
in riotous living, and robbed his brothers' patrimony.
Noble were the powers of his mind, and, like jewels,
they might have shone in his noble frame. But, alas!
their strength was all melted down in the fires of appetite and the heats of passion. At length the too
sorely taxed system began to tremble from the height
of its proud strength. Fits of pain and sickness succeeded each other at rapid intervals, like couriers
giving signal of the fast-approaching doom. Loath-
some disease infected the nerves, and loosened every
fibre. And he that was made to be an honor to his
parents, and a glory in his day and generation, mis-
erably perished when he had lived out hardly more
than half his days. Think you, fancy draws the
portrait? But still rests on the mind the vision of
that corpse!

And death is not the end of retribution, but the
signal of its more perfect reign. Death is often
piously spoken of as a circumstance in life. But it
is not a small circumstance. The time arrives for
this temple of the human body to be taken down.
What a building it is! Have you ever pondered
its marvellous construction, the fluted columns of its
strength with cunning joints, the firm bands that

move " wheel within wheel " its various circles, the
ebb and flow of its vital currents in the heart, the net
of communication with its citadel in the brain? This
amazing workmanship,—the house in which we live,
the cradle in which we sleep, the window through
which we see, the chiming bell of every tone of melody, the apt tool of every work of benefit, an archi-
tecture that shames all temples, an instrument of
infinite uses, and a beauty beyond the stars,— this is
to be dissolved. We might well believe in a day of
judgment, even from such fit preliminary as spoiling
into food for worms this astonishing arrangement
and abode of the soul !

The question is often asked, " Will a death-bed repentance avail?" Far better, one would think, might
the laborer hope to accomplish his day's work by a
few struggles in the falling twilight, or the traveller
to effect the sober week's journey by the flight of a
few hours, or the husbandman to sow and reap his
grain in the same season, than could the immortal
soul to huddle up the duties of life in the short breath-
ings of the last agony. Is repentance, then, of no
avail? Surely ; for repentance is itself resistance to
sin, and holy effort. Not a toil or tear of it shall be
lost. What its extreme agony in the expiring moments may do, God only knows. But is not God's
free mercy offered ? Truly, ways manifold beyond
our deserving ; but never, that we know, in the way
of breaking his own law, or warding off from a moral offence its specific penalty. Nay, is it not his
highest mercy that he has given us that free moral

constitution which makes suffering inevitable from sin; but by which alone the soul can gain its true glory, and which even the pangs of remorse are designed to goad to new struggles for the blessed consummation of its being? Yet is not Christ a sufficient Saviour? Indeed he is to all who take his yoke upon them, and receive his spirit within them. So that the law of retribution is not vacated by our sorrow, or by God's goodness, or by the salvation of Jesus; though all these may be to us, if we will, mighty means to the obeying of that law, and securing of its blessing. But the law itself ever operates, in many ways, more subtle and penetrating than I have specified, or can now define. It has not merely an external, but a deeply spiritual, internal working. Holding fast to our sins, it pierces to the centre of our moral being. With real and inevitable, though unknown justice, it weakens the action of the soul, subtracts from the strength of every noble sentiment, turns the tender into the callous conscience, and, as soft substances under the steady wash of the elements are petrified, converts the heart of flesh into a heart of stone. Such, indeed are fearful, as they are incalculable, processes of its fatal equity, at which the soul should stand aghast, and for its life hasten back.

Finally, — the account from Scripture presents retribution, not only as a principle thus sure and dreadful in its operations, but as a law of rigorous justice. But you know how often the subject is presented in a wild, indefinite character. No expressions are thought fit but superlatives. The infinite and eternal are set over against the finite and temporary; and to a few brief actions are ascribed consequences absolutely without bound or end. Men are divided rigorously into two classes, one of which are to be all equally and forever happy, the other all equally and forever miserable. How different all this from those just discriminations everywhere made in Scripture! Even to the dissolute king it was said, " Thou art weighed in the balances, and found wanting." Retribution shall be measured and meted out to thee in exact proportion to thy sin. Thou shalt suffer as much as thou deservest, and no more and no less. The unbounded and unqualified declarations which are so common, are apt to make us forget this just and guarded style of the Scriptures. A man is to reap exactly what he sows, of the same kind and in the same degree. Some are to be beaten with many stripes; and others, less guilty, with few stripes. And to every man will God render according to his deeds. Such perfect justice is there in the retribution that shall search us all.

Turning aside, then, from all ingenious speculations, here is the solemn fact, that should press upon our hearts, and control our lives. We must eat the fruit of our own doings, and all of it. We must receive, and it is God's justice and goodness that we should receive, down to the very dust of the balance, the whole weight of suffering corresponding to the amount of our sin. As every step we take moves, however imperceptibly, the solid globe on which we tread ; as our words are forever printed in this vast volume of leaves of air, and our deeds recorded in the very frame of nature ; so, heed it, or heed it not, every moral act we perform affects our future destiny. Oh ! were we but once thoroughly persuaded of this simple truth, what revolutions would take place in our lives ! How should we avoid every inordinate passion as a raging fire ! How should we cast all envious and uncharitable thoughts, like vipers, from our bosoms ! What immense interest would life gain in our eyes ! To sleep over our duties, to be indifferent to the moral tendency of our actions, would be impossible. How would a realizing sense of this truth startle those who are giving their lives to pleasure, as the Chaldean revellers were startled at midnight by the letters blazing from the wall !

Steadily and forever the work goes on. Subtle and strong are the cords that bind this world to the future world in fast connection. At the slightest touch tremble both the mighty spheres. Whatever we build here is builded there. Each breath, each moment here, makes a new decision as to what we shall receive hereafter. Events sweep by us, ever taking some stamp from the moral temper of our minds, the transcript of which is entered on the book of judgment. As not the smallest particle of dust is ever annihilated, so not a thought we have cherished, not a feeling we have indulged, not the most trivial act, done in the most sportive mood, shall be lost. Buried these things may be, and are, for a time, like seed in a field. The traveller walks over the smooth surface, and dreams not of the mighty process going on beneath. But, nevertheless, soon does the full harvest wave wide its golden treasure. Thus, too, the harvest-season of life shall come. Now is the spring-time of the moral year! Swiftly we scatter the seed. Like the careless traveller, we may not suspect the silent spiritual growth. Nevertheless, soon shall we see it standing high, and thick with ripened clusters. Shall it give us sweet leaves and healthful fruits, or plants of poison and bitter ashes to our taste? "Whatsoever a man soweth, that shall he also reap."

DISCOURSE XX.

IT IS JOHN.

Mark vi. 15, 16. — OTHERS SAID, THAT IT IS ELIAS; AND OTHERS SAID, THAT IT IS A PROPHET, OR AS ONE OF THE PROPHETS. BUT, WHEN HEROD HEARD THEREOF, HE SAID, IT IS JOHN, WHOM I BEHEADED: HE IS RISEN FROM THE DEAD.

CRITICS have questioned what led Herod to express so positively this singular opinion respecting the person who had begun to astonish Galilee with his miracles, and to amaze the synagogue with his wisdom. A close consideration of the circumstances shows that Herod's language is to be interpreted as the voice of conscience, and so opens a chapter in the history of conscience, which, even at this distance of time, it may profit us to read.

The story begins, as always, with the violation of conscience in a simple infraction of right. Herod takes to himself his brother Philip's wife, while Philip lived; making room for her by divorcing, without cause, his own; thus violating, not the Jewish law only, but all law human and divine. This is the first step, conscience resisted and cast down, while some lawless appetite rides in triumph over it.

23

The next point in the history is the effect of charging the wrong-doer, with his guilt. "It is not lawful for thee to have her," says John to Herod. The sincere Baptist spared not high or low, but, in God's name, levelled his rebuke even against the prince in his palace, surrounded by his guards, with all the powers of the state at his command. It was too much for the haughty sovereign to bear. He could not be so bearded on his throne. His proud honor was in arms. But what relief shall he gain from the stigma of crime? For never lived the human being, to whom this black stigma was not as a burning brand, sore within, and intolerable to be exposed without. What, then, shall Herod do? Behold here, indeed, the second step. He will shift the blame on his accuser. Yes, if Herod can put John in the wrong, that will be a healing salve to the smarting wound. And so, doubtless assuming great show of offended dignity and outraged majesty, and making a very ingenious plea of self justification, he inflicts punishment on the preacher as a treasonable or seditious, at all events a dangerous man. Is not this the second step, this attempt somehow to put our accuser in the wrong, holding true for all time, one of the subtlest devices of the wicked heart? So was it with Herod. He, like others, readily makes this cunning plan with his own conscience seem to succeed. He has but to nod to an officer at his beck, and the preacher is arrested, and conveyed by a cohort of soldiers to prison in the castle of Machærus, on the shore of the Dead Sea, where Herod was then holding his court.

Here comes the third stage, still more remarkable, and as universally true in the workings of conscience in the sinful breast, — and that is a secret respect for the right, and for the doer of the right, felt even by him that has opposed it. Man may brave it out well and boldly against just accusation; he may crush and silence, and put out of the way, his accuser; he may hope to bury one wrong in the grave of another: yet the heap, grown but more monstrous, shall seem to cry out against him, and the unrepented sin shall live and stir in the very sepulchre of oblivion, ready to spring forth upon its author. So is it drawn in our historic picture. John lies in his dungeon, and Herod rolls on in his path of splendor. The grand occasion arrives of his birth-day. Salome, the daughter of Herodias by Philip, sharing in her mother's treachery, pleases her new father by a display of her skill in the fine accomplishment of dancing. The weak-minded monarch, vain in his provincial dignity, and his imagination warmed with the luxury of the scene, makes to the dancing girl an extravagant promise, by which he swears to abide. For it was customary to crown such entertainments with donations to those whose talent in any art had furnished amusement for the hour. Salome, guided by Herodias, who thirsts for revenge upon John, uses her unlimited freedom of choice to demand the head of the captive. The king was sorry. Sorry? and why? Because he still feared the unpopularity of the act to which he was urged? No: the phraseology points to a different and deeper feeling, growing out of the secret, shuddering respect which rests, and must rest forever, in the very heart of guilt towards innocence and virtue, and can never, and by no means,—so hath God made us,—be driven therefrom. Very striking are the words of the evangelist: "For Herod feared John, knowing that he was a just man, and an holy." Feared John there in prison?—feared the helpless captive, bound and confined far from the sight of a friend? A trait how deeply true to the human soul! Yes, vice must respect virtue all the time: ever putting it to shame, countermining and insulting it, banishing it, loading it with chains, it must fearfully respect it. Is it not so, my brother? Whenever you have been the aggressor in any difference or quarrel with a fellow-man, though you may have added defence to defence, and piled vindication on vindication, have you been able, after all, to uproot a deep-seated regard even for him you differed with? When the passion and turbid commotion of the hour have passed by, has not that solemn regard subsided to the very bottom of your mind, and, in the light of transparent reflection, made you ashamed of yourself, if not caused you to stand aghast at the wrong you see scored against you, as with the point of a diamond, on the page of your own heart?

This, too, is an authentic passage in our history. So was it, indeed, with Herod. He had not got wholly rid of the prophet, by immuring him in that lonely cell, where he could hear, as he lay awake in the night-watches, only the whistling of the wind and the dull wash of the waves of the Dead Sea near the castle-walls. John had left a barbed arrow in Herod's heart, and he could not draw it out; but there it clung still, and rankled beneath his robe of gold and jewels, and mixed a sharp pang ever and anon with the sweetest of his pleasures. While, under that camel's hair and that old leathern girdle, in the prison, the pulse was calm, for no guilty feeling made it intermit; but the approval of conscience, the pledge of the approbation of God, gave unbroken peace. Which was the favored, the truly happy man of the two, — Herod, unable to drown self-upbraiding in feasting and wine; or the Baptist, with light at the centre, and a holy love there, which the cold and the gloom that enveloped him could not quench? God for him in the prison, and against his oppressor in the palace, and each one knowing the whole fact with respect to both! But Herod resisted the warning voice within, that charged him not to add guilt to guilt. Alas! one false step involves another; for guilt must be added to guilt, until the sinner can make up his mind for a frank and thorough repentance. So Herod set aside the holy grief of his better nature; and, " for his oath's sake, and for the sake of them that sat with him at meat," he gave order according to the iniquitous request.

Here opens the next passage in our history; and its title is, the motives and temptations by which the sinner suffers himself to be induced to persevere in iniquity. " For his oath's sake." And what right, then, had he to keep or make the mad oath! How

23*

much sin arises from hasty and unprincipled engagements! From the rash vow of Jephtha, down through Herod's promise, to this day, how much evil from unconsidered and indeterminate obligations! But the other motive that urged the king to wrong is still more common in this history of the moral sense: "For the sake of them that sat with him at meat." Had the king honestly consulted his own bosom, he would have gone no further in this fatal way of ruin. Had he been alone, the shadows of his closet falling around him, or could he at that moment have drawn strength from any habitual remembered frequenting of the closet, he might have broken through the toils of those wicked women, and thrown his wretched and unlawful oath, with the wild, unprincipled promise it sealed, to the winds. But no: not alone; a stranger to the closet; the gay company round about reclined at the festive board, and he at the head. The delicious viand smoked; the inebriating draught streamed out and sparkled beautifully; the red cup passed from one to another; the delights of sense absorbed the soul. To crown all, the mazy dance had just wove in its bewitching circles with the reeling of the intoxicated brain; while laugh and jest and coarse allusion seasoned the gay repast, and gave the spice to many a pleasant fancy of the mind. And in such an hour, in such a chosen hour, the whisper of Herodias goes through Salome to the governor's ear! His conscience smites him. Every thing pure and magnanimous appeals to him. Ah! he has no power of independent moral purpose, none strengthened and built up by private reflection and prayer, on which to stand, and, under God, execute justice as her sworn defender. So he looks to the faces about him, and the rising intimation of duty is not reflected back. Nothing is said to second the enormous suggestion of Herodias, no voice lifted to counsel the infamous grant. But he detects an almost imperceptible smile on the countenance of one or another that lies voluptuously near him, a shade of suppressed ridicule at his own pale shrinking and virtuous relenting. As he pauses and looks again, he imagines painted on the features of one more distant some suspicion that he is afraid to do the deed ; and, at the farther end of the table, there are two that studiously conceal their looks and expressions, as quickly they confer together. Surely they are making sport of this hesitation of the royal majesty ! Ah ! " the world's dread laugh, which scarce the stern philosopher can scorn ! " No one dissuades from the evil counsel. No one sides with any more generous feeling in the breast of Herod. Conscience, poor solitary, must struggle single-handed with aroused pride and vanity and vain-glory, and she succumbs in the contest. " They shall see," he secretly exclaims, " whether I sit not a monarch on my throne ! They shall see if I am a craven that durst not do whatever I will ! " The fatal order is given.

Does this trait of the picture fade away or become unmeaning for us here and now ? Young man, tempted from the high course of your better feeling, because your companions are not as scrupulous as yourself, answer! — putting your hand to a doubtful act, because you fear others may say you dare not, and because you prefer the reputation of hardihood to that of a very tender conscience; venturing, for a false shame at the scorn of the wicked, to sacrifice the approval of the good, answer! — wanting the courage to discountenance and disallow in your presence an oath, however loud and mighty it sounds on the tongue of presuming youth, or of more presuming and inexcusable manhood; or to disown an indecency, however the merry laughter may ring round the circle when it is vented, and force from the moral cowards in the company a smile at the vulgarity they are shocked at, answer! Would there were no young man or elder on whom I could call to answer; no cheek to tingle at the call, as memory speaks; no heart that would not feel it an indignity to have such language left upon it, and not taken back!

The true-hearted prophet, the forerunner of Jesus, yields his head to the sword; yields it as meekly as he had boldly used his tongue to proclaim God's truth; and the gory sight of the pale features and blood-stained hair, which the artist has sometimes endeavored gloomily on canvass to represent, is brought in and given to the damsel, and by her to her mother, as they gaily together tread the rich saloons of the royal palace. Ah! then, this history of ours is not of low places only, of the outlaws of society and all decent living. Sin is not a coarse and vulgar thing alone. It is not committed by the rough and ignorant and ill-mannered alone. Beauty and rank and elegance have dipped their hands in blood. Cruelty and hatred and revenge have lurked under gay clothing. The highwayman is sometimes hid in the garb of the courteous citizen. The thief may possibly somewhere still say, as he did to Alexander, "I am the small robber, but you are the great." Now, as ever, with perfect smoothness of demeanor; now, as ever, with unexceptionable politeness of deportment, with sweet smiles, and honeyed words, and soft pressures of the hand, may be the preface and beginning of volumes of hypocrisy and terrible unkindness of conduct. "The words of his mouth were smoother than butter and softer than oil, yet were they drawn swords." Happy the man who has had no experience to verify the words! In the midst of your civilized life, as we speak amazedly of the crimes of barbarous and savage life; in the midst of your fashion and your pleasure, look to your heart, examine the principles and passions that rule in your heart.

Time wears on. The event whose circumstances have been related passes by apparently into oblivion. Pleasure holds undisputed reign in the regal dwelling; and the momentary sorrow of Herod, at having enacted so dreadful a tragedy, seems whelmed and lost in the full stream of uninterrupted prosperity. But rumor at length bears dimly from afar to the purlieus of the court strange tidings of mighty works, such as no living mortal had ever before beheld. And

what a singular spectacle now! King Herod does not
rebut the account with any sneering scepticism. Lo!
a thing strange and extraordinary, — the murderer a
believer! Some of the Jews denied the genuine-
ness of the miracles performed before their eyes.
Herod accepts them at a mere hint, a dim rumor,
without ever having seen. He believes that the man
whom he had slain, and whose very head had been
put into the keeping of a Herodias's revenge, has
now got up out of his winding-sheet, in which for
months his body had lain cold and mouldering, to
perform — what? Wonderful deeds of omnipo-
tence, to which, when alive, he had never pretended.
Ah! the voice of conscience, the never quite-silenced
voice, that will speak on in the most guilty heart;
will make itself heard through all the inward stiflings
of evil passion, and all the outward smotherings
of a worldly life; will grow tender in the very spot
where it has been seared, and pure under the very
baseness with which it has been polluted! Oh!
the power of conscience, that could lay such a grasp
on the soul of a Herod, — Herod, the true son of that
Herod who, at the time of Christ's birth, had slain
the innocent children, and filled Rama with the lamentations of Rachel mourning and not to be comforted, because her children were not! Yes: the
power of conscience, I repeat; for I would that
every one might stand in reverential awe before that
which will, if not now, at some time, manifest its
power to the confusion and grief of all who do not
revere it. For who is this tetrarch Herod, now so

quick to believe in the earthly resurrection of a man
whose ghastly visage he had seen brought in, in a
charger? He — can it be believed? — is a Sadducee,
a member of that sect of whom we are told, that, like
some persons still, they utterly rejected all idea of the
resurrection of the dead, and held to the existence
of neither angel nor spirit. He it is, a Sadducee
of the Sadducees, that verily believes John the Baptist, whom he beheaded, has risen from the dead !
For an energy within him, stronger than this curious
and captious infidelity so ostentatiously paraded,
has opened all the moral sensibilities of his nature ;
and the little sceptical creed which he had built in
his speculative intellect, as a house on the sand, and
of which he had made a proud, worldly profession,
is borne off upon the irresistible tide of feeling, which
electrifies him into an admission of the supremacy
of the spirit, and of the reality of the powers of the
world to come.

"It is John." No : he was mistaken. It was not
John. John had risen, not however on earth, but
into heaven. Herod was to meet and confront him,
not in time, but in eternity. Ay, in eternity ; for the
final conclusion of this solemn history does not yet
appear, so that I can narrate it ; but in eternity shall
we read it, where, for us all, will be a resurrection
of all our deeds and purposes and mutual relations,
in the light of a moral truth more clear, and of a
conscience more awakened, than this world ever
knows. Yes, we shall all meet our consciences
there. The judgment of God and the rewards and

retributions of immortality are but our meeting with them. Our meeting with God himself (be it reverently spoken) derives from this one fact its solemnity, that our consciences will speak to us before him. And the whole history I have related is but for one question, How shall we treat here that moral nature, before which we shall be brought face to face hereafter? For, however we doubt about or disregard now God's revelation of eternal things, when these things are open in all their grand and dread sublimity, as by the unfolding of a scroll, the greatest sceptic of us all will be no more astonished than it seems Herod would have been to see the beheaded prophet stalk from the tomb to his palace-chamber.

Close not, then, your ear to the grave and warning strain. Some history of your conscience you, too, are writing; and the page shall be indelible, as it was with Herod, on the very tables of your heart. Be persuaded to examine the writing as it fatally forms under your hand. What entries are you making in that book of account which shall be opened before the throne of God? For you that apocalyptic vision was seen and recorded: "The dead were judged out of those things which were written in the books, according to their works." It is the book of conscience. It is the volume of memory. It is the written history, without one erratum, of your daily life; a plain, artless, unvarnished tale of the true and false, right and wrong, in your speech and conduct, whose relator is within the reach of no bribe you can offer. The recording angel is your own incorruptible consciousness, and you can touch with no forgery a single sentence that falls from her mysterious pen. The leaves of this book are curiously folded together, as the busy scribe of the soul, with your will or against your will, turns them over, one by one, day after day; and writes on, ever on. Of many a leaf no effort of desire can now break the seal, or bring the lines into the light of remembrance. And we may sometimes foolishly fancy the record annihilated and irrecoverably lost in the gulf of the past. No: never. The flood cannot drown it; the fire cannot burn it. No power of destruction or of the world can reach it. The body shall leave us, how shortly! but that record will remain perfect in every jot and tittle, and every link that now binds it be unclasped at once before our eyes, and in the sight of Almighty God.

24

DISCOURSE XXI.

PERSONAL RELIGION.

Deut. xxx. 14. — BUT THE WORD IS VERY NIGH UNTO THEE, IN THY MOUTH AND IN THY HEART.

MUCH is said of the importance of personal religion, as what alone is pleasing to God, or can secure human salvation. We should know the precise meaning intended in this expression; and my object will be to define it. And first, an idea is given in the text and the circumstances connected with it, — the idea that religion consists in nothing external and formal, nor in any sudden impressions made from without upon the mind. The very heavens had been opened to the Jews, and the moral law proclaimed amid terrific sounds and splendors. But the thunders had soon died away, and the lightnings vanished on the burning mount; and nothing could avail any further, save the quiet discharge of duty. The commandments, graven on tables of stone, were to be imprinted on the heart.

Moses, in his second communication from God, reverts to the circumstances of the first. He conjures the people not to place their trust in any outward display or sudden excitement. They were not to gaze upward and ask, Who shall bring down the commandment from the sky? or to look away, and inquire, Who shall transport it from beyond the sea? For what they needed could not come from abroad, but was in their very heart and mouth, in every word they were speaking, or thought they conceived.

Even this simplest and most obvious view of personal religion needs still to be urged. Many seem still to rely for salvation too much on the display made, and the excitement produced by outward circumstances. We may abound in meetings and movements; enthusiastic gatherings in field or forest may kindle all minds with a common sentiment; great revivals may bear away thousands on a torrent of sympathy: but it is all in vain, if men do not retire from the tumult to the silent culture of every right disposition and the quiet practice of every duty; in vain, unless they patiently engrave the commandments on inward tables, unless they hear a still voice in the soul, and retain a steady warmth there, when the noise has ceased and the flames have died away, as on the ancient mount of revelation.

But there is yet a stricter meaning in the phrase, *personal religion.* Our duties may be divided into two great classes; those belonging to social connections, and those included in the mind itself. To the latter, personal religion has primary respect. There are those who seem to think their whole duty is public and official. If they are faithful to every civil relation, and meet every just claim, they think their Christian character complete, and are ready with the

young man's confident question to Jesus, "What
lack I yet?" But, like him, they may have in these
outward respects acted from worldly motives, without any thorough culture of the religious principle.
Do not, then, rest contented with discharging your
outward and social obligations. There is a class of
duties more solemn still, lying within the circle of
your own being. They respect the choice of motives, the establishment of principles, the cultivation
of hidden personal graces, the cherishing of just sentiments towards the Author of your being, and a calm,
conscious preparation of spirit to meet the solemn
eras his finger has marked before you on the line of
futurity, — death, judgment, and retribution.

These duties press upon you, not only when you
sit in some chair of office, or discuss questions of
general concern, or deal with your fellow-men in the
ordinary transactions of life. The times of peculiar
fitness for their discharge are the seasons of retirement from the crowd, when the sounds of business
are not heard, when the glare of day has vanished,
when you lie awake in the night-watches, with no
eye upon you but the All-seeing. These should not
be hours of idleness, but faithfully devoted to the
culture of personal religion.

But there is a third and still closer view of religion, as a personal thing, to which I invite your
thoughts. I believe it is the Creator's design, that
religion should be in every soul a peculiar acquisition, and have a solitary, unborrowed character ; so
that Christians should not be, as we commonly sup-

pose them, mere copies of each other, but possess each one an original character. As the principle of beauty in nature shows itself in no monotonous succession of similar objects, but is displayed in a thousand colors and through unnumbered forms, so should the principle of piety ever clothe itself in some fresh trait and aspect. I say, this is the Creator's design. The view I offer may be made more clear by considering some of the proofs of this design.

The first proof that each individual should reach a peculiar excellence is, that each has received a peculiar constitution. The human system, has, indeed, a certain uniformity, as we speak of human nature in general, all men having the same members and faculties. But as, with the same features throughout the world, there are no two faces alike; so, with the same capacities, there are no two souls alike. Every man has his own powers, passions, tendencies to goodness, and besetting sins. How does this happen? By accident? No one who believes in God can think so. Is it through some fate that has travelled down to us from former times? We cannot reconcile this with God's universal justice. The only supposition left is, that God's design is to give to every man his own materials of character, and lay in every soul afresh the foundations of a divine fabric.

The church has long been rent with a controversy whether we are born pure or corrupt, a question naturally suggested by the struggle between good and evil tendencies in every heart. But is it not a

24*

vain dispute ? Can we apply such terms as pure, corrupt, to these native tendencies ? Do we not rather employ the right denomination, when we call them simply materials of character ? That these tendencies should conflict, is made necessary by the very end of our creation, which is virtue. What is virtue but resisting temptation, and choosing good in preference to evil ? But how can we resist without desires needful to be resisted ? and how prefer good, unless evil also solicit us ? But every man has his own desires, therefore his own temptations; therefore, again, a peculiar work to do, and a character of peculiar and original excellence to build up.

Accept, then, your own natural constitution in this view, and use it to this end. Imitate not the example of those who complain of their particular temperament and inclinations, bemoan the depravity and weakness of their nature, and murmur at the task-work marked out. Wonder not why on you have not been bestowed one man's gifts of intellect, another's amiableness of temper, another's perseverance of will. Send no repining sighs to Heaven that you have some dispositions by which you are sorely tried, and that certain sins most easily beset you. You are not to contemplate these things in indolent despair, but to note them as an index to the duties you are called immediately to discharge. Use faithfully the materials put into your hands. Despise not nor faint before what in them may seem rugged and unpromising. You shall find nothing in them so rough and hard, that patient toil will not transform it into shapes of wondrous beauty. The house built of light materials, though soon erected, will not stand the blast like that of marble, hewn with long, exhausting labor. Obey the maxim on the ancient oracle, "Know thyself," and you will not fail of that personal religion for which you were made.

But again : God's design, that every spirit should reach a peculiar excellence, is seen in the dispensations of providence, as well as in the facts of creation. While the general fortunes of humanity are the same, every man receives his peculiar discipline from the hand of God. He has his own successes and failures, his own health and sickness, joy and trial. And does any man's portion come by chance? No : if we believe in God at all, we must know it comes by his ordination ; and if we believe in his goodness, we must know it comes kindly meant. There is no such thing as chance in life, any more than it is allowed in the most thoroughly disciplined army or wisely ordered school. And every man should receive his own providential allotments as intended for his special training.

Deplore not, then, your situation in life, any more than the natural constitution of mind ; but use it for the building up of a character of original strength and beauty. Do not inquire, "Why was not I born to ease and wealth, to high rank and extensive influence ? — wherefore am I destined to work obscurely at a laborious trade, instead of dazzling the world by conspicuous achievements ? By what curse am I doomed to drag about a sickly frame, instead of being blessed with a robust system and uninterrupted health?" If your circumstances are peculiar, you have then a peculiar work to do, an original excellence to gain. And God is ever looking down to mark your diligence or your sloth. Be careful you waste not a single dispensation of Providence. Remember there is no exigency in which the work of life should cease. Lying helpless on your bed, you have still as much to do as he that ploughs the field, frequents the marts of business, or conducts the operations of commerce. Nay, never has the work of life been more swiftly done than often in the languid hours of sickness. Perchance you were withdrawn from your place of labor, or from the crowded street, because you were not doing enough, and special warnings were needed to urge you on your way. Whatever your state, sickness or health, prosperity or misfortune, view it with no atheistic eye, but accept and use it in the culture of that personal religion for which you were made.

Once more: God's design, that every soul should reach a peculiar and unborrowed excellence, appears in the fact, that all spiritual exercises, to be genuine, must have a peculiar character. No man can perform any exercise for another in religion. Take, for instance, the exercises of faith and prayer. Every one must believe for himself in view of the evidence he has seen, and according to the impulse of his own mind. It matters not to him that many bodies of divinity have been framed. The principle of faith is not made to operate, because he formally accepts any one of them. It matters not that a thousand creeds have been drawn up; that they have been written on paper; that they have been stamped on the holy symbol of the cross; that they have shone in illuminated manuscripts, or been blazoned on military standards. A dead and barren faith will his be with all these treasures, unless he spiritually behold the truths of religion and the realities of another world with his own eyes. And, if he do this, his faith will have a personal quality, and be marked by some peculiarities corresponding with the tendencies of his mind. No one can embrace the whole circle of divine knowledge. Every one will be attracted to some particular points. And here is the wrong done by minute systems and long confessions, to which the soul is bent in unwilling conformity. By preventing every thing personal in faith, they destroy every thing genuine. Instead of an agreement of faith, there is an expulsion of the principle from men's minds, and for it is substituted a dead, barren assent.

So, too, as no man can believe for another, no man can perform the spiritual exercise of prayer for another. In vain is the preacher's voice heard in supplication; in vain, in the use of a form, do you repeat words the most fitly chosen, unless the heart aspire to God. The soul must mount on its own wings; or the Infinite One is not reached, or communed with at all. And if the soul do thus mount, the communion will have, in each one of all the myriads that worship, a personal and peculiar character. It will spring from the individual's own feelings, from his own consciousness of want, and his own faith in God's "fulness and willingness" to supply his wants. Thus it will be not merely a decent posture in the house of worship, a reverent look, a response in solemn tones ; but the knees will bend in solitude, the heart will feel special and sudden humblings of itself before God, ejaculations will ascend from the midst of daily care and business, unexpected favors will open the soul to utter the full eloquence of devotion, and conscious guilt will kindle it with the still more moving inspirations of lowliness and grief.

Who, then, in view of these considerations, has made religion a personal thing ? He only who knows his own nature, and brings all its powers and dispositions to contribute to the building up of a good character. He only who makes all the dispensations of Providence, all events of joy and grief, conspire to guide him towards his perfection. He only whose spiritual exercises are genuine and sincere, consisting not in profession, or appearance, but expressing real convictions, springing from a strong consciousness of want, and moving the deep places of the soul.

The man who has formed these habits will continually make progress in strong, unborrowed excellence ; and when his time to depart shall come, while earth loses a precious possession, it is not too much to say that heaven itself shall gain a new treasure, inasmuch as it will receive a character of fresh, original strength and beauty. For that wondrous sphere, we call Heaven, is no more marked by a dull monotony than what we have already seen of the universe. We are apt to think of the angels as having the same faces, and wearing the same dress, and doing the same offices. We picture them in our imagination as arrayed in glittering robes, all the mere copies of each other. But, while purity and piety are universal in these upper courts, and no eccentricity of sin exists, may we not suppose there is much more of individual excellence, more various forms of beauty and displays of goodness, than even here? We know how much the delight of earthly society is increased, when all persons, equally honest and disinterested, have yet a certain difference of powers and graces, by which they, as it were, set off each other's qualities, and supply each other's defects. This promise of joy, granted now, may have its fulfilment above; and every chord in the celestial harp, all-melodious in itself, add its note to produce the perfect harmony. Does any one hope to be borne within the sound of this heavenly music? nay, to mingle his voice in accordance with, and sweeten its tones? Let him use every power and inclination, consecrate every opportunity, and perform every spiritual exercise, so that religion with him shall have a genuine character, be a personal acquisition, and display a peculiar beauty.

But what is the reliance of those multitudes that make their preparation for another world, in no such strict and solemn way as I have described? They

pass perhaps for religious men ; they think themselves such : but, it must be sadly declared, they
have no religion which is truly their own.   Their
reputation depends on circumstances and artificial
associations.   It is a very common and a dreadful
delusion for persons, neglecting to form a strong
character of their own, to trust for recommendation
and success entirely to their social connections, to
the general religious atmosphere in which they live.
They hope, that, by the good name or Christian zeal
of kindred and friends, their own idleness and folly
will be allowed to pass unquestioned, as in a pro-
tecting shadow.   But if, at Christ's coming, the
nearest relatives were separated, according as they
were willing or not to profess his religion, how much
more surely, at the judgment-day, shall they be
divided by the sharper test of personal character !

Every one must die by himself, and go to the
great bar alone ; and there all the excellence of
friends, all the fame of forefathers, will avail him
nothing.   The traveller in a foreign land often feels
sorely the loss of that character given him by accidental relations at home.   Every thing adventitious
being stripped off, he is thrown back upon his personal qualities, and must stand or fall, according to
the judgment passed upon those.   Now, how much
more surely must such things forsake us, when we
proceed, each one in his own time, attended by no
companion, leaning on no arm of flesh, a solitary
pilgrim, on our last journey to the skies !   The heir
of rich estates shall leave behind the splendor of

wealth and the flattery of retainers. The haughty lord must disrobe himself of badges and stars of honor, and be addressed no more with his hereditary titles of reverence. He that now shines in a reflected lustre from the circle of society in which he moves will soon find himself in darkness, unless he have fed the inward light of truth and virtue. Even the man who marches on in the hosts of philanthropy will soon stand alone, uncheered by the sympathy of thousands, unsustained by the stimulus of enterprise; for his secret motive must be determined, whether it be a pure benevolence, or a selfish desire of human praise and worldly advancement.

Thus, for every one, the question at last will be, not of outward connections, but of personal character; not merely what religious institutions have you supported, but how far have you made religion itself a personal thing. And we all, who now tread the populous street, passing through multiplied scenes of interest, bound in with numberless associations for business or pleasure, shall, in a few days, see all these things fade away, like those shapes in the clouds, which, for a moment, resemble rich paths and splendid dwellings, and then are gone forever. Yes, when that last trial of personal character shall come, he that rejoices will have rejoicing in himself; and, as it has been said, great as may be the multitude assembled on that occasion, whosoever mourneth will mourn apart.

If there be truth in this doctrine, every one has his own peculiar mission to accomplish, his word to speak, his labor to finish. Swiftly do the wheels of time roll on, and this life's sun sinks rapidly to its setting. Let us also hasten, with the words of our Lord and Master ever in mind, "I must work the works of Him that sent me while it is day."

I have thus presented the doctrine of personal religion. It may to some appear to be a hard and stern, as it certainly is a serious and warning, doctrine; and, while laying so much on the individual will and conscience, it may seem not to rely on, but to set aside, the extraordinary and supernatural means of salvation. The doctrine does, indeed, contradict the idea that a superhuman power, independent of our concurrence, is the only agent in our redemption. We must be saved with our will, not against it, and conspire even with the Divine influence. But the true doctrine of personal religion does not dispense with any aid from other sources, whether common or miraculous, to the growth of our virtue. It does not require us to work without material, or to create moral excellence from nothing. It rather allows and encourages us to derive help from every source, — from nature and our fellow-beings, from God's holy spirit, and the grace of our Lord Jesus Christ. In fact, these fountains of supply, so far from overwhelming our personal power and responsibility, make a mighty demand upon us, in the language of Isaiah, "to draw water out of the wells of salvation." The auxiliary and remedial forces of the gospel we must use. The gracious privilege of pardon and atonement we must apply to our need. The record of sacred writ, the example and mind of Christ, yea, even the holy spirit of God, we must appropriate to and incorporate with the development of our own soul, or to us they exist in vain. The divine resources are infinite, but cannot enlarge or bless us any farther than they are assimilated to our individual being, which the Almighty will not suffer even his own action to neutralize or overbear. The moral ability implied in personal religion not only goes into the outward life, through the work of the hands, but has a more important, though silent and invisible theatre within the soul, where we meet "Him that seeth in secret," and hold solemn sessions in the chambers of the heart, in treaty with God. The resolves and surrenders there made before the pleading and commanding Spirit are as worthy of the "name of action" as the loudest and most noted deeds done in the world, of which in truth they are the vital origin and cause.

Thus the fact of Divine influence, so far from contradicting, illustrates the doctrine of my discourse. God knocks at the door of our heart, but we must open. He calls, but we must hearken. He works, but we must work with him; nor will our working with such a one as he is, indulge us with long vacations or a settled sloth. We might as well say, that the builder of a house or vessel is exempted from toil and personal accountableness by the precious loads of timber or granite that lie hugely around him, as that the soul is excused from labor and

activity by the truths, motives, merciful offers and
invitations of the gospel. These but assign our work,
and set our holy and life-long task. They are the
priceless and invaluable stuff to be, by our diligence
and pains-taking, wrought into the substance and
texture of our characters. They are weights for us
to lift, elements for us to adjust, threads we must
arrange, and the weaver's shuttle we must throw;
else, in our supineness, even the love of God promises us no spiritual elevation, expansion, or final
perfection.

The doctrine that God alone, without our agency,
is to begin, carry on, and complete this redeeming
and unfolding process, while it is a doctrine that
seems to appeal to our humility, appeals much more
effectually to our love of ease. It is not so painful
as it is pleasant to a morally debilitated and relaxed
spirit, to be told it has nothing to do but yield itself
to a foreign impulse. Thus our magnifying of God's
power, while we subtly assume great merit and
freedom from pride in submitting to the terms of the
gospel, may prove to be but an indolent escape from
that exertion of our own highest faculties, to which,
by conscience within, and as with the sound of a
trumpet from the skies, our Creator summons us.
As we are travelling on the perhaps rough road of
duty, it may seem delightful, could some swift en-
gine come to convey us with locomotive speed, or
some balloon lift us with aerial lightness from our
feet. But no such instruments have been devised to
convey us to the celestial city. We must tread that

plain and sober path of duty with our own earnest and diligent steps, while we receive "secret refreshings" of our strength from above; not making our dependence the reason for rest, or excuse for tardiness, but the sufficient ground for never stopping in our motion, till we reach the heavenly courts at which we aim. Then we shall have guidance and support all our journey through. The providence of God will be ever working for and with us, causing all events to conduce to our progress. We shall be perpetually enlivened by an inward breathing from on high. The Son of God, who walked, never for a moment faltering, in the path of duty and trial, will cheer us on our way, as we recognize and are led by the print of his passage.

Thus every faculty and affection in our nature will be brought out in its intended power and beauty. As each kind of vegetable or animal existence shows a result more distinct as its germ is more developed, so every human soul will be more marked and individual as it becomes more perfect. It will not, as some philosophers fancy, be absorbed in God, but be in harmony with him, and will serve him better with the clearer disclosure of its proper worth and each higher stage of its personal power ; liberty and love, with equal step and parallel advance, bearing it from point to point along its endless career. But logical deduction and imagination would alike fail in an attempt to infer or anticipate the condition of glory and joy to which personal religion will conduct the children of God. In his

25*

unbounded universe, there is room for each spirit he inspires to grow without limit, and attain more than we can conceive. The fancy may be but a feeble one, that there are in heaven individual intelligences, whose knowledge exceeds the united wisdom of the human race, and to whose charge and executive talent the affairs of worlds may be entrusted. To such a sublime consummation, the weak germ of infancy, now nursed and protected by divine tenderness, may arrive! What a privilege to enter the company of such beings! Simple as they are wise, gentle as they are mighty, with more than the "giant's strength," which they use in no "tyrannous" way, but are energetic only to love, counsel, and bless those around them; while, with all their abilities and acquisitions, they can come into no comparison with or comprehension of the Infinite One.

"In vain the archangel tries
To reach the height with wondering eyes."

DISCOURSE XXII.

HUMAN NATURE.

Mark x. 14. — OF SUCH IS THE KINGDOM OF GOD.

REVELATION gives but little express and formal instruction concerning human nature, because perhaps
of the little need of any supernatural information
about that which every body may know from the
world and his own heart. The inspired writers
generally take man as they find him; assume his
character, as it appears at particular times and in
special circumstances. Those passages, whose strong
language is so eagerly quoted as decisive, are almost
always local in their application, and their force
definitely restricted by the context.

Still, not alone for speculative but practical reasons, we would know, if we may on divine authority,
— and not merely judge by experience, or reason
on grounds of philosophy, — what our nature is.
There are, to this end, some sentences in the New
Testament, whose conclusiveness I feel there is no
way of resisting. Observe that we wish to know,
not the acquired character, but the original nature of
the human soul. This nature exists pure only in the

child. This, the advocates of the doctrine of total depravity, I presume, all admit; for their language is that we are born depraved, that sin is innate, hereditary, substantial in the very essence and constitution of the mind. The soul of a child is therefore its absolute principle and embodiment. Now, we have six parallel declarations of the evangelists, Matthew, Mark, and Luke, on this very point, expressing, not what they thought of the child's nature, but what Christ thought and declared; that is, six passages giving the decision of the highest authority in religion ever in the world. The burden of these passages is, that of such as little children is the kingdom of God and the kingdom of heaven; that to be converted, and become like them, is the only and necessary title of entrance into that kingdom; that to be humble as a child makes one the greatest in that kingdom; that to receive a child in Christ's name is to receive him: and, in still another passage, he gives it as a warning against despising one of these little ones, that their angels (by which, I think, he must mean the spirits of departed children) do always behold the face of his Father in heaven. Strictly speaking, I know not that there are in the Christian records any other testimonies upon the primary, simple nature of man; and upon these testimonies I decline all reasoning.

Leaving, then, the words of Jesus Christ, it may be alleged that this is not a full and fair account of the Scripture-representations on this subject; that the Bible abounds in descriptions of iniquity, and rebukes of the ungodly; that it contemplates men as estranged from God; that its whole object, the very reason of its existence, is to cleanse them from corruption: while it may also be maintained, that the nature of a being is not to be learned from its feeble, infantile elements, but from what, when brought out and developed, it necessarily and always becomes. The Bible speaks of the wicked: for their restoration and salvation it speaks. Christianity regards men in general as alienated more or less from their Father. But how alienated? By wicked works. Their sins have separated between them and God,—not their nature; and their own sins, not another's who lived ages before them; while these, not born but actual sinners, Scripture regards as existing in every variety of acquired character, and calls each one to repent of his own transgression.

Moreover, does not the Bible speak of the good as well as the bad, commending the former even more earnestly than condemning the latter? And, in the settling of this question of human nature, are the good to have no voice or witness? Are the defective and injured specimens of any thing to be admitted to testify, and the sound, complete ones excluded? You sow good seed in the field. Some of it, deprived of its fit nutriment, or exposed to cutting blasts or biting frost, is blighted, and does not ripen. The rest is brought to rich and large perfection. Will you take and hold up the black, drooping ears to show the nature of the seed, or the sweet golden kernels? The Bible, as I said, takes human nature as it is; therefore, all varieties of excellence and unworthiness lie, as a tracery of sunbeams through shadows, on its page. And if our standard of judgment by the soul of the child is wrong, and the true criterion is in what human nature tends to become, then, in common candor, take all it tends to become, and not the worst and vilest.

But is it said, all this goodness is the result, not of human nature, but of the Divine Spirit acting from without upon it, and we see its legitimate fruits, only when it is left to itself; and these, like the apples of the Dead Sea, are always bad and bitter? I reply, it is not the constitution of human nature to be left to itself. It is constituted in this connection with God. He does not so cast it off. Did he, it would not only go astray, but perish in annihilation. There is, as Scripture says, "a light that lighteth every man that cometh into the world." There is an "inspiration" that hath given every man understanding. There is a spirit that knocketh at the door of every man's heart, not to make him good perforce, but to offer him precious aids and influences, if he will accept and use them to become good. And to say that the good fruits which spring from his acceptance and use are not the legitimate issue of human nature, is not only to decry that nature, but the author of it, who meant and made it, not to be a thorn or a thistle, but a grape-vine and a fig-tree. That only to be considered human nature which is alone, cut off from the Spirit of God! The very definition is false. Human nature, so cut off, *is* not, — is nothing.

But is there not one plain text, at least, which says, " We are by nature the children of wrath, even as others " ? Alas that men will persist in tearing out verses from their connection, to make of them universal maxims and sectarian proverbs ! Of whom does the apostle speak ? Of those who had their " conversation in the lusts of the flesh," who had " walked " in these lusts. These had come to be indeed " the children of wrath by nature ;" for custom is a second nature, especially custom reinforced and aggravated, as with them, by universal surrounding degradation. And if the word *nature* is to decide the whole question, does not the great apostle speak of the Gentiles as " doing *by nature* the things contained in the law " ? There is no room to refer to other passages requiring a similar explanation, and not one that I know more difficult, else I surely would not omit it. Save in the words I have referred to of Jesus, and the account in Genesis of man's creation in God's image, and some verses conformed to these, the Bible makes no absolute statement from heaven of what exists so plainly on earth as the nature that is in us all.

Leaving, then, the Bible, is it said once more, that observation proves the entire depravity of human nature ? There are those, I know, shrewd and observing men too, who have come to the belief, that there is nothing truly noble and disinterested in the world. All human conduct is to them but a mass of selfishness, coarser or more refined ; and systems of philosophy, I know, have been written to justify

them. Theirs is a much more real doctrine of total
depravity than was ever written in a creed, or ever
received on authority.   They have seen with their
own eyes, and know it to be so. What have they
seen with their own eyes ? The reflection of their
own hearts!   As a bright object between opposite
mirrors reflects and re-reflects itself in endless returning of the same image, so does the decided spirit
and character that shapes and controls one human
heart multiply itself, and forever return.   All other
hearts become its reflections. It is surrounded by
those it has attracted like itself. The unlike it has
far repelled. Sharp and solemn index to the inmost
temper and spirit by which we are ruled! But why
need I labor the matter ? Hear the word of God :
" To the pure all things are pure ; but to the defiled
and unbelieving is nothing pure, but even their mind
and conscience is defiled."   To these worldling-
infidels in human virtue, I trust none who call themselves religious desire to be joined.   But to those
who observe justly through an unpolluted medium,
much as iniquity abounds, I cannot doubt the good
will appear to preponderate over the evil.   There
are more true words spoken than false ; more just
actions done than unjust ; more kindnesses than
cruelties ; more affectionate husbands and wives,
parents and children, than *unnatural* ones. Were it
not so, what a world this would be ! and who could
bear to live in it ! and how would our complaints
change to heavy lamentations, crushing down our
very souls ! To this much-abused and calumniated
human nature I cheerfully so bear witness.

The appeal is to observation. And what do the acknowledged master-observers and witnesses tell us? All who read the English tongue will say, that, after the Bible, no book shows such deep and wide knowledge of human nature as Shakspeare. What, then, is Shakspeare's epitome of mankind? In his magic microcosm, he gives sad pictures of ambition, lust, and perjury. We have never seen worse men, we have never heard of bloodier crimes, than he describes. But is this all? Oh! it is not the half. How shall we thank him enough, whose eye God made keen to pierce the human breast, for those living and everlasting portraits of unblenching courage, unseducible purity, unyielding truth, before which the villain-faces that have also sat to his pencil forever flee away! Human nature! child of God! own thy weakness, and weep for thy many falls since the first temptation; but, in the name of thy Maker, take thy trophies and wear thy crown, made and woven of spotless innocence, brave fortitude, all-enduring love, — take and wear them lowly before Him who has made thee thus capable!

This nature of ours is, let us confess, sadly imperfect in the best view we can take of it. But why is it imperfect in its attainments? Precisely because it was made to attain so greatly and reach so high; because the ideas of virtue, generosity, and piety, that dawn and rise on the inward heaven of contemplation, are so broad and bright; in short, because the nature is so noble and capacious, its unfolding is so incipient and incomplete. We have not done what we can with this heart of ours. In its very beating, while I speak, it tells us we have not. We have not accomplished our destiny. The best are taking the first feeble steps on an immortal race-course : therefore let us only rebuke ourselves for our short-comings, and spur ourselves onward in a quicker pace over this eternal road ; complaining never of our nature, but of our character alone. It is the greatness of that for which we were made which is the explanation of our imperfection, and of the imperfection of all, saint as well as sinner. Far advanced in goodness as any one may be, clean from defilement as he may be, more and more clean, and farther and farther advanced forever and ever, according to the high and kindling ideal he must become.

The mushroom may shoot up and be perfect in a night. The green grass may rise and fall twice in a season beneath the summer sun. But the strong and beautiful diamond must mature in its secret caverns, while the generations of the forest, alike with those of flesh and blood, pass away. The star that glitters like God's signet, sparkling too brilliant in the clear evening air for the eye to fix its shape, sprang not into instantaneous being, but, as astronomy would now teach, began to form, innumerable ages bygone, in dim and dark mist ; revolving and condensing, and gathering pale light, ray after ray, as century after century rolled along, till what fell perhaps on the eye of Adam, as a pearly cloud in the profound remote heavens, shoots a fiery radiance now over land and sea. Even so dimly and darkly forms this human nature of ours, revolving amid unshaped elements in the spiritual firmament, condensing — if a moral truthfulness to God be taken for its law — ever into more consistent and substantial brightness, and preparing, by the grace of God and under the influences of his gospel, to shine as those stars now shine forever in the heavens, when their flames may be extinguished in endless night.

Oh ! this is a far-reaching nature of ours ; its very birthright immortality, and Christianity that birthright's seal ! All sin and folly stain and degrade it wofully, hinder its rise and progress dreadfully, but destroy it not. " Man's grief is grandeur in disguise, and discontent is immortality." Be patient, son of man, who judgest thy kind, — patient with its deviations and mistakes, as God is patient ; and believe that patient Father still made it beautiful, and for most beautiful issues, while tears mourn its errors, and faithful strivings elevate its course. He who complains of this imperfection complains of that crown which God Almighty has set on his head.

And well, indeed, is it for us, on the general grounds of divine truth, that we can so think of our own nature. For how come we to believe in any thing good and high, that virtue itself is more than a shadow or a name ? — how to believe even in a good and holy God ? We see the evidences of goodness in his works. But whence this feeling or idea of goodness (the very underpinning of the argument) to which his works are the counterpart ? In what receptive spiritual substance is stamped that material

seal which has the word *goodness* graven upon it?
God has made the necessary and only origin of
this idea to be our own nature, totally depraved
though it be called. And, moreover, a deeper philosophy is rapidly establishing the doctrine, that the
strongest and only satisfactory argument for the
being or any of the attributes of God rests primarily,
not on material nature, with all its perfections and
glories, but on the powers, perceptions, and aspirations of the human soul; that God's works all
praise and bless him, but his greatest work below,
human nature, more than all. For we cannot get
beyond our own nature, and the relations of that
nature. Nor can this demonstration be replied to,
till that be done which never has been done, — to lay
the finger on some fibre in the body, or some faculty or fundamental feeling in the soul, which is bad
or superfluous in this fearful and wonderful frame of
the Almighty's making. Then a reproach will lie
somewhere; whether on the creature or on the Creator, I leave others to decide.

I have contended for the essential dignity of human nature. But is it a doctrine of pride that I
have attempted to establish? Will you exult and
take great credit that so glorious a constitution is
yours? Oh! no: it is a doctrine of profound humility to us all. It is a doctrine of bitter shame and
confusion of face to how many of us! The doctrine
of total depravity, I know, is called one of the hum-
bling doctrines of revelation. But no doctrine can
be more fitted to inspire a false humility, and a real,

though secret arrogance. Why should it not do so? If man's nature is totally depraved, he has nothing to be ashamed of. What should he produce but thorns and thistles, corrupt fruit and bitter waters? The wonder will be if he does not this altogether. If he shows any signs of virtue, any remote glimmerings or twilight-beginnings of good affection, he deserves great commendation. Verily, if he is totally depraved, he does remarkably well to have such a proportion of truth and justice and amiableness in his words and dealings, and may plume himself on his extraordinary success with such bad means and so unpromising an undertaking. If he be a worm, as in sermons and prayers he is sometimes called, his proper business is to grovel; and it is miraculous that he can have dreamed of soaring to be an angel.

But if he has a noble nature, — if God's high chancellor of reason is in his mind, and God's vicegerent of conscience in his moral being, and an image of the Divine benignity in every tender sentiment of his heart, then may he well hang down his head, and blush from his soul that he has fallen so short, and done so unworthily. Then may he be indeed a publican, and cry, "Unclean, unclean! God be merciful to me a sinner!" Then may he tremble at the catalogue of Heathen or Christian vices that runs over the page of the Old or the New Testament. Then may he beg of God pardon for the giant cruelty that breaks forth in unjust war or avaricious slavery. Then may he put his hand on his mouth, and his mouth in the dust, for the corrupting tide of intemperance he has let flow through all his noble capabilities; and cast a thicker veil of self-abasement over his countenance, as he remembers the thousand petty meannesses of which he is guilty. Then sackcloth and ashes for our disgraceful enmities and low indulgences!

I am not blind. I see this hatred, this cruelty, this sensuality, or I should be stone-blind. I see those who commit mighty and desperate offences before heaven, and I shudder. I see those who seem, under apparently sanctified feelings and purposes, somehow to take a pleasure in subjecting to little torments and mortifications their fellow-creatures, especially those whom they suspect in some way to be above themselves, and whom they would fain in some way lower; and I grieve and am humbled for the honor of the human soul. But I see human nature, God's gift and as God gave it, rising up from behind, with sublime dignity and pathetic mien, to disavow these slights and insults cast upon her. She declares herself no self-contemner or suicide. But the will of man, the spiritual principle of the will, which God has given us to enact, or, if we please, violate, the decrees of conscience, — this will has yielded to the snares or the assaults of appetite and passion. Why, then, this appetite and this passion to be our tempters, this law of the flesh to resist the law of the mind? Precisely for this very purpose, that we may choose; not be irrational creatures, but free men; and that we may, by choosing aright, become virtuous.

This appetite and this passion are the sharp instruments which not Adam, but God, has given us, by which the jewel of transparent moral purity is to be wrought. Let us glorify the appetites and passions, too, that God has given us; for, without them, the pure and perfect diamond of excellence could not appear. They are as essential to human virtue as the spiritual nature itself. Let us not put down to the account of depravity the sallies of will and emotion in the child. Without them, he could never become the good and great man. The permitted excess, dominion, of appetite and passion is sin and ruin. Their government, use, is virtue, the very ladder for mounting up into high heaven. Does any one appetite or passion tend to excess in you naturally, hereditarily? This happens in no chance, causeless way, by no device circumventing the Almighty, far less as a curse and a doom to woe. The propensity itself is a sacred instrument. You are to check and discipline it, and, in doing this, to grow strong and spiritual. Rome grew mighty by toil and struggle. America owes to the rock and the wilderness, to bleak winter and the savage, her strength and prosperity. The human soul always owes what is great and glorious in it to the fierce desires it has, with higher principles and the grace of God, resisted; to the hard fighting it has done on an unseen battle-field, where arms clash without an echo. "To him that overcometh will I grant to sit with me in my throne, even as I also overcame, and am set down with my Father in his throne."

But it may be said, that, besides Scripture and observation, there is yet another witness in the case, whose testimony respecting human nature is conclusive, and that is, human consciousness; the sense and confession everywhere in the world of depravity. Knowing ourselves, we know that the moving spring is wrong, that our evil affections bring forth evil actions, that a black drop runs through the very circulations of our being. But this is not the whole of human consciousness. The soul of man is conscious of much else; of a vital connection with God, by which it "feels after, if haply it might find him;" of a law of right, reverenced even when broken; of good affections, though checked by evil desires; and of noble aims, though warped by the wind and stream of worldly lust and passion. Were depravity total it could never be confessed. Remorse implies some spiritual excellence; and the very consciousness of sin supposes a germ and beginning of virtue. Were depravity the total or overpowering fact in life, the reality of our experience would be worse even than Byron's gloomy fiction of human nature: —

> " How beautiful is all this visible world!
> How glorious in its action and itself!
> But we, who name ourselves its sovereigns, we,
> Half dust, half deity, alike unfit
> To sink or soar, with our mixed essence make
> A conflict of its elements, and breathe
> The breath of degradation and of pride,
> Contending with low wants and lofty will
> Till our mortality predominates,
> And men are — what they name not to themselves,
> And trust not to each other."

But were the received, so much darker, doctrine of depravity true, men not only would not name, but could not even know it!

Accordingly, the consciousness or the confession of sin exists not, or but in lesser degrees, in the worst men. The most moving acknowledgments of the plague of iniquity are not from the vile, but from the noble, when they have let their nobleness, as a white escutcheon, be stained. It is such men as Job and David, Paul, St. Augustine, and Luther, that have stood meekly at the world's great confessional, bitterly to own their transgression. The record of their lives seconds our acquaintance with good men, and our knowledge of our own hearts, to show that moral progress alone gives a perception of " the sinfulness of sin;" and that not they, who have most occasion for alarm and suspicion of their spiritual state, are such confessors, but the men who pass along with light and easy step, unaware of any thing wrong in their relations to their Maker. In the biographies of saints, it is remarkable, too, how every new advance in holiness more reveals to them the enormity of wrong-doing ; makes disobedience to God swell up into all its gigantic proportions, and discloses every lurking subtlety and evasion of vice, just as the waxing light of day shows alike every mountain and cave with the slightest uneven surface. As we become children of the light, our conscience seems to take on a heavier load ; we detect the quality of guilt in things where we had not imagined it, become impatient of habits we had borne without a wish to shake off, and are startled from exposed situations of moral disease and death where we had slept and dreamed of happiness.

Oh! no: this consciousness and confession are not evidence of depravity alone, but of a nature designed and made for all purity and worth. Humiliation and self-upbraiding are no descent, but steps on the ladder that reaches up to heaven. The cry, "God, be merciful to me a sinner!" is not the voice of an heir of perdition, but of a chosen candidate for the society of angels. Nor, in the secrets of this confessional, which stands more in the heart's chamber than in the priest's closet, does it appear to be our nature which the self-reproaching soul decries, but its abuse and perversion. The guilty, in their honest avowals, lay their burdens at their own door, and do not shift them upon their Creator or on human ancestry. Their sin has been their own consent to temptation, the consent of beings capable of loving and serving God; else it surely would not be sin, but misfortune, fate, accident or Divine infliction. Nay, but for these capabilities of lofty affections, which faintly at least stir within them, they could not morally suffer for their faults and short-comings. Their melancholy is, that the celestial in them has been betrayed to the earthly. In the conflict of the breast, the unrighteous cause has for the moment triumphed. But the struggle shall be renewed. The forces of conscience and the spirit within never entirely surrender. The prize for which the fight is maintained is too glorious to be resigned ; the shame at its temporary loss, too

burning to be endured. The conviction then of sin
before God is before the tribunal, too, of one's own
soul: the uncorrupted judge, as well as the criminal,
is there. So the consciousness is twofold, the confession is resolve.

That human consciousness in general testifies to
much moral weakness, to much actual sin, to severe
inward struggles between the mind and the flesh, no
one can deny. The poet Burns, who understood
the nature of temptation and the power of a habit,
came nearer than many a theologian to the truth,
when, in his " Epistle to a Young Friend," he
wrote, —

> " I'll no say men are villains a' ;
>   The real hardened wicked
> Wha hae nae check but human law,
>   Are to a few restricked ;
> But, och ! mankind are unco weak,
>   An' little to be trusted ;
> If self the wavering balance shake,
>   It's rarely right adjusted."

It must be admitted, God has made us fallible and
peccable beings. He has not given us a sinful nature, yet a nature through which we may be led into
sin. He designs to teach us by our very errors, fol-
lies, and falls. If, indeed, we try to overreach him
by doing evil that good may come, we shall only arm
the pleasure or malice we indulge in with a double
sting : nevertheless, from the height of heaven and
the distance of eternity, we shall doubtless recognize
his wisdom in giving us a nature liable to mistake

and transgression. We perceive in this, that the goodness of God is no superficial impulse, but, if I may so speak, a long-minded principle, planning a destiny for us so vast and blessed that it cannot be accomplished in this little day of life, but, amid apparently cross-purposes and discords, only begun.

As I have already said, not utter wickedness, but moral weakness and imperfection, is that of which we are chiefly conscious. A globe of dust, a crystal, a plant, an animal, can be made and finished, and then begin to crumble, fade, and die. But human nature, in the greatness and duration of its design, is so unfinished that it can at present hardly more than be called a promise and a prophecy. Could it show at once that beauty and perfectness which its disparagers would demand as the condition of their eulogy, it would only be ready to dissolve and pass away. It would come under Shakspeare's account of human life, where he says, " We ripe and ripe, and then we rot and rot." Having filled out its ideal, it could be put into its grave. But, considering its real, boundless aim, its imperfection now becomes more beautiful than the perfection of any thing else on earth ; and it seems a flagrant injustice to make that in it the subject of censure which is requisite to its progress, and the only pledge of its immortality. The blame is praise. Its Author, in making it, eternally saw, if he did not eternally cause, all it would involve and produce ; nor would permit its original composition to tend to vanity or ill, or to aught less than angelic and immeasurable excellence. It is the tendency of the nature, not its present condition as determinate, which we are to consider in our judgment. One might as well judge of the worth and beauty of a ship by the confusion of materials in the yard where it is building, or of a fruit by its green leaf and acrid bud, as of human nature by its first demonstrations. We are not to criticise it as we would a performance of skill, or examine it as we might a painting or statue, which have received the last touch of the brush, the final stroke of the chisel. Its experiment is yet to be tried, its divine art fully shown. It is not Saul of Tarsus that we are to look at, but Paul the Apostle; and still more Paul "departed," as he desired, to "be with Christ," and ever anew glorified. The very glory of our nature is this ideal flying before our advance like the horizon, towering over our ascent like the upper air.

There is undoubtedly a false view of the dignity of human nature, held in ignorance or neglect of facts. However we may settle the critical dispute, whether Paul writing to the Romans of the struggle between the will and the deed, the inward man and the members, meant to speak in his own person, in that of an unconverted Jew, or that of the whole race, our self-inspection is the only needed test of the truth of his words. We feel in us the conflict of laws, the present will and the absent power, the sin that slays and the holy commandment, the sore strife of the flesh with the spirit, which he so vividly paints. As attention is fixed exclusively on either

27

side of this twofold picture, an erroneous view of human nature in its present state arises. One party exaggerates, in its statement, the law of the members; another party, the law of the mind. Both parties are carried aside from the truth. If, according to the first, human nature be fatally subjected to the law of the members, the helpless sport and hapless victim of appetite and passion, then to talk of human sinfulness at all is a fiction of speech. A machine cannot sin. Sin is wicked, unlawful choice. Necessity has no choice or law; and mankind, instead of being thus convicted of their actual transgressions, are universally absolved, and made as innocent as the animals in obeying their irresistible instincts. Thus a great objection to the doctrine of total depravity is, that it takes a light view of sin, a technical and negative view, from which the sinner easily escapes. Under the semblance of a severe, it is really a licentious doctrine.

But the doctrine of the now perfected dignity and divinity of human nature is alike faulty in fixing our regard simply on the law of the mind, the authority of conscience, the good affections, the rich endowment of capacity in every heart. The advocate of this doctrine sees human nature, not as it is, but as it ought to be. He overlooks existing wickedness, and is blind to, or contemplates with a venial eye, the inordinate propensities rushing on, heedless of the boundaries of virtue. Thus, as much as his opponent, though in a different way, he may make sin a nullity; as certain of our philosophers, in fact, hold it to be

only privative, an absence, a shadow, a negation,
which will disappear by the simple development of
human nature. So alone the pantheist and optimist
can understand it, maintaining that God is the only
will, and an all-inclusive necessity of the divine decrees ; and certainly the pantheist and optimist have
this advantage over the Calvinist, that their necessity
only blesses, while his carries also a broad and blast-
ing curse. But sin, the wilfully wrong action of the
mind, cannot thus be disallowed, without losing at
the same time the mind's righteous choice of virtue
and excellence. God's power to create a free being
is moreover denied, by merging the soul in the absolute essence, instead of regarding it as formed to be
an individual and deathless force.

In fine, when human nature is thus magnified, as
having all the germs of goodness and correctives
of evil within itself alone, any interposition of the
Most High for its redemption becomes superfluous.
It needs no word from the heavens, and no laying
bare of an almighty arm, to help or rescue a nature
armed in its own right with an irresistible genius.
This would contradict the ancient maxim, that the
Deity does no useless work. Is not here the secret
of the scepticism of our day? Professing to spring
out of critical difficulties respecting the records of
our religion, the uncertainty of human testimony,
and the incredibleness of miraculous works, does it
not really spring out of a notion of the independent
self-sufficiency of the human mind? If human nature
can go alone, it needs nothing to lean upon ; and if

the voice of reason and conscience suffice to keep it
unfaltering and undeviating in the high road of virtue, no superhuman influence to guide it in the right
way, or arrest it in the wrong, deserves praying for,
or is worth accepting. But is this *actual* human nature? Is the inward light so bright, steady, and
uneclipsed, that the day-spring from on high serves
not any more than a flickering candle amid the
beams of the rising sun? See the bondmen of sin,
the workmen under base desire, the multitudes falling below their own idea, the individuals impotently
subject to some overgrown inclination, struggling by
fits with their master, and then driven along; and
then take your notice of others as the key and cipher
of what transpires in your own breast, before you
answer. The "commandment" of God "is exceeding broad." It gives sentence, not only against
abandoned characters, guilty of gross vices and
chargeable with overt crimes against society, but
levels its blow against all sloth, selfishness, neglect
of personal improvement and of opportunities to do
good; against unkindness to the feelings, injustice to
the motives, and disparagement of the claims, of
others; against envy, that carps at and would drag
down transcendent merit; jealousy, spiteful at de-
ficient regards and civilities; vanity, standing on
hollow pretensions; ambition, that would rise over
ruined reputations; avarice, worshipping gold, careless of the temple of a devout, benevolent heart,
which "sanctifieth the gold;" revenge, perhaps
handling no weapon but the stiletto of delicate de-

traction ; falsehood, deceiving for the cheapest gains ;
hypocrisy, putting the garb of an angel of light on
mean and unworthy feelings; impiety, with blas-
phemous tongue and irreverent deeds, such as drew
into hands, never employed in self-defence, the
scourge of small cords, signal of God's judgment, —
a numberless brood, an endless progeny of spiritual
sins, growing out of each other, nestling close together, and polluting the sanctuary of the soul.

Moral evil is indeed not a thing that superficially
happens in the world, but which the human heart
consciously knows to be planted in itself.   It is not,
as some would seem to consider it, a slight, passing
disease, but a chronic affection of the human will.
The wrong institutions of society are not careless
heaps, as of wood and stone loosely piled up on the
surface, and, as the reformer may fancy, to be easily
or at once overthrown ; but, like the primitive trees
of the forest, they have deep and ancient roots.
How persistent, how inconvertible often, is nature !
There is not, indeed, as theologians fancy, a universal nature and uniform race alone, much less an
utter, invariable wickedness of man ; but different
persons have peculiar native idiosyncrasies and constitutional leanings.   Depravity is neither total nor
constant, and the imputation of original *sin* would be
morally unjust, were it not philosophically absurd ;
sin being voluntary disobedience.   So far as, in various manner and degree, that inclination to offend
and break God's law in his word and in the heart,
allowance of which constitutes actual sin, is a herit-

27*

age transmitted from parent to child, God's wisdom and justice to each one will unquestionably appear in the foreordained, though now untraceable results. Yet even here we can see the unambiguous purpose of these constitutional tendencies to evil. They are meant by God for the occasions and provocatives of our virtue, to discipline our principles and sharpen our good resolutions. They are our badge as soldiers of Jesus Christ, our divine commission on the enterprise and expedition of holiness, even the heraldry of our salvation, and the very device of that " whole armor " we are to put on "against the wiles of the devil ; " like the signals engraven in shield and breastplate of the ancient knight, of scenes of perils encountered, obstacles surmounted, and fierce foes overthrown, things of good omen, things of good cheer.

Meantime, let us with deep compunction own every positive transgression or short-coming that can be included in the largest enumeration of faults under the divine law.

When such a delineation is offered to demonstrate that human nature is totally depraved, we can, indeed, in opposition to the dark troop, array a heavenly host, all love, friendship, honor, purity, self-denial, and devotion. We can specify many a bias to good, as well as to evil. We can point to the mother, in her unconsciously fatigued and famished watch over her child ; to many a father, besides him of old, who would have died for his son ; nay, to the instinctive promptings of humanity, by which

a common person, as if doing but a common thing,
plunges into the fire or flood to save the life of a fellow-creature, — as the miner, who lately fell down the
shaft, had no voice for himself, but only with the cry
of "Below!" to warn his companions out of the way;
to philanthropy, at her disinterested toils and charity,
pouring out, as from the horn of plenty, her benefactions; in short, to every form of service for God and
man that makes the world habitable and beautiful.

But if the moral defects and difficulties of men
do not make out the case of essential wickedness,
they do establish that of moral weakness, and want
of help, such as the gospel affords. And this required
help is not of mere law, but moreover of the divine
mercy. The blood of self-sacrifice, freely shed by
Christ on the gentle height of Calvary, speaks louder
to us than the thunders that rolled through the
rugged clefts of Sinai; and the dove of God's spirit,
descending on the air at his baptism, moves to obedience more mightily than the heavy tables of stone
that were let down into the hands of Moses. The
method of God's grace in our redemption is not to
draw up in terrible distinctness a list of his violated
commands, while the awful finger of the offended
Judge points from the broken precept to the offender's doom; but it is the Judge himself bending in
fatherly compassion from his eternal throne, speaking in pity to his delinquent children, and sending
from his bosom the Son that had never displeased
him, as though Almighty Power would sheathe its
thunders, and Infinite Justice had become fond.

That heart, must be harder than the nether mill-stone, or rotted through with the pollutions of vice, which can resist this appeal. The forgiving love of the gospel will soften the stone which the hammer of the law could not break, and the balm of long-suffering kindness search into and stir the sensibilities which the pains and penalties of disobedience could not probe. The blood of the atonement will wash away the sins and inveterate spots which the moral will could not alone remove ; and the spirit of him, from whose sacred form it flowed, temper the heart to a celestial strength and fineness which natural conscience could never reach.

Herein lies the importance of receiving Christianity as an express revelation, to convince us that such is God's mind towards us. Strip off from Christ his peculiar character, discredit his miracles, deny his authority ; and the law of Jewish or Gentile morality, with the hard precepts of the philosophers' schools, returns upon us in cold, stoic austerity ; nature, that never pardons, resumes her sway in the domain of mind as of matter ; and the assurance of that which is more glorious than nature, with all her general laws, God's unquenchable love even to the sinner,— its superhuman seal broken,— vanishes into conjecture and doubt. But, thank God, no human hand has yet proved strong enough, or can ever suffice to break that seal. It stands in uneffaceable characters, the pledge, through Christ, of the exhaustless riches of the Divine goodness. It is a certain sign to secure those definite views of revealed religion, without which the gospel would at once have sunk into the grave of oblivion.

The divine foresight and equity in the time, place, manner, and spread of this revelation, need not our vindication. In these, as in all things, God will make good and put beyond cavil his own procedure. He prepares the fulness of every time; he administers his truth and providence to his family's need; he shapes the spiritual and organic elements, and furnishes the stimulus and discipline of every individual being; he works in a thousand ways which we cannot measure or define; when old instruments are worn out, he supplies the fitting substitutes; and, in eternity, will clear up the justice of all his words and deeds. In eternity we shall see more of his purpose in this human nature which he has formed and inspired. Then we shall understand how baseless was every objection to his work. We shall perceive how every liability, with which he first constituted man, or severally endued his offspring, was in wisdom, and every fundamental feeling and instinct designed to yield its ennobled or restrained strength to the everlasting growth of human virtue. We cannot, indeed, fully know this at any specific period in our future way. There shall be no end to expansion, no cessation of fruit, no term of progress, no summit of ascension, no limit of blessedness, no silence of our song of praise. But the issues of mortal life will at least begin. Existence will have taken its course, though forever to widen its stream. Ever-increasing production will point back with incessantly heightening significance to the seed God himself planted in the human soul.

To this lengthened discussion must be added, in closing, some distinct consideration of the practical influence of the doctrine I have maintained. Individual opinions respecting human nature have, in the same general class of believers, now reached to so wide a difference, that one, belonging to no theological sect or denomination, may express his judgment on this subject wholly apart from any theological odium or envy. The conviction of sin is thought by many to be the grand basis of all spiritual edification. That it is a necessary element in the foundation of character, one pillar, if not the corner-stone, of the building, cannot be fairly denied. But this solid support is to be found in a conviction of actual, not of a fancied natural, sin; while a conviction, not only of the sin in our heart, but of the goodness, too, which there solicits us, is requisite to any lofty endeavor or achievement. The moral evil of our own soul, as well as the injurious evil inflicted by our fellow-men, we can overcome only with good. Jesus said to his disciples, that the spirit he should send would "reprove, or convict, the world of sin, of righteousness, and of judgment." Wonderful instance of his penetrating wisdom, of his divine inspiration, that he would have men convicted, not only of wrong-doing, but of holiness too! It is not sufficient for God's purpose respecting us, that we should be repelled from iniquity, but that we should moreover be kindled with the generous flame of excellence, being baptized "with the Holy Ghost and with fire." While we come to spurn at vice, to take the distance of disgust and be removed from it by the power of repentance, something lofty and magnanimous, positively pure and worthy, must as it were descend from heaven to lay hold of, inspire, and lift us. As the lives of the bad do not so greatly bless us as the examples of the good, so dwelling even upon our own faults and mistakes is not so profitable, as to contemplate and become vitally possessed with wisdom and virtue. If only the "unclean" demon is expelled, "seven other more wicked spirits" will take up their abode in the empty house whence he is gone out. But give occupation and lodgment in the breast to the Holy Spirit, and, though the evil temper have been as a strong man armed, a stronger than he shall take from him "all his armor," and "keep his palace."

Reason and God's word, Christ's method and our own heart, together attest the superior power of goodness to win, over that of vice to warn us. The little child gets a better benediction from the biography of the good, than from the histories of transgression and all the diaries and morbid exposures of impurity and deceit. The experienced teacher of the young, with the practised reformer of the erring and prodigal, bears witness that touching the better feelings of the heart is more effectual, to guide or reclaim, than pointing to the precipice of ruin, or pouring out the vials of wrath. Demand what is noble and good; draw the line of high expectation; in your whole tone

and deportment presume and require your fellow-
creatures to walk upon it; cast out into practical
scorn, absurdity, and impossibility, the base and
unmanly part; put it into the region of your own
ignorance, let it be to you only a shock and sur-
prise as coming from them; and they will be apt to
make an effort to come up to the mark and place of
your standard. A moral magnetism will draw them
into blessed captivity; as Christ's own life attracts us
into the imitation of his spirit, and obedience of his
law. The language, "England expects," could
nerve with double force every heart that throbbed to
the sound. A writer of fiction well describes a poor,
degraded creature who had led his life in the vilest
parts of the social walk, as being stirred even to
inward renewal by the words addressed to him,
Heart and honor! Animals themselves seem to feel
something like a moral impression from man's treatment of them. If he gives them a bad name with a
curse and a blow, even they are degraded. They
know when their race is persecuted, and are thus
made mean and vindictive. A higher, and, we are
almost tempted to think, more than mortal nature is
brought out in them by kindness, confidence, fellowship, and sympathy. Before the at once commanding and confiding eye of their keeper, the
fierceness even of the lion, leopard, and tiger sinks
and ebbs away into the low and remote channels of
their bosom, and the awkward but affecting tokens
of intelligence and good-will come out in their gro-
tesque motions, and gleam upon their harsh or rug-

ged features. And it is wonderful that *human* nature, considering how it has been denominated and treated in time past, can bear so clear indications, as we may distinguish in it, of goodness and hope. But a wiser and better day is dawning, when the sins into whose commission it is tempted will not be regarded with any less serious disapproval, yet with a more considerate and profounder judgment; while its frame from an Almighty hand for a glorious virtue will be discerned and acknowledged, exercised and vindicated. May God hasten that day; for it is the day of the coming of his own kingdom of light and holiness and love!

DISCOURSE XXIII.

HUMAN NEED.

Rev. iii. 17. — BECAUSE THOU SAYEST, I AM RICH, AND INCREASED WITH
GOODS, AND HAVE NEED OF NOTHING ; AND KNOWEST NOT THAT
THOU ART WRETCHED AND MISERABLE AND POOR AND BLIND AND
NAKED.

IT is commonly supposed to be the apostle John
who thus addresses a church of Christ, outwardly
prosperous and flourishing, but spiritually poor and
destitute. Whether this outward prosperity con-
sisted in numbers and handsome ecclesiastical ap-
pointments, or in worldly riches and grandeur, or,
as is very likely, in the union of a rich estate with a
pompous ritual, does not certainly appear. It is
only manifest, that, under some sort of splendid
external show and conceited self-satisfaction, — the
Laodicean church being, as we learn from history, the
wealthy metropolitan church of the neighborhood,
— the real life of religion was faltering and dying out.
And so the apostle represents their condition as one
of need and poverty, though they themselves felt
they had need of nothing. He would make them
sensible of their need, that they might seek for it a
supply. It is no slight attainment for us all to
become thus sensible, and thus to seek. Prosperous

and flourishing though we, like the Laodiceans, may, individually or collectively, think ourselves, we shall not lack room for meditation on this point; for man is by nature the neediest of all beings.

Nor is it, as some might maintain, his disgrace and the signal of his inferiority that he is thus needy, but rather the mark of his native glory and pre-eminence. For it points to the number and greatness of his faculties. Our need answers to our capacity. We might indeed construct a scale of existence on this principle of need. The lower the creature, the less his need; for the more feeble his sensibilities, narrow his powers, and torpid his desires. The shell-fish yonder needs but to draw in from the beating waves, or through a slender aperture in the muddy bottom of the sea, a little water, and then expel the same through those stony valves which are at once his defence and his dwelling. His finny swimming superior, with a more versatile power, needs a somewhat richer nutriment. The insect, with its still finer organization, needs to fly in the air, and to feed on the sweets of flowers. The beast, of structure more complex, and increased capabilities, needs a still greater variety of support; the cravings of each kind of animal nature multiplying according exactly to its additional susceptibilities of sensation, intelligence, and affection; from the creature that is satisfied with a green leaf, and, that consumed, creeps slowly and lazily to another, to the fierce or kingly birds that cut the air of a hemisphere, and seek their prey on the far mountain-top, or " where the carcase is " in the lonely valley.

But, from the most sagacious and strongest of the animal tribes, how vast the difference, in capacity of intellect and feeling, to man! And no less vast the difference of need. He draws from the earth, from the water, and from the air, to satisfy his appetites and to satiate his curiosity; he ransacks every kingdom of nature for his comfort and aggrandizement, and is not content. His restless and changeful wishes are ever roaming abroad for something new, something better, something greater. He cannot stay attached to one place, " like the limpet to the rock." He cannot stop with one sort of food, like the bee that roves among the blossoms. He does not, like the ruminating animal, stand still and peaceful in his own reflections. Nor, though he should leave his anchorage on the ground, soar into the sky, and, for his clumsy balloon, substitute the wings of a dove, could he even then " fly away and be at rest." He is uneasy, he is needy, he is craving and discontented still. It is because his faculties are so many and so great, because his desires are so ardent and so infinite, that his supplies must be manifold and huge.

Is there, then, no satisfaction for a man? Are we alone in the universe made to be thus uneasy and discontented, like peevish children wanting what we cannot have, and crying for what is beyond our reach? No: God has not made his noblest creature for a wretched failure and a miserable want. Let him bring into light all his abilities and desires, — they are not too many or too strong; those of the

higher nature as well as the lower; those that tend
up to God himself and heaven and immortality, as
well as those that tend downwards and abroad to
earthly things.   Let him unfold them without fear.
The vast supplies from the foreseeing Creator, in
the treasury of his truth, are ready. Let him appropriate them to his need.   And the fish that cleaves
the liquid sea, the insect that revels in the cup of a
flower, the beast that browzes in his pasture, or the
bird that darts through the yielding air, shall be no
more at home or content with its lot than he;
while the lot, he is content with, shall be as much
superior to theirs, as "the heaven and the heaven of
heavens" are above the earth.

Man is a being that does not need daily bread and
clothing and shelter alone; but he needs truth, needs
duty, needs love, needs God.   The mistake is in
trying to gratify fully his nature with such outward
things, neglecting the spiritual.   But, though he turn
his bread into luxury, though he turn his clothing
into splendor, though he turn his shelter into palace-
like magnificence, he cannot succeed.   He may
seem to succeed.   He may even persuade himself
he has succeeded.   He may go on with his pleasure
and pomp, with "his uppermost rooms at feasts, and
greetings in the market-place," and think lightly of
or even despise the joy of devotion, and the glory
of heavenly things that we talk of.   But his happiness is a frail structure, a house upon the sand.   At
the first assault of the blowing wind and the beating
rain,— which God has garnered in his providential

28*

treasures, even as he has the winds and storms in the air and the sea, — it will fall.

It is just this foolhardy and hazardous assurance of satisfaction in outward prosperity, that, I apprehend, the author of our text means to expose. For it matters not whether it be a whole church or an individual soul that says, " I am rich, increased with goods, and have need of nothing," when, in fact, it is so limited and cramped, as, in comparison with what it might enjoy, to be " wretched and miserable and poor and blind and naked." Well may such a soul, in the eloquent scorn of the apostle's figurative speech, be counselled to " buy gold tried in the fire," that " it may be rich," " and white raiment " that it " may be clothed." Man, — whosoever thou art, wheresoever thou standest, whatsoever thou pursuest, — content with sensual good and clinging to outward treasure,—that is not " the bread of life " which thou eatest. That is not the true gold with which thou fillest thy coffers. That is not the durable raiment with which thou art clad. There is food that satisfies. There are riches of goodness for the heart. There is a wedding-garment of purity for the soul, which shall never fade or crumble away, but be the " white robe " thou mayest wear in heaven, when the gay dress is moth-eaten, and the spotless shroud, too, earth's last apparel, which thou shalt not put on thyself, but which shall have been put on thy limbs, hath mouldered in the tomb.

To sustain this exhortation, it is not necessary to speak in the exclusive ardor of one idea, but the

sober proportion that takes in man's whole estate.
Though, in the highest sense in which our Saviour
once spoke, " one thing is needful ; " yet, considering
man in his whole nature, — mixed dust and spirit, a
member of society, an associate in civil polity, and
a link in the training up of new generations, in short,
an inhabitant of this world as well as a hoper for
another, — he doubtless needs many things. Nor
will I push the claim of religion with that extravagant urgency which would shut out his other interests and claims. He needs, by various education,
to get possession of all his members and faculties.
He needs, according to the primal command, to subdue the earth, and have dominion over it. He needs
to understand, and perfect its productions ; as, even
in his original, unfallen state, he did to train the plants
of Paradise. He needs, like Tubal Cain of old, to
dig into the ground, and bring up the metals for his
arts, using the more precious ones for his exchange,
and to turn the forest into his utensils, houses, and
ships. He needs to fabricate, needs to manufacture,
needs to discover and invent, needs to trade, needs
to accumulate ; so that every industrial faculty may
be brought out, every hand employed, every talent
put in motion, — nay, so that the community itself
may not fail and sink, but be civilized and refined,
and, with its corporations and capital, its genius and
skill, undertake every useful enterprise for the individual and public good. In setting before you a
moral and spiritual need, I certainly do not forget
these personal, social, and political necessities, nor

would shove them by an inch from their place ; but, admitting the latter, maintain the supreme importance, the predominating position, of the former.

Let the soul within us become our solemn preacher, and speak in its own person, according to the dramatic representation in our text ; and what would it say from the breast of each one of us ? — " I need the air of heaven for outward breathing ; and I need the light of heaven for sight. I need the bodily sustenance on which the vigor and clearness even of my own operations depend. I need the decencies of a customary appearance and deportment in my external association with men. I need that exemption from galling and ceaseless labor which shall give me opportunity to develop my understanding. But " — and is not the tone in which it speaks deepening, and the accent more thrilling ? — " I need other, greater things. I need, oh ! I need inward peace. I need ' a conscience void of offence towards God and man.' I need a religious courage, and a trust which the fluctuations of the world, on which we are borne as a little boat on the sea, cannot unseat, nor its sudden changes of life and death, severing the closest cords, overthrow. I need objects vast enough and holy enough to absorb into themselves these yearning affections, content with no created good. I need to live, not for mere eating and drinking and clothing, and passing selfishly through my career ; but I need — oh! how deeply ! — to be endeared by sentiments of love, and deeds disinterested, to my fellow-beings. I need to make the world better that I have lived in it, to leave some other monument and memorial of myself than a grave-stone, or a flattering epitaph cut by the hand of friendship in its cold surface. Verily I need, — God knows it, and my heart knows, — I need to bless those around me, to be united to them, not by ties of blood alone, or transient convenience, but by deep, indissoluble, immortal bonds. And in order to all this, I need Christ, the Son of God, for my Saviour, and God himself for my friend."

If the soul speak not thus within us, it slumbers, or is "dead in trespasses and sins." If the soul speak not thus within us, we have not encouraged it to speak at all. Or if, from within, the soul utter instead the voice of worldly contentment and of old self-complacency in the text, it hath faculties,— faculties from God, and which it must answer for, but "hath never used," — and needs it does not "know."

The dull caterpillar may be content with lying upon the ground, hardly appearing animated, like a lump or brown leaf, when the wings are actually folded up within, to bear it into the sunshine and among all the blossoms of the landscape. So a man may be content with a low, earth-bound life, a state of half-manhood, because unconscious of the heaven-bestowed capacities by which he might live above the world. But the mere force of nature will not unfold the man as it does the insect. He may discourage and keep down these wings of the soul. He may, by sin and his rebellious will, wound and

mutilate them as they instinctively strive to expand.
Yet he cannot remain forever unconscious of their
existence. He cannot exercise them in the mean
ways of the world in which he treads. Lacking
their true element and use, they will pine and wither
with dissatisfaction and remorse, and his upbraiding
spirit turn away from the sources to which he so
confidently carries it for supply, as the lean, travel-
worn, thirsty camel turns in gaunt despair from the
empty well in the desert. We need the principle of
devotion to God and others' good. We need the
practice of the two great commandments of love to
God and man. We need to be humble, need to be
patient, need to be meek, to the Father above, and
our brethren below. We need these dispositions,
not only as paying our debt to them, though they
are our debt, but as the indispensable requisites of
our own well-being. Our Saviour said no strange,
unnatural thing, when, after long abstinence, to his
disciples' request that he would " eat," he answered
that he had meat to eat they knew not of, " to do the
will of Him that sent him, and to finish his work."
For the deepest need of every one of us will not be
supplied, till to omit daily prayers, and daily services
of good-will, shall be like taking away our daily
food. Service, the communication of benefit as a
child of the All-bountiful, is indeed the solemn and
uncompromising demand that human nature — say
what we will of that nature, disparage it as we may
— makes of itself; is what, whenever it truly knows
itself, it requires itself to do. Yea —

" The poorest poor
Long for some moments in a weary life,
When they can know and feel that they have been
Themselves the fathers and the dealers-out
Of some small blessings ; have been kind to such
As needed kindness, for this single cause,
That we have all of us one human heart ! "

It is said that the priest and familiar counsellor of William the Conqueror, when asked by his master respecting the rewards he would have for his advice, in turn asked him, " Dost thou not love fame for the sake of fame ? " And the baron replied, " Yes." Then, turning to the minstrel, he asked, " Dost thou not love song for the sake of song ? " And he replied, " Yes." — " Wonder not, then," proceeded the religious scholar, " that the student loves knowledge for the sake of knowledge." And not till we love truth and goodness for the sake of truth and goodness, not till we hold them as the breath of our life, live in them as the inspirations of our soul, and pursue them as the very terms of our spiritual existence, shall the great need of our nature be appeased ; all its faculties, which God gave and Christ came to satisfy, opened ; and our true place vindicated on the scale of being. But then indeed we shall have learned, that the needy are not one particular class, but the whole of God's family ; and we shall satisfy the need of the poor and unfortunate, and our own need, by the same generosity of word and act.

DISCOURSE XXIV.

OBJECT OF HUMAN LIFE.

Eccles. vi. 12. — FOR WHO KNOWETH WHAT IS GOOD FOR MAN IN THIS LIFE?

WHEREFORE am I alive? What is the object or the use of life? This is the problem of our text, and of the whole book in which the text is found. Certainly it is the most interesting of problems, and one that must have occurred to every serious mind. What is the use, the meaning of my life? for what purpose was it given? to what end shall it aim? I can trace uses, adaptations, in other things. One part of the world is suited to another, and the whole world is made to correspond to my senses and organs; but for what were my senses and organs themselves, all my powers of body and mind, bestowed? Is there, above the little tasks and tradings in which I am occupied, any single presiding object, or only a swift succession and blind complication of small, shifting aims and designs? Is life an instrument ministering to some solid purpose, or a fleeting phantasmagoria, that leaves no lasting result? Such, substantially, was the inquiry of the preacher three thousand years ago, and which demands an answer still from every new generation and living man.

It would seem that the author of the book of Ecclesiastes entertained this inquiry, not so much theoretically as in the way of experiment, making various actual trials for its solution upon his own body and soul. His first essay or exploration is "to seek and search out by wisdom concerning all things that are done under heaven." Speculative knowledge, intellectual curiosity, storing the mind with all various information,— this is his first experiment; and he succeeds in surpassing all others in this kind of enterprise. But he does not seem to himself, after all, thus to have adequately solved his problem. There are many things he perceives done under the sun which it is vanity and vexation of spirit to study, and madness and folly to know. There are crooked things in the world which the student cannot straighten, and "wanting" things which he cannot number. With the width of his survey is the growth of his perplexity. Grief and sorrow come in with the increase of wisdom, and he is forced to conclude that to be a knower and a thinker is not the satisfying end of human life.

The next thing he subjects to the test, tries in the court of his own experience, is pleasure. He proves his heart with mirth and laughter, with wine and music, with houses and vineyards, with gardens and orchards, with silver and gold, with servants and maidens, with men-singers and women-singers, and more things beside than I can now mention. He

29

evidently is one that does nothing by halves; so he plunges into the stream of outward display and sensual indulgence, keeps not his eyes from whatever they desire, withholds not his heart from any joy. Yet, after tasting the depths of this seductive stream, and having drunk the cup of pleasure to the dregs, with renewed bitterness from the tribunal of his soul, he pronounces upon this trial the sentence of failure and disappointment greater even than in his first experiment.

For awhile he seems now to come to a stand, to despair in his search, and to fancy that there is no one great object of human labor, but the best thing is simply to eat and drink from day to day, and enjoy all he can as he goes along, bearing, with what philosophy is at his command, the inevitable travail and unrest of his days. He appears even to relapse into fatalism; becomes a stoic before the school of stoics arose; says there is a time appointed for every thing, which man cannot alter or so much as comprehend, but only submit to and endure. But the activity of his own will soon carries him out of this stagnant pool of a dead necessity, to make another adventure for the supreme good, the grand object of existence on earth. Having tried knowledge, the exercise of the mind, and tried pleasure, the gratification of the senses, he tries the moral quality of things, as fitted to the sense of right and justice in his own soul. But lo! here, too, he is balked with a sorer baffling than ever before. For he sees wickedness in the place of judgment, and iniquity in the place of righteousness; all things happening alike to all, or the just perishing and the wicked prospering, and death coming speedily in to sweep the stakes from the table where men, with so unfair winnings or losings, play the vain and trivial game of human life.

The solution of his problem still escapes him; and this king over Israel in Jerusalem, driven from royal rank to philosophic knowledge, from knowledge to worldly pleasure, from pleasure to earthly justice; alienated by disgust, and pushed by iniquity from resting at the so-often abused bar of human judgment, flies at last to God, to religion, to confidence in the equity of the great disposing Power. This, he says, is the conclusion of the whole matter:— "Fear God, and keep his commandments; for this is the whole duty of man. For God shall bring every work into judgment."

I have thus traced some of the preacher's steps; but I do not profess to have condensed into such brevity the entire scope of a book which has employed the patience and produced the lengthened commentaries of scholars. It is enough for my purpose, if I have suggested the main drift, and found a key to open, not so much this sacred composition, as the chambers of our own hearts. We, too, my friends, unless content to live an ephemeral insect-life, have asked for the object of our existence in this world; or, if we have not, it is time we should; and, if we have asked, we cannot too solemnly remind ourselves of a right answer. Let me at least propose the point distinctly to every hearer. Have any of you been willing to go on, without settling, or even starting, this great query; willing to sail in this frail boat of our mortality down the stream of years, without knowing whither, or desiring any port? When design is written on the whole frame of nature, from the star that punctually takes its place in the evening sky to the drop of dew that sinks down to the root of some little flower, have you looked for no design or final cause in your own being? Or, when your outward frame is, beyond all human art, the most skilful contexture of fibre, nerve and limb, have you been incurious as to the significance of that life which it guards and covers? If you reflect, you cannot proceed in this ignorant and accidental way; your existence like a column of smoke dissolved in the air, a wreath of foam melting in the wave, a whirlwind of sand dispersed over the desert. "Commune with your own heart," and you will not be satisfied, till some object rise broad as the horizon before you, embracing all lesser occupations and pursuits in its glorious compass, and enabling you, by clear and continual reference, to shape every daily trifle and detail, otherwise worthless or perhaps unmeaning, towards its accomplishment. I pray you, and to this single point I would hold your attention, to decide whether such an object be yours; for in the want of it lies, if anywhere, man's great fault, fatal error, unpardonable sin. What particular transgression against the great Designer can be so radical, what depravity so total, as an objectless life!

But a doubt may here arise as to the fact. "Who," it may be exclaimed, "leads such a life? Are not men busy and earnest enough, each in his own line of desire and attainment, which, it is to be presumed, each one has chosen with a ground of preference in his own case, as satisfying the purpose, at least, of *his* being in the world, whether it be riches or knowledge or honor, or any special success." I answer, no : this opinion or assumption in the case is not so plainly just. Ask the greatest miser whether he is making money, because he has satisfied himself with that as the object of life, — has rationally judged, consciously chosen, resolutely pursued, the pelf as such an object? If he thinks, he will hesitate, he will stammer, and confess perhaps that he has not considered what the object of life is, or whether there be any object. He is drawn on, enslaved by a particular propensity; but his life, his whole life, has no object that seems clear and worthy even in his own eyes; and, on reflection, he would be as bitter, nay, always has been as bitter, as was the preacher against *his* experiment of vanity and vexation of spirit. Ask the voluptuary, as he looks back on the excesses into which he hasted so greedily, and as with yet keen relish he looks forward on imagined excesses to come,— ask him, to give every advantage in the argument, before his constitution is broken down, or his heart of innocence rotted out of him, if he considers sensual enjoyment the object of life. Chained to his appetites, it is what he has followed, and is whipped or dragged after still ; but,

29

so far from having intelligently judged it to be the true object of his existence, or with a peaceful conscience pursued it as his proper aim, his self-shaming reproaches, if he can be prevailed on to stop and consider, shall return to the other side of the world, across the space of intervening centuries, to him that there uttered it, the old exclamation, that "Laughter is mad," and the old question of "Mirth, — what doeth it?"

No, again I answer: none of these limited ends, which the preacher specifies, and arraigns in the court of his experience for trial, and which the multitude now as then seek, — none of them calmly, deeply, contents any man: in the trial-balance of the soul, they are found wanting; their presentation in the preacher's self-questioning method, even to the heart taken captive by them, brings back no clear resonance of firm satisfaction. No: I fear our first inference is just; and that the difficulty with most men is, that they do not live for any comprehensive object, but as the serfs of their own inclinations,— the worst, as it is the most common, serfdom in the world; the changeful and transferred subjects of imperious and conflicting passions, between which they are tossed and sold from one to the other.

So my intention in this discourse will be answered, if I can prevail on you so much as to define such an object to your own thoughts; for I know, that, if you but admit the inquiry, no man, woman, or thoughtful child, could adopt or propose any amount of gain, honor, pleasure, or earthly knowledge, as filling the grasp of their wishes; but every sentence of vanity from the preacher's mouth would be re-echoed, till that sublime conclusion, "Fear God, and keep his commandments," came alone to fill the idea of this capacious soul. Decide at all upon living for an object, choose something to which you soberly consent to devote your existence, and you can hardly decide wrong, or take an object that is false and unworthy; but will be constrained, like the preacher, to determine on the right, to choose religion, obedience to God, and confidence in the final demonstration of his justice, whatever for the present may seem to be wanting, or to go awry. To express this, cherish it, and use earthly time and opportunity to build it up as the vital principle of our being's health and growth, is indeed for man, woman, and child — for even the child can understand it — the object of life.

The principle may be put into various forms of statement. You may recur to the old preacher's language, or you may say with the modern catechism, that the "chief end of man is to glorify God, and enjoy him forever." You may speak in the phrase, rightly understood, of the philosophy of our time, "Self-culture;" or in the phrase, profoundly interpreted of the philanthropy of our time, "Reform." All these mean essentially the same thing, requiring in the analysis the same elements. Shame on us, my friends, if, in that old preacher's time, when the soul's immortality only doubtfully darkened and glimmered, like the first struggling twi-

light of the morning, over the dim horizon of the
grave, he could resolve to live for such a holy end
as pure religion, and believe in the rectifying, somehow, of all earthly wrongs ; yet we, in the noon-day
splendor of revelation, and a future life brought to
light, cannot do as much !

This solution of our problem carries us into no
fanatical austerity. The adoption of so grand an
object of life, taking in our whole career, does not
abolish the minor callings and aims of activity, of
study, or traffic, or mechanical skill, in this world.
It but leavens them with a higher spirit, and turns
them to a nobler influence. It polarizes the wandering and aimless affairs of time and sense, makes
all our dealings not only serve temporary purposes,
but, in their effects on our hearts, point to permanent
results ; and, while we sail over the sea of life,
touching at every slight occasion of human service
and success along the shore, it steadily, as a great
magnet, draws us ever nearer to a blessed eternal
destiny. It puts a new question into our mouth,
which the changeling slave of temporal expedients
and little ends does not think to ask, — a question
that rightly comes up with every transaction we
engage in, every conversation we hold, every plan
we form, every measure we execute, — Are we promoting here in this very thing, however great or
trifling it may look, the object of life ? If not promoting, but defeating this object, it bids us beware
and abstain. It does not shut us up in a narrow
place of hermit stiffness and seclusion, but goes with

us over the broad ocean of worldly business, only asking that it may stand a divine pilot at the helm. It lays no bar upon pleasure, tasted with an innocent moderation, — as the preacher himself, after being swept clean away by the gulf-stream of excess, solemnly judges it best to taste it, — but it converts pleasure itself from the foe into the friend and servant, as it well may be the true friend and faithful servant, of virtue. It does not condemn the acquisition of wealth as a means which may accomplish the very ends of religion; but it inquires with a searching whisper at the very confessional of man's spirit, and which, beside God, only the man himself can hear, whether the heart is given to wealth, delighting in it, hovering round and settling down over this sweetness of gain, which it would hive, with supreme habitual desire; or, on the contrary, as a steward regarding it as God's loan, as a worshipper proffering it for his sacrifice; while, on the wings of its chief and ardent aspiration, itself ever rises to him as the Infinite Good, takes the breath of his Spirit in return for the incense of its praise, and, from the elevation of its prayer, brings down the counsels of his majestic law upon its mortal conduct.

Have you discerned and adopted such an object of life, ye advancing men and women in the human generations? Are you pursuing such an object, or do ye drift towards eternity? They that drift are sure to be cast away; and only they are safe whose chart is large and complete, reaching to the farthest shore they must visit. Ye, too, that are young, have you stretched your thought, as you well may, to conceive that God gave you existence for a great object, which you may continually pursue by reverent, trustful doing of his revealed will? But we all, young, old, and middle-aged, have a surer proof than argument, or even Old-Testament authority. Jesus, our great exemplar, many hundreds of years after the author of our text, without the process of his embarrassing search, repeats and embodies his conclusion. He felt he was born for an object, "to bear witness to the truth." "He came eating and drinking;" but he said, his "meat was to do the will of him that sent him, and to finish his work." He, the sinless one, had a baptism of painful, perfecting experience to be baptized with; and how was he straitened, losing no time or strength by the way, till it should be accomplished! How he pressed on, without a deviation, through gladness and grief, entering into the marriage-festival, passing by the funeral bier, going with his disciples when they plucked the ears of corn, or bearing his cross alone, still on to the object of life and the end of his being! We talk much of his nature, and our relationship to him; but, my friends, when we follow him, then only do we truly commune with, or even understand, him. And we can see to follow him, only when the same master-light of religious duty illumines our path, and reveals the whole, however circuitous, track, through which Providence guides, as the nearest road to heaven.

So far as we surrender ourselves to this divine

leading, the problem that tried the sage king in Jerusalem, carrying him into the labyrinth of thought, and the still deeper labyrinth of dangerous practice, loses its perplexity. The object of life is disclosed more plainly as we proceed in reference to it, as the mountain on the landscape towards which we travel widens and heightens on our view. It is disclosed in the harmony and constant enlargement of the powers we use faithfully, in the growth of the holy affections towards God and man which we cherish, in the ever-easier reduction of all events and deeds to the great scope of our pious design, and in the stronger assurance, so thrilling to the human heart, that continually gains upon us, "refining as we run," of immortal expansion in a boundless sphere, to which our human life, with its preliminary culture and discipline, with its crosses and changes, delights and hopes, joys and desolating sorrows, will seem as fitted as one kingdom of matter is to another, as the whole world is to our mortal senses, or as the thought of God and the sentiment of duty are to the human soul.

DISCOURSE XXV.

NOW I KNOW IN PART.

1 Cor. xiii. 12. — NOW I KNOW IN PART.

THE Scriptures abound in reflections upon the weakness and short-sightedness of the human mind. Now, it is observable that the atheist and sceptic have taken up the strain of Scripture, and striven to turn its weapons against itself and its friends. " How blind and weak, how poor and miserable," they repeat, " the creature to whom you yet assign so splendid a destiny ! You speak of the immortality of this worm, as you yourself call him ; of this ignorant being, whose comprehension a grain of dust baffles ; this impotent being, whom heat and cold, light and darkness, wet and drought, play with and scorn ; this wretched being, whom sickness prostrates, and misfortune depresses, and sorrow dissolves in tears ; the most helpless of all creatures at his birth, the most unsatisfied of all through his life ; you prophesy for *him* ' glory and honor and immortality ! ' "

I accept the issue which atheism and infidelity thus present. I will reason for the magnificent prospects of man on the very ground here taken, of his weak-nesses and diseases, his griefs and fears. I will show that there is no incongruity in holy writ, when in one breath it tells of man's miseries and vanities, and in the next of his unending life and glories. For, " *I know in part :* " what does this mean, but that I have an idea of more knowledge than I actually possess, believe myself capable of greater acquisitions, and see the domain of wisdom stretching out beyond my present reach, and inviting my further pursuit ? Why be straitened in my limits, but that my true element is the unbounded ? Knowing so little, why not rest content with this small modicum ? Why, indeed, *know* that I am ignorant ? Ah ! it is this knowledge of my ignorance that contains the seed of my immortal aspiration. The brute, grazing in the field, is ignorant too, but dreams not of any insufficiency of information, aims at nothing more. But man's intellect puzzles itself ever upon new doubts and difficulties of investigation. Nor will I be sorry that there are points he cannot reconcile, questions he has reasoned upon for ages without settling, and sciences still imperfect and ill-understood. They are the promise of food for his eternal activity.

Could we glorify man's present spiritual advances, and celebrate the complete beauty of his intellectual furniture, the argument for immortality would not be so strong. We might think the mind had drunk its fill here, and accomplished its destiny. This crying at every point for something further and more is the very principle of its endless being. " Away, away ! "

exclaimed one on hearing a rich strain of music:
" thou tellest me of what in all my life I have not
found," pointing to a purer state of existence and
sensation.

The same argument might be pushed as to all the
limitations, sadnesses, and defects of our nature.
We will admit that the human being is everywhere
sadly incomplete, and nowhere has finished his
work.   There is, for example, truth in the melancholy lament so oft repeated at the death of friends.
They were interrupted in the midst of their useful-
ness.   They were taken away in " the dew of their
youth," or withdrawn in the increasing fruit of their
age.   They were stopped before the accomplishment
of their designs.   With what a wreck of plans and
hopes, enterprises and calculations, is the shore of
eternity strewn !   If the soul's measure be in this
weaver's shuttle of time, with no threads woven to
reach across the span of earth, death is untimely
and the tomb premature.

Look out upon all nature, and see the exquisite
perfection of every object there.   From the blade of
grass to the everlasting stars, there is no deviation
from the law of order or the line of beauty.   Everything is still, as at first it was pronounced, good.
Everything seems to accomplish its work, and fulfil
its design.   In the plant you see the end reached in
the unfolding of the petals, or the ripening of the
product.   There is nothing more to be wished or
expected, and no tendency to anything further, save
to drop the seed of the same species through suc-

cessive ages. In the animal there is a like definite organization, all its powers corresponding to the present world, or with only dim, uncertain signs of faculties suited to another. The same completeness appears in the globes on high, as they roll in precise orbits,

> " Forever singing, as they shine,
> The hand that made us is divine."

The astronomer detects no lawless course, no really, however for a time apparently, irregular or straying motion. So perfect is nature, from the fine dust of the balance to the revolutions of the sky.

But the human mind rises up the vast, lonely exception to this hair-breadth completeness of the world. Recognizer of the perfection of all things else, itself alone is imperfect. It is allowed on all hands to be imperfect. God and Christ, believer and infidel, demoniac tempter and good angel, here consent. It conceives of a knowledge transcendent. It conceives of a purity shaming its pollution. It conceives of a blessedness to which earth's joys are but glimpses of light and breakings in a stormy sky. Now God, the perfect One, deals not in fragments, like some weak human artist who may overlay the walls of his chamber with attempts at an entire beauty. This universe, the room he works in, is filled with perfect shapes, and tints all-beautiful. With him, however it may be with inferior artists, a part always implies the whole. But if this human soul, in the very beginning of its aspirings, in the unabated stress of its strivings, is to cease at death, then there is a fragment indeed, one colossal frustration and stupendous anomaly ; and that in the crown of nature, which God with his own hand has fashioned and set.   Man, whom he made the lord of the universe, is the broken column, while everything beside is whole !

It has been common with pious men, contemplating the excellent capabilities of the soul, to say it is greater than the material universe.   And it is a sober saying, alike a rational and scriptural judgment. For we may conceive of any part of visible nature as passing away.   It exists, not for its own sake, but as a servant.   And so the Bible speaks of the heavens being wrapped together as a scroll, and the elements melting with fervent heat ; while the human spirit, for which they were ordained, shall survive, witness of the dread dissolution.   It is a singular coincidence, that some modern astronomers have almost reached this very point.   Bringing immense distances into their field of view, upon data which it is needless for me to enumerate, they have supposed themselves to ascertain the gradual formation of distinct systems out of vast nebulous masses ; annexing the probability of their gradual decline too, as of flowers in the field, after each one shall have fulfilled the purposes of Him who calls them into being.   But what metaphysical astronomy, prying into the inner firmament, hath measured the capacity, what calculation hath predicted the orbit, what discernment hath detected the seeds of decay,

of the human soul? While the body is committed
" dust to dust," doth not that soul, from every high
power and affection, respond to Scripture, and cry
out, " From glory to glory "? Doth it not sit by
the broken sepulchre of Jesus, repeating his words,
" Whosoever liveth and believeth in me shall never
die "?

Were there any sign of the soul's filling out its
defects and putting away its limitations, the argument would be less strong. But its growth, marked
at any point, followed in any direction, requires still
a lengthened being. A late traveller observed in
the city of Jerusalem the fragment of an arch on the
wall of the temple ; and, tracing it according to the
principles of its construction, concluded it must have
been designed to spring as a bridge across the ad-
joining valley. So, if this little arc of the human
mind, which we can here trace, be constructed upon
true principles, it must mount over the dark valley
of the shadow of death, the stream of time must flow
away beneath it, while the course of an immortal
destination opens before it. Else, denying this, we
charge the Supreme Architect with fault.

I would, then, found an argument for immortality
on the apostle's declaration, "Now I know in part."
I would found it here, even in the unbeliever's scorn,
making atheism and infidelity themselves unwilling-
ly prophesy. I would found it here more strongly
than even in man's religious nature, simply considered. For, though man have a religious nature, yet,
could he become satisfied with its exercise, could he

30*

know as much of God and praise him as much as he desired here, and did he not long with this out-stretching desire to " dwell in the house of the Lord forever," his destiny might naturally conclude on earth. But when he pants for him more and more, would awake from the sleep of death " in his like-ness," and " drink of the river of God, which is full of water," the argument becomes irresistible. Even did I adopt Hume's philosophy of universal scepti-cism, I should still say, the intellect is *made* for truth, and must have time for its inquiry and doubt to end in the satisfactions of knowledge.

I know this is not the commonly accepted mode of reasoning. I know it is usual to draw religious argu-ments from man's positive abilities; but I would draw them from his vast defects. It is usual to draw them from his great triumphs: I would draw them from his signal failures. It is usual to draw them from his vigor and joy; but I would draw them from his weakness and grief. It is usual from his wide knowledge to predict a splendid destiny; but I would predict it from his wider ignorance. It is usual from his shining virtues to celebrate his end-less claims: I would see him lifting his moral victo-ries out of the abysses of conscious degradation, and observe his dignities springing from the depth of his decays. Even in the horror of death and anni-hilation, so peculiar to man, and unshared by the animal, I would see the sign of immortality. In the very sharpness of domestic grief, I would note a like indication. The brute parts from its companion

without a pang, or with but a brief and indistinct
sadness. But the days of man's mourning for the
dear departed are never accomplished. Wherefore,
but that the tie is in the undying soul? Rejoice, then,
that you do sorrow. Hope because you lament. If
you could commit the precious remains to the ground
without emotion, you would lose one token and proof
of your destination to an eternal being. Your very
sighs breathe of immortality; your groans preach it;
your funeral rites bespeak it. For truly has it been
said, " Man is a noble animal, splendid in ashes,
pompous in the grave."

The train of reflections to which our text has
led, accords with the whole tenor of Scripture.
The gospel of Christ speaks no flattering words to
our vanity; it paints in no high colors our powers
and acquirements. It rather digs beneath the high-
blown pride, fond fancy, and vain self-complacency
of the human soul, to lay the foundation of that
structure, which shall reach to heaven, in its feeling
of weakness, in its confession of ignorance, in its
sense of unworthiness, in its pangs of grief, and
prayers for Divine aid. These support its heavenward hopes, when the towering Babels of its proud
speculation have all crumbled away. Its infinite
expectations rise not from the transient forms of
human enjoyment and the fleeting plans of earthly
adventure, but from yonder beds of sickness, from
chambers of sorrow, and from the tombs. Yes,
build on the tombs, — the tombs, whose marble
walls hold the ashes of those you love and vene-

rate, whose dusty vaults of old fitly protected the worship, and nursed the eternal life, of the hunted followers of Christ. The pyramids, the grandest structures man has reared on earth, and pointing nearest to heaven, were tombs ; — so reared, were they not? with the obscure consciousness of immortality. As the portal and entrance to an infinite progress in virtue and joy, does not the tomb bear always, even on its dull and gloomy front, a charm of beauty beyond the richest and loftiest edifices which the hand of art can raise and adorn? In eastern lands there is a city of the dead, made up of graves carved in solid rock, enduring while the palaces and dwellings of famous towns have, under the trampling of change and revolution, sunk in ruin ; standing thus as a silent witness to the duration of the soul, while the material garment is dissolved. The sepulchre of Jesus, the most glorious fabric and solemn temple ever hewn by mortal hands, is the firmest basis of the imperishable hopes of humanity. You may support thoughts of eternity well and clearly on the low resting-places where lie the bodies of those at whose names your hearts still throb. You may inspire steady anticipations of heaven from sober reflection on your own not distant grave.

DISCOURSE XXVI.

AUTUMN: LIFE'S CONTRAST.

1 Pet. i. 24, 25. — FOR ALL FLESH IS AS GRASS, AND ALL THE GLORY OF MAN AS THE FLOWER OF GRASS. THE GRASS WITHERETH, AND THE FLOWER THEREOF FALLETH AWAY; BUT THE WORD OF THE LORD ENDURETH FOREVER.

THE form of thought here used illustrates a common principle in the operation of the human mind, — that principle of contrast by which one thing suggests its opposite. The withering grass and fading flower, emblems of the short life and declining glory of man, are mentioned only to have set over against them the word of the Lord that endureth forever. Life is made up of contrasts. In all things they vividly affect us, and are made to supply much both of our happiness and wholesome discipline. A sunny day after a dreary storm, or a bright flower wrought on a dark ground, excites an emotion, gives a delight, which we do not receive from uninterrupted sunshine, or from unrelieved ornament. Sickness imparts an exquisite sensation to returning health, which the uniformly robust cannot know; prosperity never shines so brilliant as on the retiring cloud of misfortune; sorrow gives birth to

a joy only the afflicted can taste ; and long fear and
anxious suspense end in a rapture, in the hour of
hope, which makes us almost think God had been
grieving only to make us happy. All the darkness,
indeed, of this world, is but to show off its light;
all its frailty, to direct us to almighty strength ; and
all its short-lived scenes, to prefigure what is undying and eternal.

The secret of this influence of contrast lies in
man's twofold nature, allied on the one side to the
frail and perishing, on the other to the stable and
enduring ; one hand grasping dust and ashes, the
other seizing upon the very throne of God ; the outward eye seeing only what fades and passes away,
the inward eye beholding glories which nothing can
destroy or dim. There is no season at which we are
more under the influence of the principle I have suggested, more in the mood of feeling indicated by the
text, than the fall of the year. The autumnal change
brings to mind at first only melancholy thoughts of
blight and decay. More persons are said to be
discouraged and dejected, to mourn over their ca-
lamities, and come to loathe life itself, in the dark
November, than at any other time. The frost smiting every green thing; the dull, heavy, weltering
storms fast succeeding one another; the sun lowering his mid-day track, altering his points of rising
and setting, and looking cold and askance upon the
gray earth ; all the life and beauty of nature laid low,
or with a death-like hue in the leaf not yet crumbled
into dust ; the ocean sending only a groaning sound

to the ear, as its waves are more frequently lifted by the strong wind ; the air pinching and inclement ; our bodies shrinking, and needing new guards, against the chill blast ; — all these things dispose the mind to think of loss and privation, of what vanishes and quits our hold. We are sad at the departing glory that leaves our earthly habitation so naked and desolate. The sepulchre, too, of man becomes a more distinct object to our view, as the flowers that were planted fade, and the leaves wither around it. Our dead appear to us, in outline more marked and impressive, drawn on the pensive and brooding imagination of the soul. We think of the coffin under ground, and of the dust mingling with its kindred dust. We feel more our own feeble tenure of life and nature ; and the grave, that has swallowed up so much, yawns for all that remains of existence, affection, and beauty in the world.

But God has not made us to despair. At the very point of the trouble, he provides the relief. This very tone of feeling or train of thought naturally, as in the apostle's mind, suggests the opposite, and turns the soul, by contrast, to what is firm and abiding. "But the word of the Lord endureth forever." There *is* something beyond the reach of change and decay and mortality, — God's truth, as it has been revealed to man ; God's word, which from the infinite, unfathomable heavens, he hath spoken ; God's promise, which by his Son he has made ; — this cannot fail. It will outlast all the forms of outward life, and all the splendors of nature ; and, though

heaven and earth pass away, it shall not pass
away.

The connection of the text makes it more em-
phatic. The apostle had been speaking of Christ's
resurrection, and of the faith and hope which this
fact excites; and he alludes to the wasting away of
all material things, so as to fix attention more joy-
fully on the soul's undying nature. He leaps from
the vessel, that is sinking with all earth's treasure in
the sea of time, to the firm shore of immortality.
Let the grass then wither, and the glory of man
fade away. God willing, we would not have the
present scene to be our permanent dwelling. We
desire not to live forever in this gate-way and vesti-
bule of God's wondrous creation, but would enter
into the interior vastness and amid the richer splendors of his universal temple, whose solidity and
endurance shall be as deep and sure as the forms
of this earthly abode and of these fleshly tabernacles
are frail and fleeting.

The transient and the abiding in the nature and
experience of man — this is, indeed, a contrast which
it well becomes us to consider. The great mistake
that human beings make is in regarding perishable
things as though they were imperishable, and so
fastening on them the feelings and expectations
which belong only to the imperishable. Christianity
does not forbid us to have any regard for what is
perishable and passing away. Jesus Christ brought
no ascetic religion into the world. He came eating
and drinking, looking with pleasure on the lily of

the field and on the whiteness of the harvest, glad-
dening the marriage-festival, as he turned water into
wine, and dignifying with his presence the social
table and endearing intercourse of domestic life.
Nor can one trace of any thing austere or morbid be
detected in his whole conversation and career. And
he does not bid us dig a cave, and hide ourselves from
all that is bright and gladsome around us, fleeting
though it be. He is not morose at human gaiety,
even though every sound of it must die away in the
grave ; nor misanthropic at aught of grace and
beauty that the eye can behold, though the moth
and worm shall quickly have it for their legacy.
But what he and his apostles insist on is, that we
shall graduate and proportion our interest in all
things according to their worth, making a right
valuation, bearing with a due interest on the passing
connections of time, yet resting our whole weight
only on what will surely to the end support us,
taking strongest hold of that we can keep hold of
forever. Do we not need this counsel ?

To put in its right light the contrast, I would bring
out, suppose some inhabitant of that upper world —
as it is thought departed spirits may — to lift the
curtain, and look in upon these scenes in which we
mingle. To one whose eye looks from his high station, how small and obscure this lower world, the
dim, narrow entrance-way to the more glorious
mansions of the Father's house! He knows that
authentic tidings of the great region, he dwells in,
have reached the ears of that crowd of mortals who

31

move along through this entry of the spiritual world. As the sickly generations of creatures advance, the angel-spectator scans the occupations in which they engage. What a thrill of amazement shoots through his breast to observe such multitudes living as though these narrow earthly steps to the great temple beyond were themselves the whole universe, studiously averting their eyes from the gate that leads to the immense splendors of the inner sanctuary, and spending all their thought and labor upon adorning and making comfortable the porch they are so rapidly passing through, strangely dreaming that they are not rapidly passing through it; and even working themselves into the practical belief, that they are not to pass through it at all; and, though the door of that eternal world is not for one moment at rest, as soul after soul, with instantaneous and uninterrupted succession, goes along, these ranks just in the rear, with astounding coolness, seeming busy only in putting around themselves all the fixtures of a permanent abode!

One is wholly absorbed in giving free scope to sense and appetite and superficial fancy, thinking only how the passing hour may be most filled with amusement, heedless of the concerns of the vast futurity, if the moment may but sparkle with pleasure; his whole course fitly symbolized by that of the man of whom we read, who delayed preparing a grave-stone, that he might finish a marble toy!

Another seems taken up entirely with swelling his

pile of gold. He bends steadily down over it, and, as he stoops, gives up the lustre of heaven for its glitter. He grudges every atom which benevolence begs from his heap. He smiles with new satisfaction at his increasing revenue, as his cheek grows evermore pale and his health withers, and employs his last feeble strength to drag his treasure to the very edge of his mortal term, where he slips suddenly down, and his riches remain coldly shining for his eye no more. What a contrast is this! The wealth of mind and heart, of ever-growing worship and love, given up as the mere purchase-money of his accumulated dross!

But yet another sight that angelic witness as surely beholds, and, oh! there is not a pleasanter sight beneath the sun than that of a man rich for this world and for the world to come; the favored son of fortune, but still more the humble child of God; his purse of gold not closed, but turned into the horn of plenty; his eye not hard to the suffering destitute, but soft with melting charity; his hand not shut with the avaricious grip, when religion asks aid to sustain her institutions, but lavish to every good cause; yea, of a man who rejoices, more than an old alchemist over the supposed discovery of the philosopher's stone, at the opportunity to transmute his temporary into everlasting treasure. Here surely the principle is illustrated aright in a contrast just and holy.

This, then, without further illustration, is the lesson of our text. Be not deceived in your estimate.

Distinguish the things that differ. Observe the contrasts that God has established. Is the New Testament true ? Shall these great scenes of judgment
and doom, of weal or woe, according to the deeds
of the flesh, be soon ushered in ? Make not, then,
the enormous miscalculation of leaving so vast an
element out of your account. Even in this life, the
contrast between things earthly and things heavenly
sometimes demonstrates itself in striking results.
The distinct consequences of diverse characters are
especially marked, as men advance in life towards old
age ; and the rewards and retributions already bestowed seem to anticipate the judgment-day. With
the old man whose aims have been worldly alone,
see how object after object that has engaged him
fails, or the passions that sought them are worn out ;
and the wearied, uninterested soul, having laid hold
of nothing but what was sublunary and crumbling,
lingers out the wretched remainder of earthly existence, with fading hope and declining strength, weak,
objectless, irritable, and remorseful, to an ignoble
end ! How different the case of the old man who,
through all his pilgrimage of years, has trusted the
word of God, has believed in the realities it reveals,
and has acted with daily reference to them ! His
faltering footsteps but indicate his drawing near to
where the road rises up to heaven. The whiteness
of his hair seems to come but from the light of that
glorious world, falling more directly upon him. His
ever-increasing affections contradict the infidel's idea,
that mental decline runs parallel with bodily decrepi-

tude. An earthly crown of glory is placed on his hoary head, prophetic of that which God shall place to rest there forever.

As I walked through the lanes of yonder growing forest, on our beautiful common, the dry leaves crushing under my feet, and the sinking sun taking his last look at the bare boughs of the trees, I met a man on whom the blow of grief had descended as sorely as upon any, and with oft-repeated stroke. A new sorrow had just fallen on his gray head, and long-diseased, emaciated frame. While I approached, he was slowly eying the setting sun. As he turned his face towards me, I looked to see the marks of deep, uncomforted sadness wearing mournfully in upon his features. But no: not a trace of trouble in that eye which had so often looked on death in the forms of those he had most loved. His vision gleamed as though a light beyond that of the setting sun had fallen upon it. He spoke; and now, thought I, the secret melancholy will peradventure come forth, and mingle in the tone, though this unnatural excitement be kindled in the eye. No: pleasant was the voice, without one plaintive note. He spoke of faith. He spoke of loyalty to God and duty. He spoke of heaven as though it were near. He said nothing of being hardly dealt with, nor hinted aught about not understanding why *he* should be selected for such trials, but seemed to think there was nothing but God's mercy and kindness in the world. He bore a staff to support his drooping limbs. But he seemed to me, as I looked upon him, to have an inward stay that would hold him up when all earthly props had fallen to the ground. He was a Christian believer; and, though prospered of God in this world, he said, "The riches we think so much of gathering together, are nothing in comparison with the better portion that rich and poor alike may attain." We parted; and as I walked alone again among the fading, rustling leaves, which had been expounding to me the text of this discourse, they took up new eloquence of meaning. The bare, cold ground, the gray, chilly sky, and the long shadows, that told of the lengthening night, seemed beautiful — yes, pleasant and beautiful — to my soul; more beautiful even than the herbage and balm, and long, long sunny hours of the enlivening spring. For once, the contrast between earth and heaven was revealed to my mind; and the dissolving emblems of mortality under my feet, and the cold, shifting mists over my head, were transformed from sad tokens into symbols of hope and joy.

So let the season speak, not mournfully but cheeringly, to our hearts. Let gladness breathe upon us in the sigh of the autumnal breeze, and consolation be traced for us in the furrows of the dead, exhausted earth. Let all that is dark and disappointing in this world but set off the brightness and expectation of heaven. Let the gloom that settles down over our earthly scenes and prospects be but the background of a splendor from the sun that never sets. Then shall we turn the principle of contrast, which God has so wisely inwrought into the constitution of our minds, to its true, intended use. Successive seasons and years shall but find us farther advanced on the way to a blessed destiny. And when the curtain of death is drawn over our eyes, as the curtain of night over the landscape, like that curtain it will reveal above more glory than it conceals below.

DISCOURSE XXVII.

RECORD OF THE YEAR.

Ezra vi. 2. — AND THERE WAS FOUND A ROLL, AND THEREIN WAS A
RECORD THUS WRITTEN.

THE record here referred to was of what had been
done for the house and service of God. It was a
religious record, such as I propose we should now
read of the past year. The recorder and the actors
concerned in that ancient memorial, the parchment
that was unrolled to be read, and the so solid and
splendid temple it described and celebrated, have all
sunk under that monument of dust which outlasts
all monuments of marble and brass, and have left
no tangible relic or remembrancer on earth but this
sentence of our text, written on a frail leaf, though
a leaf perishable only in the last fire. Records and
recorders of mighty and mean events have, for more
than two thousand years, fallen beneath the same
wasting mortal fate ; the space since they flourished, occupied in the world's history, being but a
space, so far as they are concerned, in eternal destiny. We, in our turn, stand up awhile on this
little plot of ground, to read from the book of our

experience ; hoping in God's mercy, that, by what the finger of his providence has written on our past condition and action, we may be made wise to eternal life.

Records are made of changes, of what is altering from day to day in that great empire of change, of which we are all subjects. This law of change is often considered and spoken of as a melancholy law, a dreadful necessity stretched over us, ordaining that no lot we attain to can long abide, but we must be unfixed from every quiet posture, and hurried on by a remorseless hand to an untried condition. But is this an unhappy doom ? No : it is the decree of growth and progress. It is the ordinance of escape from old limitations, and the impulse of rising to new stages of life, to gain, as we are dislodged from our nests of ease and comfort, fresh energy of thought and will ; continually nearing the grave indeed, but travelling, if faithful in the use of our privileges, towards an existence to which this is but lowness, poverty, and distress. A state of sameness and immobility would be, in truth, a wretched doom. Nor is the record of any year, which we may read together, a record of sadness or decay alone, even as respects this world, but very much of delight and advancement.

Its first opening chapter, that I shall venture to read to you, is a large one, of blessed meaning. It is of new being, birth and growth. Not with careless levity of feeling, but with all the solemnity of devout regard, it is to be noted how many houses, during this year, have been made the scenes of holy gladness by the gifts of God's creative and inspiring power. What trust so great to our hands as that of a living spirit, with its own individual nature, distinguished from all other rational intelligences, and with capacities for a peculiar development of intellectual and moral strength ; in short, a new character in the universe of God, and a fresh candidate for immortality ! With what a reverent, sober, trembling sense of responsibility it should be received ! What office that men crave and strive for is so high in rank, so great in opportunity, so large in patronage, or susceptible of good, with such hope and fear, promise and menace, wrapped up in it, as this parental office ! What expanding of outward nature, or unfolding of earthly policy and ambition, is really so grand and affecting as that of an undying soul ; as we see intellectual animation flow by such subtle degrees into the countenance, and ever-added expression beam from the features ; as thought wakens after thought, and feeling after feeling, to take their place among the lines and motions of every trait and member ; as the will plays, it may be at first rashly and capriciously, with its new-found, but soon to be mighty sceptre, on its little throne in that slender breast ; as the kind affections come out to cling to us and tame childish waywardness, while the conscience, too, begins to assert its lordship, and the dawning idea of God, the greatest that can visit the mind of man or archangel, with its majestic authority, subdues disobedience to the laws of righteousness and truth !

No changes of material growth, of splendid seasons and solemn spectacles, can equal this.   The
record is not on paper only, or in the friendly observer's eye, but within our throbbing breasts.   It
is a record of overrunning and unspeakable gratitude for what no publicity celebrates, no mention
attempts to do justice to, and no stranger intermed-
dles with.   Day by day lengthens it out.   It makes
the purest inspiration of love ; it turns self-sacrifice
into a pleasure ; it converts watching into rest ; it
plies the inventive faculties with all knowledge and
wisdom to provide for the beloved object ; it draws
the mind into long foresight of its benefit and improvement ; and, by the force of mingling filial and
parental communications, exalts the soul to a perception of the relation of all to Him who is the
common Father.

Life's record, then, as we read it, is not all of
gloomy change, of dwindling strength, of wan and
pining existence, and irreparable privation, but of
strength enhancing, existence renovating, and of
new possession.   The cradle overbalances the grave ;
and even that feeble hand, stirring so faintly in it,
points through the tomb, threatening, as with gigantic might, to turn its dark portals for the entrance
of that which is life only and forever.   The record
of birth and growth — while we read it, let our
fidelity and Christian training secure that it shall
be a record, not of dishonor and sin, but of increasing virtue with increasing years.   And let the sacred
dedication we may make of our offspring to God

and Christ beneath the roof of the public or the private sanctuary, by our sincerity and steady conspiring with its purport, be indeed a rite of blessed influence and inextinguishable hope.

But I must turn this bright, this illuminated leaf of the record, on which I have lingered so long, to a page veiled in shades, perused by the dim light of darkened windows at curtained bedsides ; read not aloud, but in the whispers of those who tread with noiseless footsteps. It is the record of sickness and decline. "Behold he whom thou lovest is sick," was the message of the sisters to Jesus. And how simple, yet heart-moving, a message to us all ! coming the oftener as our circle of kindred and friendship is wider, and calling us to minister with such words of comfort and preparation as we may to those languishing in pain and disease, under the cloud of dim uncertainty whether life is to fade away, or brighten again into a new lease of years.

This is a record of change, indeed ! The vigorous frame, of late so erect and sprightly, now prostrate ; the eye that beamed and pierced with such lightness of movement and spontaneous force, as though the immaterial spirit in very truth had there in it the seat which has been vainly sought for, now heavy and lustreless ; the elastic limb relaxed ; the firm and rapid utterance clogged, and broken into dull and lifeless tones, expressive only of a faint or wandering mind ; and all the forces of nature expended in a struggle against the unbracing powers of decay ; — this is a dark and ill-boding altera-

tion, going on in many a chamber we pass, thoughtless of the agony it may hold. And what shall we
say of this change ? We cannot make our record
all pleasant and cheerful if we would. The skele-
ton, that the Egyptians carried to their banquets,
will intrude upon every feast of our earthly joy,
and fling its ghastly shadow both across the avenues
of our immediate thought, and along the vistas of
our farthest recollection. But, my friends, I shrink
not from the reading of this record, too. I fear not
to hold it up in the light of God's providence and
plain designs, and read all it contains. I have seen
too much the gracious work that sickness, with all
her sharp instrumentalities, does, to wish to close
my eyes on, or pass slightly over, her entries in the
book of life. She is the angel who comes not alone
and unattended to the body and soul of man. Herself dark, she comes with a bright retinue. Patience,
resignation, spiritual thoughts of God and of futurity, come with her. Penitence, flying back over
the past, yet the pardoning mercy of the gospel
flying with her, and shedding rays of heaven on
her mournful way ; resolution, pluming herself for
a better course ; good affections to the Father above,
and the brethren around, often unfolding more strong
and tender than they had ever done before in health ;
these are the attendant spirits and close companions
of sickness, to whose presence and precious agency
we can all testify. And so this page of our record
shall be to us no page of fell chance or dark misfortune, but written with the finger of God, not in the

train of outward circumstances merely, but, for enduring instruction, on the tables of the heart. For
as the most blazing effulgence of heaven sleeps
within the black cloud, so in this lowering darkness
and eclipse of bodily suffering often lies the very
brilliance of a spiritual and divine glory.

But we must read still further, as we turn the last
leaf of our record. It ends, like all earthly records,
with death. This is the final word of every one's
known history. For how many, during the year
that is now closing, that final conclusion has been
made! Elder forms and infancy, youth and maturity,
childhood and manhood, from the broken cords of
every kindred relationship, have been let down into
the grave. The list of the departed falls under my
eye. And is this brief register all that remains of
those that occupied such room in our daily life and
religious associations? All shrunk to this cold statement, and these scanty lines? The presence, the
countenance, the greeting, the long, friendly converse, the co-operation in kindly arrangements and
benevolent plans, all reduced to a cold catalogue of
names and years? What a change, indeed! how
great! how deplorable! The new-comer from the
eternal regions, that made a revolution in the house,
greater and happier than that in kingdoms and dynasties, gone again with how speedy return! Infirm,
yet honored age, more loved and cared for, the
more it lingered, the centre of the domestic picture,
at length retiring; the very head, unity, and soul of
the family seems lost. Fond companionship, for

which all the nearer ties of life seem ordained, has fled, leaving some sad and weary to grope along their path alone. With each extinguished existence, what a light has gone out! what a fountain has been sealed up! what a music of the heart has ceased forever on earth!

How take off the burden of sadness that settles down on a record like this? God, my friends, by his Son Jesus Christ lifts up even this burden. He lifts it up in the assurance that they are not dead, though their mortal frames are dissolved; that they are not silent, though by our dull ears their voices are unheard. They praise him yet, though not in the faint tones of this our humble worship. Their virtues live and grow, still sacred in his care, though canonized in no human calendar. Nay, they are not only themselves immortal, but they keep alive, or create, the faith and sense of immortality in our hearts. They have made a path with their feet into the blessed land: they have filled up and bridged over with their hallowed dust the separating gulf from time into eternity. To the meditative and prayerful soul, they send back their appeal. Being dead in the body, they yet speak for truth and goodness with louder tone and more persuasive pathos than when their words fell on our outward hearing. They have gone, that they might awaken our virtue. They have gone, that they might chill and discourage our worldly lusts. They have gone, that, from their purer, spiritualized being, they might sanctify our motives, and touch with a thrilling and arousing, though invisible, hand our better nature. Like the mysterious stars, though with a warmer attraction, they lift and beckon us up. The light burns on, the fountain flows, the music sounds for us.

Neither, then, is this final change and record in the providence of God the ground for lamentation and repining. It is rather the declaration of our native dignity as his children. It is the announcement of our glorious destiny. It is a call to us to live worthy of that destiny, and not forfeit our heavenly birthright. It is a summons to us to gird up our loins, trim our lamps, watch, and be ready.

DISCOURSE XXVIII.

ETERNAL LIFE.

John vi. 54. — WHOSO EATETH MY FLESH, AND DRINKETH MY BLOOD, HATH ETERNAL LIFE.

1 John v. 13. — THAT YE MAY KNOW THAT YE HAVE ETERNAL LIFE.

IT has been said, that the single word *eternity* could not be justly pronounced in a congregation of persons, without its sensibly affecting them; the human soul having a native attraction to its vast and solemn significance. It first instantly lifts the mind to God, translates it from this fleeting scene to a calm and solid state beyond the waves of earthly tumult, shaken no more by human passions than the upper air and the silent stars are by the dust and turmoil of the earth. Yet eternal life is not in the Scriptures limited to God as an incommunicable attribute or essence, nor to the angels even, as a possession shut up within the walls of heaven; but is spoken of as something that may be conveyed to and shared with men.

What, then, is this eternal life which we are called to "lay hold on"? To most persons, the chief meaning of *eternal* seems to be continuance without end, simply lasting through a limitless succession of seasons and times. But surely it is not because God has lived, or is to live, through such a succession ; because he has passed over an immense series of ages, and sees other huge intervals stretching before him, that he is eternal. No such accumulation of years or centuries could make eternity. It is not made up of time. The very idea of time is suggested by what is material, changeful, and perishing. On precisely the opposite account, God is eternal, because his life is *not* measured by days or years, but "a thousand years are as one day, and one day as a thousand years." He lives in "the dateless and irrevoluble circle of eternity."

So, again, we believe that, to the blessed spirits before Him, there is no such change as our day and night, summer and winter. Our measures of existence do not hold with them. Heaven is an eternal morning ; heaven is an unfading spring. Birth and death, outward growth and decay, waxing and waning moons, mark not that glorious life, nor break that peaceful, soul-felt progress. Should we reach that holy rest, we shall need no more the hands of the clock, or the shadows on the dial-plate, to mark the divisions and periods of our existence. We shall live, not the life of mere time, but of eternity. What, then, the question again arises, is this life of eternity, if it be not simply a life ever extending in unlimited degrees ? I answer, that eternal life is the life of the spiritual nature, the life of sentiment and affection, of moral and religious principle. Indeed, in the New Testament, many phrases might equally

well be translated either *eternal* or *spiritual life;*
as, for example, " No murderer hath eternal life,"
hath spiritual, holy, religious, divine life, "abiding
in him." No murderer hath the life of love, of God,
of duty, abiding in him. This evidently is the
meaning. It is remarkable how often eternal life is
spoken of in the present tense.

Moreover, that eternal life is not simply enduring,
or literally and only everlasting life, is plain, because
we never speak of the devil and his angels as having
eternal life, though it is supposed in our theology
they have a life that endures through all the future,
contemporaneously with that of Divinity and seraph.
The bad surely do not live the eternal life, though
they have before them the same unbounded prospect
of existence with the good. Theirs is a state of
eternal or spiritual death. When the good affections
shall be waked up in them towards God and man,
when a pure rectitude shall have become their law,
and disinterested desires for purity and peace their
inspiration, then only will they have that eternal life.
No otherwise could they have it, though countless
æons of duration should circle over their heads, till
the sun's lamp were burned out, and every measure
and instrument of time were broken. Eternal life in
God is the life of absolute goodness, purity, rectitude,
and truth. Eternal life in man is the life of justice
and love, of fidelity in all his relations. It is a right,
holy, and becoming life. There is thus deeper meaning than is commonly suspected in that ancient sentence of the Bible, " Honorable age is not that which

standeth in length of time, nor that is measured by
number of years; but wisdom is the gray hair to
man, and an unspotted life is old age." When
we are elevated above selfish and trifling cares into
noble thought and generous feeling, our life, so far
from having the character of a life that simply endures or is to endure for a long succession of time,
seems no longer concerned with time at all, but to
have risen above it. In this exalted frame, when we
are contemplating the Infinite Excellence, when the
wings of adoration bear us up, when a pure flame
of devotion to the will of God and to the good of
man burns in our breast, and when righteous purposes of magnanimity and self-sacrifice form in this
inner sanctuary, the hours hang not heavy on our
hands, but pass unnoted by. Time, which, when we
steadily regard it, moves slowly, now flies and disap-
pears. Eternity is present; and eternal life, the life
of God, stirs and glows in the heart. Days and
weeks are no longer the terms of our existence;
but thoughts, emotions, dictates of conscience, impulses of kindness, and aspirations of worship, —
these make the eternal life, because we feel there is
something really fixed and impregnable in them,
which neither time can alter, nor age wrinkle, nor the
revolutions of the world waste, nor the grave bury,
but the eternity of God alone embrace and preserve.
In the language of the beloved apostle, "We know
that we have eternal life," not look forward to and
expect it, but already possess the principle that cannot die. As God chooses for the most expressive

title by which he can be described, "I AM," and required his servant to say, "I AM hath sent thee," showing forth his eternity not as a mere prolongation of time, but as existing every instant; as He is not to *be*, but ever is eternal; so the eternal life in the souls of his children has a present and immediate character. It is felt every moment. Time, whose intervals of weeks and years, to the little child with undeveloped powers, seem very long, and one day of which may to the insect be as considerable as our whole life, — as our energies of thought and affection are brought out more and more, — continually contracts its spaces, and threatens wholly to vanish away. We are possessed with those realities which

> —— " have power to make
> Our noisy years seem moments in the being
> Of the Eternal Silence.
> Though inland far we be,
> Our souls have sight of that immortal sea
> Which brought us hither,
> Can in a moment travel thither,
> And see the children sport upon the shore,
> And hear the mighty waters rolling evermore."

It is true, that in that life, as in the absolute and perfect Spirit of God, is involved also the quality of permanence. The pure, loving, righteous, and devoted heart feels its own imperishableness. Its immortality is secretly whispered to it in a great assurance. The Spirit bears witness with it to its incorruptible nature. The dust claims no kindred with it. The elements ask not to dissolve it. Inwardly alive, essentially vital, it "says," not "to corruption, 'Thou art my father,'" nor "to the worm, 'Thou art my mother and sister;'" but is conscious of a bond with the Almighty Parent, and has its pledge, security, and irrefragable tenure of life in his love, in his very being. Yea, day and night may come and go; the seasons may change through their annual rounds; the mortal frame may grow old and decay, and generation after generation pass along; but that filial heart, in harmony with the holy One on High, shall not decline or wither, but ever advance, and swell in its communings of immeasurable worship and joy with its Inspirer and Source. Nor shall the everlasting hills stand, nor the mighty rivers flow, nor yonder brightest star in the crown of night sparkle, so long as it shall love and adore. Even here, rising above the earth, "nor feeling its idle whirl," it shall vindicate its superiority to all that is material, as it drops the flesh, and takes the celestial body.

But the heavenly and indissoluble life begins in this world. Jesus Christ had it here. For who thinks of him as any more immortal after his resurrection and ascension than before? He had his eternal life in the clay, and bore it about in the world, as "the candle of the Lord" shining in human dwellings with the same lustre which it should cast through the upper mansions. Jesus Christ, the only perfect possessor on earth, is accordingly the great and incomparable communicator, of this eternal life. To him, especially and above all, we are to go for it.

So certainly did he himself know that he was its fountain, so clearly did he see his disciples' dependence on him for it, so well did he understand that no other principles than those he taught could impart it, that, in a metaphor of almost unparalleled boldness, he declared to them, "Except ye eat the flesh of the Son of man, and drink his blood, ye have no life in you. Whoso eateth my flesh, and drinketh my blood, hath eternal life." His doctrines and precepts, his mind and temper, what was most vital and spiritual in his soul and conduct, are to be taken up as food by our inward hunger and thirst, and incorporated with the inmost frame of thought and motive and disposition. Then will be unfolded and experienced the proper "eternal life;" the life not employed and expended upon the outward world, like that of animal instinct, but retiring into a holy rest and safe refuge from all material working and decay; the life which is akin, and knows it is akin, to that intelligence, justice, goodness, which, abiding immutable at the centre of all, forever as a glorious luminary rays out beams of light and life to countless ranks of happy creatures, — creatures clad like us in these perishing robes of matter, or advanced into the lines of cherubim above; but all feeling, though in different measure, the same eternal life.

So, too, looking down from those rising orders of blessedness into the empire of darkness and antichrist, the eternal death or punishment spoken of in the New Testament has not sole or primary reference to the mere duration, but to the nature, of the lost soul's evil doom. It is death in the spiritual frame, man's nobler part, or, as the Scriptures elsewhere express it, being "dead in trespasses and sins." It is not a hideous, arbitrary torment, unmercifully inflicted through periods without end. It is the insensibility, inactivity, sleep, stupor, of those affections that seek the Invisible, and rise heavenward. These being overlaid by worldliness, overridden by the passions, and left, through dull unconsciousness and cold neglect, in the lonely, unfrequented, tomb-like places of the heart; while the love of gain, of pleasure, and of earthly power, spurs hotly on; the eternal, spiritual, or, as it is sometimes called, second death has place. It is not something to occur in, or be imposed by, a future retribution alone. Here and now, all around us, it enters into the sinful breast; and palsy and dumb forgetfulness pass over and penetrate every generous desire and capacity for real excellence; a numbness of heart and soul, to endure coeval with the ill temper and conduct which are its cause, in a connection locked fast and forever.

How pass from this worst, this real death, unto life! "The way," if not the only way God has ever revealed to his children, yet the way for us chosen, and the best ever opened in the world, is intimacy of faith and love with Jesus Christ. He who is, as we have seen, the great communicator of spiritual life, is also the Restorer and Redeemer to resuscitate and raise the dead. Those that are in the graves of sin, hearing his voice, will come forth.

Those who, feeding on the husks of the prodigal, have pined and starved, will, by eating his flesh and drinking his blood, revive. Their sunken spirits, assimilating the bread from Heaven, will become alert and rejoicing in the divine, the eternal life. In him is that eternal principle, derived from God, above the world, triumphant over time, commanding its past as well as coming cycles ; so that in its infinite majesty he could stand, look back over thousands of years, and say, " Before Abraham was, I am ; " while, as he looked forward too, the bars of death broke, and the gates of heaven flew open, at his glance.

They who have kept his company, and breathed in that eternal principle from his spirit, have the same pervading reality and consciousness of life ; even as the material elements of bread and wine from his table, flowing through every circulation of the body, are an emblem of those with which he, the moral Enlivener of the world, quickens the soul. Before this eternal life, the outward and temporal death, so terrible and absolutely destructive to the sensualist and the worldling, lowers its ensigns of victory, and loses in a flitting shadow all its power. I have seen the face pale and worn with consumption, ready to yield all that was of the flesh as the prey of the boastful conqueror, yet serene and smiling, with the sense gleaming out there of something that conqueror could not touch ; with a beaming of Christ-like expression, as the pledge of alliance with him to whom, as we read in his own language, it had

33

been "given to have life in himself;" the immortal
soul itself almost visible through the thin spiritual
features, and preparing to fly, and leave in the last
enemy's hands only a little dust and ashes for all his
spoils.   Verily, we may say with the apostle, "This
is the true God, and eternal life." Yea, this is the
assurance of an existence stable, though the earth
burn, and the heavens be wrapped together as a
scroll.   This is the title to a seat among the elders
of the Most High.

Shall this spiritual or eternal life become at length
universal throughout the intelligent and moral creation ?   From different denominations of believers,
this question would receive various or opposite
answers.   Some would maintain, that the restitution
of all things, and the subjection of all things to God,
which are spoken of in the Scriptures, mean nothing
less than the salvation of every individual soul, and
the complete harmony of the moral world.   Others,
on the same basis of holy writ, contend for a doom
of endless woe to a large portion of the souls of
men ;   implying, of course, a literally everlasting
repugnance between God and Satan, saint and demon, the powers of good and the powers of evil.
Still a third party, on the ground of God's word,
connected perhaps with the reasonings of their
minds and the humanity of their hearts, hold that
there is to be an annihilation of the wicked, and
admit the perfect triumph of good in this way.

The theme is perhaps too great for the comprehension of the human mind, nor is it even by the light

of inspiration so cleared up that we can hope for an entire agreement respecting it among equally wise and good men. To the idea of a spotless purity and painless bliss in the whole universe, many would object, that it is but the spiritual Utopia of a sentimental fancy, that it merges the claims of justice in the feeling of a weak fondness, and makes of God's pure love a weak, doting sensibility; that it overlooks the incalculable and perhaps interminable purposes of suffering in the Divine providence; that it exchanges a moral freedom for a somewhat mechanical and necessary joy; and, in general, exercises too boldly the "liberty of prophesying" as to the actual condition of things which may obtain at any fixed point in the works and among the creatures of God. To the doctrine of hopeless torment it may be objected, that it is a contradiction of the Divine goodness; that even the Divine rectitude, which the doctrine magnifies, is affronted by the supposition that God should suffer the whole existence of any being he has created to be a curse; that the will of man, though having the ability to choose, is yet a pendulum that must somehow swing in an arc of God's own power; and that, on the psalmist's principle that the great Maker's " work is perfect," we cannot admit in his greatest work, the human soul, any hopeless check or irretrievable ruin. In fine, to the theory of annihilation it may be replied, that, for the soul of a man to fall, like a fruitless flower, would be a baffling of the Almighty in the failure of his most serious design ; that, while in the uni-

verse a grain of dust is never lost, or a particle of
light or heat extinguished, it is absurd to imagine
the absolute destruction of reason, conscience, and
love in an individual soul ; and that, though in the
hypocrite and sensualist, the spiritual principle
seems lost in empty falsehood and the dissoluble
flesh, and ready to disappear in the senseless clod,
yet even in them it is not wholly dead, but, by
right applications, may be relumed to burn again in
token of an essential immortality, and rekindle our
conception of something which the dust of the
valley cannot cover, but the air of heaven forever
fan and sustain.

Such considerations at these several points of view,
hinting how difficult, if not impossible, it is for us at
present to decide this matter to the conviction or
satisfaction of all, present at least a dissuasive from
dogmatism, and teach us that we should not take
any opinion on such a subject for the primary article
of our creed. Better is it that we should, by all the
motives and sanctions, hopes and fears, of the gospel,
try to awaken the moral and spiritual nature in our
own and in others' hearts, than that we should exercise the fancy with predicting the fortunes to arise in
the coming ages. It is enough to show, that the
horrible hypothesis of a predetermined, ceaseless
anguish to individual souls, either for their natural
bias or for their temporary transgression, is groundless ; while we suggest an interpretation of sacred
language in which the wise and good of different
names may unite, without doing violence to God's

word, or to his oracle of truth and mercy in their own hearts. The doctrine of everlasting torments seems peculiarly to have distinguished the theology which has prevailed in this country : a fact prominent, to mention nothing else, in the debates of the late Evangelical Alliance. The adoption and able re-statement among us of the great and good John Foster's well-known repudiation of this doctrine will do much, we may hope, to modify and improve the popular belief. Meantime, as followers of Christ, we may well affirm, that his own treatment of outcasts and sinners admonishes us not to despair of our kind, or of any fellow-creature, but with all our might to apply the divine truth and love to the regeneration of the world ; to hope and strive that the eclipsing cloud of evil may pass away before the light, the rebellious war of sin find its prophetic end of peace, and every discord which it has introduced die at last in the hallelujahs of the redeemed.

Do not the actual triumphs of Christ's church in the kingdom of darkness encourage the hope of such a consummation ? When one who has been the subdued and fallen victim of appetite, or the sorely beset, though flying, object of its pursuit, yet, by the grace of God, rises, resists and repels the foe ; when we see in the eyes of such a one, instead of a sensual, unholy gaze, the look of eternal rest and the light of celestial serenity, and hear from his lips, not the profligate or passionate word, but that speech of heavenly truth which is the very soul and expression of harmony ; when the tribulation of iniquity and of

33*

present avenging circumstance breaks and wears for
him a path into the kingdom of God, and the robes
that were stained with pollution are washed "white
in the blood of the Lamb;" then, seeing what God,
through his Son, can do, must not our hearts be forgiven for swelling with a boundless expectation?

Nay, has not the most remorseful personal experience shown the demon of despair chased away before
God's angel of hope? Musing on my condition as
a creature of the Infinite Might, I walked forth amid
the beauty and grandeur of the world. The order
around me seemed to rebuke the chaos not yet
wholly banished from my soul. Law, fulfilled at
every point whither my eye could rove, appeared to
raise its menacing finger, and point at law violated
in my wishes and designs. The pervading purity,
cleansing so soon into sweetness every spot of earth's
corruption, warned me of the stain that lingered on
my imagination, and sunk into my heart. The sublime equity, the overflowing bounty, all around,
stung me with the memory of every wrong or ungenerous act. Feeling my weakness, conscious of my
sin, out of harmony with my situation so magnificent
among the works of God, and but so feebly connected with those works, I fell into melancholy and
vague alarm. "How unworthy," I exclaimed,
"and how insignificant is my being! As a fly
creeps by the hollow valves of his feet along the
ceiling, so alone cling I to the creation. Or, as I
gaze from the green and wooded land over the blue
and misty sea, my life, like a diffused breath or odor,
seems gliding off, through the vast expanse, to

oblivion and loss of self in nature or Deity. So the guilty and contemptible jar of my will with the frame of things shall be swallowed up and disappear." But from this self-reproach, from this dumb forgetfulness of my being, and pantheistic absorption in superior Power, a voice of God in the heart, and through the gospel, out of the miraculously parted and unveiled heavens, wakes me. It declares, "Thou art a child of my family. I have made, I have inspired and taught thee. Call no man father on earth, as thou so callest me in heaven. Beyond thrones and principalities runs back thy lineage. Further, too, than any mortal descent, runs forward my gracious purpose concerning thee. I have spoken to thee by my beloved Son. As thou repentest and believest, will I forgive and accept thee. Clothe thyself in the dignity becoming my offspring. So will I preserve thee in the changes of nature, prolong thy being through all the forces of wasting and desolation, and nourish the spirit that is in thee from my breath, even unto eternal life."

Is this an imaginary voice, or one which has been really heard in many an erring heart? Is there a breast so obdurate that it must forever exclude, or so insensible that it can never come to heed it? Do the passions within any make such a noise, that, in no lull of their tempest, they will hearken to God? Can a worldly mind so close up and fortify our bosom, that, with the call for our surrender, he finds, in his holy siege, no listening ear, or avenue of approach? Is self an usurper too strong and boastful to yield the throne to the command of its rightful

king ? or is sense the blind wall through which even
the divine glory may not pierce, or the message of
grace and pardon sound ? Is there not in every
breast a holy apostate from the powers of evil, who
can be reached by this tempting offer, accept this
precious invitation of eternal life, and open the way
to the universal triumph of Divine love ?

Let those, however, who affirm such a triumph,
beware lest they forget that it consists in a moral, not
in a sensual, life and salvation. It is a comparatively
low end for us to come at last to enjoy ourselves,
and be perfectly happy. Our nature, in its nobler
aspirings, owns not, but scorns, such an aim. It
demands, beyond passive bliss, a sphere of exertion, duty, and self-devotion. Pleasure is but
incidental ; progress is proposed ; and any views
are injurious which would sink, even upon the line
of farthest futurity, the prominence of this sublime
endeavor. Heaven is no plain or valley, but an
upland region ; and our joy is to be in climbing its
everlasting hills. The heroic martyr-spirit waives
not, but claims, all the preliminary toil and agony
that could fit it for the glad ascent. Even the guilty
heart, in true self-knowledge, asks not to be excused
from that purging fire whose rage is not quenched
while any inner fuel remains. It would not have
the heavy consequences of its impurity carried away,
but bear its own load ; and, by its expiation of sin,
and satisfaction of justice, be nerved for holy achievements ; blessing God in Christ for its deliverance,
not from the results, but from the very essence, of
iniquity. Only a low carnal sentiment fixes its

regard on felicity and luxury, even though it were
the felicity and luxury of the soul's exalted imaginations and thoughts, as the heavenly portion and heri-
tage upon which we are to enter. Our rest above is
not sleep or indolence, but divine, harmonious effort.
The song and harp there are not the mere utterance
of sweet voices, and the twanging of melodious
strings; but our very action shall be music, and our
life a hymn. God's own love to us in this world is
not a feeble indulgence of our inclinations, and hu-
moring of our childish desires. It is no fond wish,
but an eternal principle. It dispenses, not only
smiles and gladness, but, for our good, darkness and
frowns; so that we, in some of its manifestations,
call it *wrath*, though it is still love perfect and alone.
We should pitch our affection, our esteem and effort,
on the same holy key, and lift it into the same god-
like strain, as we contemplate the condition, and
strive for the perfection, of ourselves and our fellow-
men. We should enter into sublime sympathy with
our Father in the tasks and sufferings he appoints;
in the hard, long scourging he lays on the impenitent
and impure, that he may open a better fate.

In fine, the inquiry, whether that fate will at any
fixed period embrace every creature, and there be
literally no such thing as sin or suffering in all God's
universe, seems not within our power clearly to solve.
We know not the origin of evil; we know not its
end; we cannot measure the purposes which, under
God, it may subserve; we understand not how
extensively through the creation his training of
erring and peccable natures is used, or how many

souls of his inspiration must pass through stages of weakness and folly, before attaining to wisdom and moral strength. To make any definite prophecy of the time when his plans shall be accomplished is a greater presumption than to predict the end of the world. Indeed, will his plans ever be accomplished, and nothing left for him to do? *One* space, we believe, is free from sin and remorse : *that* we call heaven. To our imagination and hope, as they expand in the light of Scripture, it is an ever-enlarging space. It may not only take in soul after soul, but reach from planet to planet, and from star to star. It is a space of spiritual existence. It is the fulfilment of the dream of a perfect society. It is a true community, and a moral harmony. As it spreads and advances, the regions of gloom dwindle, and the rebel forces of wrong diminish and retire before its predominant power. . It is a pure and divine contagion of virtue. It is the adjustment of the spiritual and material worlds. It is the love of God, as a positive, manifest, and overcoming energy, adopted and exercised by his children, servants and saints. Reversing the application of the wonderful words in "Paradise Lost," it is *hell* " ruining from heaven." It is *eternal life.* Could we, with our faculties, conceive of a period or state when its tendency would be fulfilled, the universe would be *all* heaven. But our business is not a vain and foolish struggle to raise our speculation to a level with that of the Infinite Mind, but it is an unceasing endeavor to live the eternal life of God's spirit in our souls.

DISCOURSE XXIX.

CHANGE AND GROWTH.

Acts iii. 19. —REPENT YE, THEREFORE, AND BE CONVERTED, THAT YOUR SINS MAY BE BLOTTED OUT, WHEN THE TIMES OF REFRESHING SHALL COME FROM THE PRESENCE OF THE LORD.

WHAT is the main principle or necessary condition of the Christian life and experience? Is it change, a change of heart? or is it growth, a growth of nature? Theologians and religious denominations have been much divided on this point. The Orthodox sects have commonly insisted, that the needful process is change, suddenly expelling from our nature an evil, and introducing a good element. The Liberal party has in general contended, on the other hand, that growth is the law; that the nature which God has given us needs no alteration, but only right development, by a method of orderly progress and gradual sanctification. Which party is right in this controversy? May not both be right, and both wrong? To the true Christian life and experience, are not change and growth alike requisite, and equally recognized in the Scriptures? The real point is not to decide between these two principles, but to assign to each its just relative position. Let

us do this, not as identified with, or speaking in the
name of either party, but hoping rather for the day
when Christian believers shall no longer be styled
Liberal or Orthodox, but Liberal *and* Orthodox;
strict in truth, and catholic in love.

To proceed with our question. The liberal believer, in holding the Christian character to be a
process of growth, relies much on the analogies of
nature. "See," he says, "every living thing that
God hath made, how it grows! — in the vegetable
world, the flower by just degrees developed from a
tiny seed, and the oak developed from the acorn;
in the animal world, every creature rising, with no
sudden starts, but by a perfect series of gradations,
out of the very rudiments of existence. Why should
not the same law be observed in the spiritual world,
and all that is good and holy in character be evolved
from a primary germ in the very nature of the soul;
to use our Saviour's own analogy, 'first the blade,
then the ear, after that the full corn in the ear'? —
growth, being, in fact, the law of the universe." But
to this it may be replied, that, if growth be a law
of the universe, change is a law too: the light, the
air, the earth, the water, changed into the plant;
the body growing by change and assimilation of its
daily food; the worm becoming a butterfly, not, as
is imagined, by simple growth, but by transformation, as the waxing light and heat of heaven rend
away the old covering, and alter the very mode of
existence; every thing that has life brought into
the world by mighty alteration; the earth itself, on
which we dwell, reduced to its habitable condition

through a succession of vast variations; its surface, in every rent and chasm, hill and valley, a record of convulsions; its crystalline interior the product of continual shifting, and its whole sphere the very empire of change; we ourselves the subjects of change in life, and to pass through an unquestionable change at death. Change, surely, as well as growth is the law of the universe; for nothing is unchangeable but God, who can neither change nor grow.

So stands the argument from analogy. But the soul of man is a peculiar existence, having laws and operations of its own, beyond all the analogies of material things. It can and does grow, gradually advancing in every capacity of thought and feeling. But it is free in its nature, rapid in its thoughts, often quick in its decisions, capable of going on, or turning upon its track, liable to error, subject to compunction, seeing lofty visions of excellence, which pour scorn upon its base attainments, and stimulate it to preternatural efforts; nay, still more, open to the working of God's truth and Holy Spirit, and called with his high calling in Christ. And shall not blessed and glorious change, as well as slow, patient growth, be possible to such a nature? nay, if a man be a sinner, *must* not the law of change operate on him, before the law of spiritual growth can come in? If he grows simply, he grows in sin, and increases ever into a more monstrous size of iniquity. There are, indeed, perhaps a very few whom we might be content to see simply grow. There is in them, even from early years, such conformity of temper to

34

the will of God, the currents of all divine and human
love flow so purely in their humble breasts, that they
seem, in the quality of their mental frame, perfect,
and need only the perfection of growth. But these
are rare persons. The great majority need to be
changed. And we should not feel sadly, as though
this necessity were some hard thing, pointing to the
degradation and depravity of our nature. It is rather a great privilege and a blessing of God *in* our
nature that it can repent ; that it is not like many
material things ; not like a leaning, crumbling edifice, which, when it has once begun, must continue
to lean and crumble till it falls ; not like a decaying
plant, which must go on decaying till it dies ; not
like a diseased body, driven on in disease to utter dissolution ; — not like these things, but, by God's
mercy, it can recover itself, become erect and healthy ;
and, like the angels, as Milton describes them, "vital
in every part, cannot but by annihilating die." It is
God's blessing, too, that this need not be the slow,
well-nigh interminable work it is sometimes represented, as though the sins one has committed in the
past, perhaps in the sanguine, heedless, tempted days
of his childhood, must dog and curse him forever,
and the grim spectres of memory haunt him through
all eternity ; but, by the regeneration of God's truth,
and the reconciliation of God's love, he can put them
away, and be no more chased with their whips and
stings as of scorpions. "Come now, and let us
reason together, saith the Lord : though your sins be
as scarlet, they shall be as white as snow ; though

they be red like crimson, they shall be as wool."
Wasteful, hungry, and weeping wanderer from the
Father's house, drop your ill burden, and take Christ's
easy yoke; "put off the old man, and put on the new
man," explaining the apostle's meaning not by a commentary, but by your life; change the habit of lust,
anger, pride, vanity, selfishness, or envy, and graft
into the stock of your nature the first principles of
meekness, purity, humility, and love; and then you
may *grow* to the content of your own heart, to the
approval of God, and to the blessing of your fellow-
men.

It is a serious question, What is the first step we
should take? Is it of change from evil, or of growth
in good? Have we all, according to the noble
thought of a late theological writer, and to the gospel's undoubted design, *grown up to be Christians?*
or have we been bred in, or invented for ourselves,
a nurture so imperfect and unspiritual, that we need
to be changed? As it is best for a nation to proceed,
not always in the way of growth and development,
but sometimes, on account of its evil condition, in the
way of change and revolution; so do not many of us
need to be revolutionized, constituted anew, with
better principles, and governed by better laws? I
know it is sometimes thought, that spiritual regeneration is not wanted where Christianity has been fami-
liarly learned from youth, but only in those heathen
lands where it is for the first time promulgated. But
how imperfect the real operation of our religion, even
in the domain it has overrun and apparently conquer-

ed! It is not only the hundreds of millions of men who are ignorant of it, that you must, in measuring its triumph, strike off, but also the millions who understand and grossly violate it; then those who practise only its decent moralities, without being controlled by its loftier spirit, in business, society, and domestic life, — what gulfs of ruin open at every word! — till, coming down to a Christian city like this, perhaps as good as any in the world, you behold thousands living in the direct light of the gospel, heedless of its influence; and still again, contracting your field of observation, enter a Christian assembly, and honestly own how much change must be preliminary to a true growth. Nay, even in the Christian's own solitary regenerate heart, what conflict, what room still for change!

Oh that we might reach to that fountain of renewing strength which would change us from all that is low and unworthy, from the inordinate love of pleasure, love of possession, and love of the world, into the very image and inward forming of Jesus Christ! What a transformation, without as well as within, would then be witnessed, in the zeal of our worship, in the warmth of our fellowship, in the *true* growth that would succeed, in the overflow of our numbers, and the still better enlargement of our hearts!

Is all right with us now? Are we content to go on in the old, beaten way of tolerable respect for religion, or of formal monotony of worship? Would some little access of zeal, some working of the revival spirit, hurt us? Ought there not, in fact, to be something like an exchange, in this regard, between the different portions of the Christian church? Some congregations have, by appeals of unmitigated excitement, been burned and blasted into a deadness of conscience to common duties. Might they not well, as some of them are beginning to feel, borrow the pungent, moral strain? Are not others in that general course and latitude where they need an awakening to their religious relations? Might not *we* well pray and strive for such " times of refreshing " as Peter, in the text, predicted, and lived to see fulfilled ; pray and strive, not in displays of fiery intolerance and high conceit, but " of power and of love, and of a sound mind " ? These times of refreshing may come, indeed, not in any proud and blazing demonstrations, but in our domestic privacy, or in the social gathering. The refreshing of God may run into our hearts, as we peruse his word, and ponder his gracious, spiritual providence. It may flow to change our stubborn will, and melt our frozen affections, as we listen and think and praise in his house. It may break like a healing flood to alter and exalt our purposes, as we meditate in the solitude of the closet. It may mingle in with the torrent of sorrow that has burst over us, or fall noiseless, as a reviving dew, upon the prostration of our sickness. Everywhere, and in every hour, let us welcome its access, entreating that it may change and " turn " us "from darkness to light, and from the power of Satan unto God," till we " grow unto an holy temple in the Lord."

DISCOURSE XXX.

PERFECTION.

2 Cor. xiii. 11. — BE PERFECT.

To most persons, this is discouraging language. It does not furnish a very frequent theme of preaching, except among a particular body of Christians, who, struck with its commonness in the Scriptures and with its neglect, have associated themselves on its special basis, and are styled Perfectionists. But the idea is, not that we should grasp perfection as an immediate result, but make it our aim ; and this, so far from discouraging, only inspires. Is there no reason in the condition of the church, as well as authority in the Bible, for urging the precept, "Be perfect"? Is there not among us much more of a contented and barely respectable virtue, than of the thirst and aspiration after excellence? How many are satisfied to be as good as others, to reach the current medium of reputable character, to stand with the majority, that potent talisman in our community, and seek to accumulate fancied morality enough for a passport into the gates of heaven! To such men the gospel is a sealed book; nor can one gleam of its real meaning penetrate their souls, till the perfection it proposes dawn upon them, and they pursue it as their glorious end.

But what is this perfection? First, it includes all the virtues. It suffers us not to rely on some good qualities to the neglect of others, or to hope that we can, by a partial innocence, compound with God for the commission of any sin. In the scales of his justice, generosity will not atone for intemperance, irritability, or dishonesty; but the virtues least congenial with our temperament, or most trying to our resolution, he requires us to cherish with the greatest care. Again, perfection requires that each quality should be free from taint, like the Jew's unblemished offering, and without debasing alloy. Lastly, perfection requires that all the graces be expanded to an unlimited degree. As the seed contains in spotless purity every part of the plant, as the infant's frame is perfect in every member, as the child's harp may be no less harmonious than the great organ, or his tiny trumpet mock in its note the alarming blast of battle, yet all these things are of imperfect size or power; so how many faultless yet feeble characters need unfolding towards the perfection of moral stature and strength!

But, immeasurable as perfection is, shall it not be our aim? See how every thing great and good on this earth has grown out of the aim at perfection.

Its fruits, if not in religion, are everywhere else around us. Why do we live in such comfortable dwellings? Because men were not satisfied with a cave in the ground, or a rude fabric above it; but aimed at perfection, till the lowliest of our abodes surpass those once occupied by kings and princes. Why that proudest monument of architectural skill careering swiftly between continents, through the waste of waters? Because men were not satisfied with the creaking raft, slowly pushed upon the quiet stream, or with the timid boat that crept along the coast; but pressed on to perfection, till they came to span the breadth of the seas almost with the punctuality of the revolutions of the globe. See the Eastern caravan, once, with flocks and herds and merchandise, plodding its dull way through the desert: by the thirst for improvement, the aspiring to perfection, it is now transformed into a self-moving train, bearing through hills, over rivers and plains, greater multitudes and stores, as on the wings of the wind. Behold there a pale student, bending in tedious toil over a manuscript, which he is transcribing upon parchment by a process so expensively long and laborious that a few books exhaust a fortune. But progress is made; perfection is aimed at; and now the word of God is printed as in a moment, and the shelf of the poor man lined with treasures of knowledge that would once have excited the envy of monarchs.

In yonder village a painter paces, in quiet meditation, his little room. Beautiful pictures has he sent

forth to charm every beholder; but he alone is not
satisfied.   He draws some grand theme from the
mighty chronicle of the Bible.   He would turn
the words of the rapt prophet into colors.   He
would hold up to the eyes of men a scene of the
divine judgments, that should awe down every form
of sin, and exalt every resolve of holiness in their
hearts.   The finished result of his labors is shortly
expected.   But the idea of perfection has seized with
an overmastering grasp upon him, and it must give
him pause.   How shall that awful writing of doom
be pencilled on the plastered wall?   How shall that
finger, as it were of a man's hand, and yet the finger
of God, be revealed?   How shall those voluptuous
forms below, that have been all relaxed with the
wine and the feast and the dalliance of the hour, be
represented in their transition so swift to conscience-
stricken alarm, prostrate terror, ineffectual rage,
and palsied suspense, as they are confronted by
flaming characters of celestial indignation, which
the soothsayers, with magic scrolls, and strange garb,
and juggling arts, can but mutter and mumble over,
and only the servant of Almighty God calmly explain?   How shall it be done according to the perfect pattern shown in the Mount of Revelation of
God's word?   The artist thinks and labors, month
by month, and year after year.   The figures of
Babylonish king and consort, of Hebrew seer and
maiden, and of Chaldee magician, grow into expressive portraits under his hand.   The visible grandeur
of God the Judge, over against the presumptuous

sins of man, approaches its completeness. The spectator would now be entranced with the wondrous delineation. But the swiftly conceiving mind, which shapes out its imaginations of that dread tribunal so suddenly set up in the hall of revelry, is not yet content. The idea of perfection, that smote it, smites it again. The aspiration after a new and higher beauty, that carried it to one point, lifts it to another, and bears it far aloft, in successive flights, ever above its own work. Yet still, on those few feet of canvas, the earnest laborer breathes out, for the best of a lifetime, the patient and exhaustless enthusiasm of his soul. He hides the object, dear as a living child to its mother, from every eye, and presses on to the mark. If he walks, he catches a new trait of expression, some fresh line of lustrous illumination, to transfer to this painted scripture which he is composing. If he sleeps, some suggestion of an improvement will steal even into his dreams. In weariness and in sickness, he still climbs slowly, painfully, to his task. In absence, his soul turns back, and makes all nature tributary to his art. And on his expiring day he seizes his pencil to strive, by another stroke still, after the perfection which runs before him, and leaves his work as with the last breath of his mouth, and movement of his hand, upon it, to show, amid unfinished groups, and the measured lines for a new trial, that, if absolute perfection cannot be reached here on earth, yet heights of splendor and excellence can be attained, beyond all the thoughts of him whom the glorious idea has never stirred. What a lesson for us in our moral and religious struggles! What a rebuke for our idle loiterings in the heavenward way! What a shame to our doubtings about that perfection to which God and Christ and apostles call!

There, again, is a man who has toiled in loneliness and secrecy upon the strings of a musical instrument, till he has concentrated all the sweet sounds of nature into that little space, and can draw forth liquid melodies and mingling harmonies, the voice of birds, and the flow of streams; now the sounds of laughter, and anon the sobs of prayer, to the astonishment of assembled thousands. And shall Christians debate whether it is a possible or reasonable thing to make a perfect piety to God and charity to man their standard? No: there is no other aim worthy of your immortal natures. There is no perfection so glorious as that of moral and religious goodness. There is no example in other modes of perfection so clear and inspiring as that in spiritual things of the life of Jesus our Lord. Satisfy yourselves no longer with moderate attainments. Pause no longer upon the level where others may rest content around you. Pursue, each one, the peculiar and individual perfection which your Maker has marked out. Press every power of thought and feeling to this end. Labor till every color in the living picture of your excellence become true, and all deformity sink into just proportion. Tune over and over again the strings of each feeling in your breast, till every discord that jars there melt into harmony of love

and praise.   At least, so aim and so endeavor,
and the Perfect One himself, who has so commanded, will grant you his blessing ; and, from all
the short and broken accomplishments of earth,
will take you to the joy of higher and eternal
progress, with the spirits of the just made perfect
in heaven.

The Romantic Tradition in American Literature

An Arno Press Collection

Alcott, A. Bronson, editor. **Conversations with Children on the Gospels.** Boston, 1836/1837. Two volumes in one.

Bartol, C[yrus] A. **Discourses on the Christian Spirit and Life.** 2nd edition. Boston, 1850.

Boker, George H[enry]. **Poems of the War.** Boston, 1864.

Brooks, Charles T. **Poems, Original and Translated.** Selected and edited by W. P. Andrews. Boston, 1885.

Brownell, Henry Howard. **War-Lyrics** and Other Poems. Boston, 1866.

Brownson, O[restes] A. **Essays and Reviews Chiefly on Theology, Politics, and Socialism.** New York, 1852.

Channing, [William] Ellery (The Younger). **Poems.** Boston, 1843.

Channing, [William] Ellery (The Younger). **Poems of Sixty-Five Years.** Edited by F. B. Sanborn. Philadelphia and Concord, 1902.

Chivers, Thomas Holley. **Eonchs of Ruby:** A Gift of Love. New York, 1851.

Chivers, Thomas Holley. **Virginalia;** or, Songs of My Summer Nights. (Reprinted from *Research Classics,* No. 2, 1942). Philadelphia, 1853.

Cooke, Philip Pendleton. **Froissart Ballads,** and Other Poems. Philadelphia, 1847.

Cranch, Christopher Pearse. **The Bird and the Bell,** with Other Poems. Boston, 1875.

[Dall], Caroline W. Healey, editor. **Margaret and Her Friends.** Boston, 1895.

[D'Arusmont], Frances Wright. **A Few Days in Athens.** Boston, 1850.

Everett, Edward. **Orations and Speeches,** on Various Occasions. Boston, 1836.

Holland, J[osiah] G[ilbert]. **The Marble Prophecy,** and Other Poems. New York, 1872.

Huntington, William Reed. **Sonnets and a Dream.** Jamaica, N. Y., 1899.

Jackson, Helen [Hunt]. **Poems.** Boston, 1892.

Miller, Joaquin (Cincinnatus Hiner Miller). **The Complete Poetical Works of Joaquin Miller.** San Francisco, 1897.

Parker, Theodore. **A Discourse of Matters Pertaining to Religion.** Boston, 1842.

Pinkney, Edward C. **Poems.** Baltimore, 1838.

Reed, Sampson. **Observations on the Growth of the Mind.** *Including,* **Genius** (Reprinted from *Aesthetic Papers,* Boston, 1849). 5th edition. Boston, 1859.

Sill, Edward Rowland. **The Poetical Works of Edward Rowland Sill.** Boston and New York, 1906.

Simms, William Gilmore. **Poems:** Descriptive, Dramatic, Legendary and Contemplative. New York, 1853. Two volumes in one.

Simms, William Gilmore, editor. **War Poetry of the South.** New York, 1866.

Stickney, Trumbull. **The Poems of Trumbull Stickney.** Boston and New York, 1905.

Timrod, Henry. **The Poems of Henry Timrod.** Edited by Paul H. Hayne. New York, 1873.

Trowbridge, John Townsend. **The Poetical Works of John Townsend Trowbridge.** Boston and New York, 1903.

Very, Jones. **Essays and Poems.** [Edited by R. W. Emerson]. Boston, 1839.

Very, Jones. **Poems and Essays.** Boston and New York, 1886.

White, Richard Grant, editor. **Poetry:** Lyrical, Narrative, and Satirical of the Civil War. New York, 1866.

Wilde, Richard Henry. **Hesperia:** A Poem. Edited by His Son (William Wilde). Boston, 1867.

Willis, Nathaniel Parker. **The Poems, Sacred, Passionate, and Humorous, of Nathaniel Parker Willis.** New York, 1868.